T0312482

DRAMA DRIVES INTEREST

THE WEB SUMMIT STORY

Catherine Sanz

HarperCollins*Publishers*

HarperCollins*Publishers*
1 London Bridge Street
London SE1 9GF

www.harpercollins.co.uk

HarperCollins*Publishers*
Macken House, 39/40 Mayor Street Upper
Dublin 1, D01 C9W8, Ireland

First published by HarperCollins*Publishers* 2024

1 3 5 7 9 10 8 6 4 2

© Catherine Sanz 2024

Catherine Sanz asserts the moral right to
be identified as the author of this work

A catalogue record of this book is
available from the British Library

ISBN 978-0-00-864697-4

Printed and bound in the UK using 100%
renewable electricity at CPI Group (UK) Ltd

All rights reserved. No part of this publication may be
reproduced, stored in a retrieval system, or transmitted,
in any form or by any means, electronic, mechanical,
photocopying, recording or otherwise, without the
prior written permission of the publishers.

MIX
Paper | Supporting
responsible forestry
FSC
www.fsc.org   FSC™ C007454

This book contains FSC™ certified paper and other controlled
sources to ensure responsible forest management.

For more information visit: www.harpercollins.co.uk/green

CONTENTS

To grasping the nettle

PREFACE

I used to tell Paddy Cosgrave that it was only a matter of time before he turned on me.

I thought that by saying it out loud to him it would prevent it from happening, because Paddy hates being regarded as predictable. He made it into a running joke.

Back when I first started intensely reporting on Web Summit in 2021 after a litany of lawsuits involving the three co-founders brought an ugly row into the public domain, most things with Paddy felt like a joke. Until they didn't anymore.

After a series of amusing but increasingly tense engagements, a heated argument at the end of last summer largely spelled the end of our contact, which by then had been ongoing for over a year. I think Paddy appreciates being confronted with a different point of view, but he has become so entrenched in his, it can be impossible to find common ground. It should be clearly stated, too, that Web Summit, and Paddy personally, were contacted to discuss the content of this book, but they declined to engage or did not reply.

As for the other co-founders, they have had multiple opportunities to be interviewed for this book.

Writing a book about a business that has built an empire around holding space for powerful people to share ideas has raised questions about whether that is a way to wield a power of its own.

And sharing this story about a businessman who, after years of courting controversy without serious professional repercussions, crosses the line while you're writing it, has been absolutely surreal, to say the least.

Along with this drastic narrative shift, the process has been additionally complicated by Paddy's online attacks and repeated claims that he is writing his own book. I don't think many non-fiction writers have to deal with issues like these but, as you may already be aware, Paddy is not like most business people.

The grief I have absorbed from some characters involved in the story has at times paled in comparison to that which has been directed at me from others. Emotions ran high at various points, such as when, standing in Tesco on Baggot Street, I was shouted at on the phone by a rival business journalist who told me that I wasn't 'tough enough' to write this book.

I am acutely aware, after speaking with so many people who shared their experiences when they had no obligation to, that there is a lot of hurt in this story. The lawsuits are only one aspect of that.

It is frequently said by those who know Paddy that the difference between him and the persona he has cultivated online is extremely large. That is true, but it doesn't negate the pain that many have felt at the hands of either character.

Paddy himself also appears to regard his private and online self as two distinct entities. In 2022, despite privately complimenting me that a piece I had written 'nailed' him, he posted online that it was riddled with inaccuracies, and he was going to respond with a legal letter.

When asked why he felt the need to attack, his response was to send a screenshot of the number of click-throughs his post had received, saying 'drama drives interest ...' I knew then that there was more to this story.

Web Summit came of age in the 'hustle' era of the early 2010s, when churn and burn was par for the course on the road to success, and when everyone thought they were only a few ideas away from being the next Facebook or Twitter.

It capitalized on the zeitgeist of its time, when pop culture and user-experience driven technology were just beginning to fuse into what they are today; when the tech world was trying to reinvent itself as a force for good, despite being marred by a greedy and indifferent reputation.

For these reasons and many others which will unfold on the pages of this book, I truly believe this is the most compelling Irish business story of my generation.

Catherine Sanz, June 2024

Chapter 1

SHITSTORM

It's just after 4 p.m. on a Monday in November and a swarm of lanyard-wearing techies are beginning to descend on a strip of land to the east of one of Europe's oldest cities.

White tents with bright swatches of purple, blue and pink dot Lisbon's Parque das Nações, which is unusually lively today, notwithstanding the warm winter sun that has been beaming all afternoon. The park sits on the mouth of the River Tagus, which ends its over 1,000 kilometre journey through Spain and Portugal in the Atlantic Ocean around the bend from the capital city's coastline. Featuring twenty-first-century architecture erected to help rejuvenate and urbanize a formerly industrial part of Lisbon, the park includes a museum, a concert hall, and an oceanarium which is typically a tourist-magnet of the area.

But the thousands funnelling through checkpoints and waiting drone-like in line to have their lanyards scanned by smartphones are not here for penguins and sharks; they're here for an annual tech conference. It's Web Summit 2023 and four days of watching, listening, drinking, eating and 'connecting' await these eager attendees, some of whom got their tickets for free while others typically paid between €1,000 and nearly €5,000 for entry.

Leaders of companies big and small will take to more than a dozen stages to have their positions in life, their so-called expertness, endorsed by the presence of those in attendance. Many more will watch content from the event online in the days, weeks and months afterwards – perpetuating the idea that what happened over a week in Lisbon was fun, engaging, valuable and, most importantly, worth participating in.

Web Summit is theatre. It plays out under bright lights, is threaded together with choreographed interludes and encourages attendees to suspend their disbelief for the notion that what happens there will change the world, or at least their world. This may be among the loftier ambitions held by the team behind the conference company, but some of those filing through the gates as the sun sets on a Monday afternoon believe it too. And they are eager for the show to begin.

Absent from crowds buying hot dogs and mozzarella fingers, or the blacked-out cars stalling behind a VIP tent, are the three men who founded the company behind this spectacle in Lisbon. Notably missing is Paddy Cosgrave, who resigned in a storm of controversy just three weeks prior to this November evening following comments he made online. His resignation may have been swift, but it was not enough to stem a flood of sponsors and high-profile speakers from departing the event's line-up. Also absent from this year's event is Daire Hickey, who left the firm nearly seven years ago and has since established a new company, and David Kelly, who resigned two years ago.

Paddy, Daire and Dave are no longer friends. They are typically only named together in a sentence when describing Web Summit's beginnings or when detailing the tangled web of lawsuits each of them is embroiled in against the other. Paddy sued David, then David sued Paddy, then Daire sued Paddy, and relations have gone from bad to worse to extremely ugly. The rows centre on alleged director duty breaches and shareholder oppression claims surrounding three stakes in a company believed to be worth hundreds of millions of euros.

Web Summit has been an enormous Irish success story – from modest beginnings in 2009, it has grown to employ over 300 people across two countries and holds events in multiple continents. It has also welcomed guests like Elon Musk, Jack Dorsey, Eva Longoria, Al Gore, Olena Zelenska and countless others. Before it moved to Lisbon in 2016 it was based in Dublin, where it was founded, until a high-profile row with the Irish government unfolded and a more lucrative offer abroad beckoned.

Wind the clock back just a month before this sunny winter's day in Lisbon, and you end up in Doha, where Paddy was on a trip ahead of the conference's first ever Middle East event: Web Summit Qatar.

On 7 October 2023, hours after more than 1,200 people were massacred in Israel by Hamas fighters, Paddy tweeted a graph assessment of the number of deaths by both Israelis and Palestinians in the conflict since 2008. Many said he attempted to downplay the massacre, which was the 'worst single-day killing of Jewish people since the Holocaust', in this and other tweets. Toward the end of the following week, he shared a post which received huge levels of engagement online. 'War crimes are war crimes even when committed by allies, and should be called out for what they are,' he said.

The backlash was swift as the tweet went viral. He was criticized for taking days to show sympathy to those killed in Israel while he posted critically about the country, and later bragging that Web Summit had sold more tickets to that year's event.

In the aftermath of his comments, Intel, Google, Stripe, Amazon, IBM, Meta, Volkswagen Group and Siemens were among the companies to say they would not be participating in Web Summit's flagship event the following month. Key speakers, including Gillian Anderson, Nick Clegg, Scott Galloway, Amy Poehler, Tim Berners-Lee, and senior Stripe executives, also withdrew from the conference.

Some did so quietly, with their names removed from Web Summit's website in the hours and days after the controversy erupted. Others, like Galloway, who the company had been courting to speak at the event for over a year, were vocal about their reasons for doing so. 'His narcissism has overwritten his obligation to his employees,' Galloway said.

Some of those who had paid for tickets demanded and were granted refunds. Staff were in damage control mode, but it became impossible to put a brake on the exodus. Initially, Paddy had tried to stem the tide of fleeing sponsors, delivering a rallying speech to the Web Summit troops in which he apologized but said he would remain as chief executive and that the company had enough cash to go on until 2026. But the pain behind the scenes was palpable for staff – some of whom watched the names of speakers or sponsors they had spent months getting over the line disappear from internal spreadsheets as the hours and days unfolded.

The episode was also an onslaught for the PR team who were essentially powerless as tweet after tweet appeared from increasingly well-known figures distancing themselves from the company.

'I refuse to appear at Web Summit and am cancelling my appearance,' said Garry Tan, President and CEO of Y Combinator.

David Marcus, former PayPal boss, said he was saddened by Paddy's 'ill-informed stance ... You could've taken a more nuanced one, condemning these atrocities and calling for restraint. That would've been acceptable. You chose to support terrorists. As such I'll never attend/sponsor/speak at any of your events again.'

In a WhatsApp group for tech founders and VCs who dubbed themselves alumni of Web Summit, the fallout from Paddy's tweets happened in real time. As some of the conference's most well-known industry figures, the cohort are regarded as among those of most value to the conference.

'Does anyone have concerns about this or have any thoughts?' a San Francisco-based VC asked the group, posting a link to one of Paddy's tweets on the subject.

'Oh jeez,' was among the initial replies.

What unfolded in the group over the next few days was like its own microcosm for what was playing out in public on Twitter, LinkedIn, and Instagram.

'Positive intent, perhaps. But poorly crafted messaging from a guy who should understand the impacts of poorly crafted messaging. The recent Web Summit Qatar solicitations certainly add fuel to this fire,' one tech founder said a few days later.

Another founder and CTO weighed in, describing how he thought Paddy was a great guy after he met him but the recent 'Twitter shitstorm' made him 'honestly ashamed and disgusted' that he ever appeared onstage at Web Summit.

On 17 October 2023, after spending days in damage control, Paddy apologized for his tweets. 'I understand that what I said, the timing of what I said, and the way it has been presented has caused profound hurt to many. To anyone who was hurt by my words, I apologize deeply. What is needed at this time is compassion, and I did not convey that,' he said. He also compared himself to Anthony Blinken, the US Secretary of State, who he said he was trying to emulate in his remarks. 'Like the US government, Web Summit believes in working with regional and global partners – including Qatar – to encourage the dialogue and communication on which peace depends, and to strive for a just and lasting settlement to the underlying questions facing the region,' he added.

Some of those in the founder WhatsApp group were unconvinced by the apology. 'Sounded a lot more like a justification for the Qatar summit than a heartfelt apology,' one said.

What was remarkable for many were the tweets that led to the furore. This was especially so given that he had previously tweeted serious allegations about numerous individuals, including former employees, and had public spats with numerous high-profile figures in Ireland.

For those unfamiliar with his style of engagement on Twitter, Paddy has frequently engaged in self-described 'trolling'. Very few things have been off limits in his criticism, which frequently features him mocking and name-calling those he disagrees with or using the catchall term of 'cronies' and 'cretins' to describe them. In his pursuit of a self-styled retribution, he has also thrown countless people to the mercy of his more than 95,000 followers, some of which have taken up whatever cause he rails against on a given day. Paddy's animosity for Ireland's ruling political parties is palpable in his utterances, and he has repeatedly said he regards his online antics as part of an attempt to right the wrongs he perceives in the world.

The other consequence of this geo-political débâcle was that it added fuel to the already roaring fire of the scorched-earth style lawsuits that Paddy has with his co-founders. All three men face the prospect of a hefty seven-figure legal bill when all is said and done.

Remarkably, on the same day that Paddy was coming under intense criticism over his comments, and effectively being 'cancelled' in the so-called digital town square of Twitter, his legal team were opening detailed allegations against Daire in the High Court. And when the media reported on these claims – something Paddy had been waiting two years for – he wasn't even able to take his usual victory lap online because he was in a mess of his own.

At the heart of the founder lawsuits are men who used to be close confidants but who have since irrevocably fallen out. The row involves the things business disputes between founders are always about: money, control, and how the past is remembered for years to come.

As the majority shareholder, Paddy Cosgrave owns the biggest slice of the Web Summit pie. He does not hold a slight majority either – his stake measures at a whopping 81 per cent. Dave Kelly, who joined the company in 2010, has around a 12 per cent stake while Daire Hickey, who also joined that year, owns 7 per cent of the shares. At stake for Dave and Daire are sizeable payouts – if Paddy decides to or is forced to buy them out. But he would not be able to do that with the company's most recently reported cash reserves, so he may need new investment, to sell part of his own stake, or a sizeable windfall from new contracts. A number of well-placed sources have said their shares could be worth €40 million or more, depending on what Web Summit is valued at. Paddy wants a steep discount applied to their shareholding and he has his own $10 million claim against Dave.

It's not just the three men who have been embroiled by the lawsuits. Numerous sources in the tech community in Dublin said the litigation has led to many awkward encounters as sides were chosen or not chosen. Current and former staffers are named by various parties in the filings, and some face the prospect of being called as witnesses in the case. The litigation has also complicated relations with firms who had maintained ties to both Web Summit and 150 Bond, the PR company Daire founded following his departure, and within Paddy's wider friend group.

The allegations contained in the lawsuits are ugly. Paddy is accused of making financial decisions without consulting shareholders, using company money to help fund 'vendettas', inducing a panic attack in an employee and threatening those who cross him. Web Summit is also accused of settling a complaint of bullying against Paddy by paying a 'substantial' sum of money to a female employee.

Daire is accused of soliciting hundreds of thousands of euros in 'secret' fees, and Dave is accused of breaching his fiduciary duties to the company by allegedly secretly establishing a venture fund. The claims, of which there are over a dozen more, are denied.

On 17 October 2022, just over 12 months since the lawsuits began, Paddy was already claiming victory. 'The easiest way to win was to show that there's no oppression … and now that we've won and there's lots of money, now I can go on my vengeance tour,' he said.

Exactly one year later to the day, he issued his apology statement about his tweets and resigned from Web Summit. What happened in between was a rollercoaster of its own, something the trio were all too familiar with at that stage.

Chapter 2

THREE'S COMPANY TOO

Paddy Cosgrave, Daire Hickey and Dave Kelly were not just resentful business partners: they were pals who messaged each other on thousands of occasions over the years when they were close. They fought and reconciled countless times before they ended up in court, all while Web Summit grew into a successful enterprise which now employs hundreds of people. The depth and longevity of their relationship is evident in the salacious allegations that they have also levelled against each other. To understand how things ended up, it's essential to understand a bit about the men who founded Web Summit.

Since 2009, when he cobbled together what became the genesis for Web Summit, Paddy Cosgrave has been synonymous with the company. He played MC at events, was the face of the brand and cultivated a vision for how the company would evolve. He has also repeatedly been a person to make headlines for stoking controversy in manufactured and accidental ways.

In many ways, especially in Ireland, Paddy's reputation has become louder than Web Summit's for online behaviour that involves him taking aim at politicians, journalists, business people and social media accounts he disagrees with. His style and tone of online engagement has frequently involved a series of choice vocabulary to describe people he disagrees with politically and morally, a group he refers to with the catch-all term 'cretins'. He has also referred to the country's media as 'toadies' and 'lickspittles', people of various professions as 'shills' or 'gombeens' and those he deems to be the elite as 'scum'.

Paddy is unlike most businessmen in Ireland because he campaigns with a vitriol rarely used by public figures in Irish political discussion and rarer still among those in business. His use of Twitter has led to him being accused of bullying, spreading misinformation, and doxing. Mercurial and, occasionally bored, everything is a game to Paddy. And he is playing to win – perceived or otherwise.

His social media behaviour is just one example of that, where cruel and hurtful commentary is blasted out with the stated intention to 'needle' certain people. And while he has in the past recognized errors, as evidenced by deleted tweets, or on rare occasions apologies, it seems many of these are reactionary as opposed to remorseful.

As a leading business figure in Ireland put it to me: 'It's not personal – that's the bizarre thing – and yet it is very personal. That's where I think Paddy failed … he thinks it's okay to say something according to his perspective, he doesn't realize that people are living in different universes and thinking of the world in different ways … I think he does it for another purpose, [of] not being serious but you have to realize that's incredibly serious for someone.'

Despite admitting that many of his attacks are not personal, Paddy is well aware that they can be hurtful. In describing them to me, he has acknowledged his commentary has been mean but referred to it as 'fun'. And in conversation with some of his friends about the lawsuits he's involved in, he described his sense of fun as 'more expensive and oddball than most'.

'Any scandal?' is a typical greeting he uses when meeting a friend or acquaintance. A long-time former staffer once remarked to me that Paddy must have felt frustrated that no one ever had any scandal, so he went out and created his own. 'He keeps his own life interesting,' they said.

Paddy also embodies a string of contradictions: he is both shameless and thin skinned, disgusted by power in his immediate orbit but enamoured by it elsewhere, and prideful yet insecure. More than anything else, Paddy wants to be relevant because, as he sees it, his constant crusading against whatever issue he has taken up in society, or against society, is making it better. In Paddy's mind, he could do 'it' better – with 'it' often being whatever cause he has taken up that month, week or year.

In what I think embodies the best reflection of how he sees himself in the world, Paddy told me once: 'I think it's very difficult to sort of bend the world or a tiny part of the world to how you see it. If you think that everybody else's cakes aren't good enough, and you can make better cakes, you're kind of going to offend people with that level of ambition, in the cake community.'

Someone once said to me that in Paddy's ideal world, his wealth and status would allow him to become emancipated from society and able to stand over it, pointing out various flaws. As of yet, he does not seem to possess enough liquid cash for that to be a reality, but to be taken seriously as an intellectual, as opposed to being exceedingly rich, appears to be the goal he is working toward.

Paddy carries himself with the confidence of someone who has never had to worry about money. He is nearly 6 ft 4, well-spoken, and well-read. He frequents exclusive tennis clubs, was an avid sailor in his youth and mixes with some of Dublin's wealthiest families. As a result of his affluent upbringing, he is polite to the point that it seems to sometimes pain him when engaging with those he dislikes. When in mixed company, Paddy will rarely meet even his fiercest adversaries without a forced smile.

As part of the many contradictions he embodies, his infallible self-confidence frequently clashes with his physical and social awkwardness. Paddy seems itchy in his own skin, but convinced it is skin of the finest calibre. He likes to be funny but his jokes rarely land, so instead he has settled on revelling in the awkward tension he creates by making them.

If you are in his favour, he will reward you with a book recommendation, and if he is really invested, he will bring you his own copy of a book to read. Among the insults he has levelled at people, he expresses disappointment in is that they are 'not well-read'. He can be generous with his compliments in a way that can feel both disingenuous and disarming – it displays a knowledge of how to leverage people's vanity for his own gain.

Tennis, a real passion of his, has led him to rubbing shoulders with the wealthy, who he attends Wimbledon with while tweeting about the ills of Ireland's ruling class. Someone who has played tennis against him said he was 'very good', but had a fatal flaw that often worked to a rival's advantage. 'He lacked self-control and patience. He had a powerful serve which could potentially blow an opponent out of the water, but if you held your own for the serve, he would often slip up afterwards. I don't know whether that's a metaphor for him in real life, but it might be,' they said.

Paddy lives in an ecosystem overloaded with information and has stuffed his brain with so much of it that, to a listener, it seems to swirl around into a sort of confusion soup. But Paddy doesn't feel confused – in fact he feels that he is among a shrinking cohort of people who are truly awake to the realities of the world. The sheer volume of information he consumes, which he has repeatedly used to target those he perceives as having wronged him, has contributed to him seeming extremely paranoid in conversation.

He speculates on the presence of spies in Irish newsrooms (he claims to have a 'former British intel guy' as a source on this), enjoys discussing the activities of Western intelligence agencies, and has described the genocide of Uyghur Muslims in China as 'incredibly discredited propaganda'. These are just a smattering of the topics that he enjoys of late, as he completes a turn away from some Western nations and embraces other countries to solidify Web Summit's prosperity.

Paddy has made no secret about his geo-political beliefs. He likes fighting, and will flit between subjects, especially enjoying pointed questions about himself. Often a victim of his own 'main character energy', Paddy has an explosive temper and can vehemently hold a grudge. Once he has decided on something, he will stop at nothing to vindicate himself, and as a result many people I approached for this book were fearful of speaking. Reticence to speak also applied to those who are currently his friends, despite some of them asking me to attempt to convey him positively.

Paddy was raised in a large house in County Wicklow, a sprawling expanse of forests and mountains about a 45-minute drive south of Dublin. His father was a farmer, computer aficionado and captain of the Wanderers FC, a rugby club in the upmarket Dublin 4 neighbourhood, in the early 1980s. Paddy has described his father to me as someone who has fought against what he regarded as financial criminality.

His mother, who previously worked as a hockey coach in Our Lady's in Templeogue, attempted to take a High Court case against An Bord Pleanála, the planning board, in the early 2000s over a proposed landfill near their home. After a six-day contested leave hearing she was refused permission and faced a legal costs bill of more than €200,000, according to media reports at the time.

Paddy has tweeted that his grandfather (Don O'Connor, from his mother's side) ran the so-called Ansbacher accounts, a secret banking system used by wealthy Irish people to lodge money in Dublin which was held offshore. O'Connor had a house on Heir Island, County Cork, and Paddy referred to him as being 'at the heart of FFG crony-ism', referring to Ireland's main political parties Fine Gael and Fianna Fail. Thus making Paddy, as he called it, a 'crony insider'.

'It's family, it's deep,' was how someone phrased his rail-ing against Ireland's ruling class.

After an exchange programme with a school in New Jersey in 1999, the headmaster wrote to Paddy's parents to congratulate them on raising an 'affirming, warm, and considerate' human being. He sent me a copy of this letter after I interviewed him in 2022 and described how he was 'into improving queues' in school.

He also shared a 2014 Facebook post issued by someone he knew in college who recalled Paddy, at 18 years of age, leaving Chomsky notes lying around a lecture hall so that others would pick them up 'and unwittingly absorb it all'. Paddy has shared the same screenshot on Twitter and with many others over the years.

After years in a south Dublin house share, Paddy lived on a farm in Donegal but has since moved his family into a nearly €2 million mansion near Rossnowlagh Beach, a beautiful sandy stretch which backs up onto cliffs at its southern end. Tending to the gardens and rearing the livestock is still among his stated pastimes.

Faye Dinsmore, his model turned knitwear designer wife, lives there. Stunningly beautiful and initially the more famous of the pair, she graced fashion show catwalks around the world before she settled down into married life with Paddy. Her €750 jumpers, which she states cost that much in order to pay knitters a living wage, are a staple of Paddy's wardrobe. Someone who worked for him for years said he had long been cultivating a 'faux humbleness' – 'wearing Aran sweaters and being like I don't care how I'm dressed, but then the ego is huge'.

At best, Paddy enjoys exaggerating his achievements or bending the truth to suit an argument, and at worst, he lies. He has told me a number of untruths and, after being confronted with the fact that they were not true, has passed them off as a joke. In years gone by, he has referred to something called 'future truths', or things which were not yet true but which he said would be true, to others.

Although he has not always been a pirate-flag wielding, anti-establishment warrior, he has long been an astute marketeer. In Trinity College Dublin, where Paddy met Daire Hickey, he honed these skills in his role as President of the Philosophical Society (the Phil). He was also an avid debater, which is obvious to many who engage in conversation with him.

Paddy was extremely popular at college, although those who knew him said he often 'rubbed people the wrong way' because he was outspoken and arrogant. As President of the Phil, Paddy forged a new path for one of the college's oldest societies which had typically stuck to the traditional way of doing things in its over 300-year history.

Some of his college contemporaries thought he would go into politics. When *The University Record*, as the college paper was then known, compiled a list of the 50 most powerful students, Paddy came in at number two. 'He was very driven,' a former classmate said. 'His behaviour was very sociable, looking for any advantage he could get the society. It makes sense, a lot of sense, for how his career tracked. He was good at figuring out a situation and using it to the advantage of the institutions he was working in, as well as himself.'

During this time, Paddy also sharpened his skills at orchestrating controversy and used the print-dominated Irish press as a means to make that happen. Media in the early 2000s was frequently sexist and garish. Tabloids capitalized on reality TV stars as the world's newest breed of celebrity and female pop stars were frequently oversexualized, then blamed for being sluts. Ireland was not immune to these tropes, as evidenced by the so-called '03 team' of 20-something women the *Sunday Independent* splashed, in at least one instance topless, on full-page spreads about subjects such as holiday romances, spa days and dieting.

Throughout his involvement with the Phil, Paddy often wrote press releases and sent them to news desks in order to get coverage for the society. A *Daily Mirror* piece in April 2004, headlined 'Feminists force Trinity College to scrap speech by TV beauty Gena', described how 'sexy *Baywatch* star' Gena Lee Nolin was dumped by the Phil after feminist students protested. 'They demanded the gorgeous blonde be banned from giving a talk at Dublin's Trinity College because they wanted "brains not breasts",' the article stated. It featured numerous quotes from Paddy, who was then secretary of the society. 'It's a victory for them,' he said, referring to the feminists. 'They got their way, but it's sexist to think just because she was on *Baywatch* that she's not intelligent.' The story, which appeared in other Irish media as well, said that 'left-wing author Naomi Klein' was invited instead. Klein never attended.

During Paddy's tenure as president and secretary, the Phil played host to a range of extremely impressive and unusual guests, including John McCain, the US Senator, Kayleigh Pearson, then *FHM* magazine's 'High Street Honey of the Year', Archbishop Desmond Tutu and Ron Jeremy, the world-famous porn star. The latter did spurn protests from women's rights groups, with one telling the *Irish Times* that there was a 'deplorable practice of wasting funds on porn stars, glamour models and page three girls that is, we feel, insensitive and insulting'.

Another controversy during Paddy's time in college occurred when the entire print run of *Piranha!*, the college's satirical magazine, was withdrawn from publication after one of its articles used the 'n'-word to describe Arabs. Paddy, who said he was in charge of advertising at the time, has maintained that there was an investigation and no sanction was levelled at him as a result.

High-profile speakers allowed the society to attract media attention and thereby solicit sponsors. Each newspaper article acted as free publicity which helped it fund more exclusive parties. One gimmick used to recruit the guests was to send out hundreds of letters, printed on 'nice paper', with an incredible story of its history, featuring a tale about how the society was where Oscar Wilde first sparred with Edward Carson, who went on to indict him, and that people like Bram Stoker of *Dracula* and Winston Churchill had graced its halls.

Daire Hickey's tenure as president of the Phil, which occurred a couple of years later, was also a star-studded affair, with guests including Al Pacino, David Hasselhoff, Oliver Stone and Ruth Bader Ginsburg.

Also ambitious but from much more modest upbringings, Daire was raised in Ballincollig, a suburban town to the west of Cork city. He went to a local school and came out as gay to his parents – who he is extremely close to – in college. His father Tom, a sub-editor with the *Irish Examiner* for over four decades, has spoken extensively about living with a facial disfigurement which occurred after he was burned as a child. A close confidant and mentor to Daire over the years, Tom penned a 2015 blog entitled 'Why I love my son Daire'. In it he describes how in the early years of Web Summit, Daire was 'way out of my league at that stage' but 'still anxious for my opinion'.

'I loved him for including me,' he wrote.

Tom has also written about the pain of losing a child following the death of Daire's brother Alan. He said the family buried Alan on Christmas Eve 1989, when he was just 22 months old, after being born with spina bifida, a birth defect of the spine. 'I carried his coffin up the aisle that day and the memory still haunts me in a way my facial disfigurement never did,' Tom wrote. His blog is sincere and well-written.

Unlike Paddy or Dave, Daire's upbringing was not affluent or well-heeled, but he took to the world of celebrity like a duck to water.

In describing how he met Al Pacino on the tarmac of Dublin airport because he was 'flying private and it's a whole other world', Daire recalled how the Oscar-winning actor does two funny things. First, he drinks a triple macchiato over the course of five to six hours, from the morning to afternoon. And second, he brings his bed sheets from home with him everywhere. 'He said that everybody does things for him and one of the things that he likes to do for himself to make him feel just a little bit grounded, is to make his own bed every day and to put on the sheets,' Daire said about Pacino.

Daire loves money and has always wanted to be rich. He has previously described how his first understanding of money came when he went into a store with his mother and asked her to buy him a Lego pirate ship. 'And she's like, it's too expensive, you can't have that. It was like, I don't understand. She's like, well, you need to collect a lot of money to go and buy this and I was like, Aha, I see. Money. How do I get this money thing?'

Luckily for Daire he has since fallen into money after allegedly making a double-digit million windfall selling crypto in 2021 that he purchased from a PR client years earlier. He is a connoisseur of luxury bedding in five-star hotels and delights in the proximity to celebrity he has enjoyed over the years. A master self-promoter, Daire knows how to spin a story and then how to think on his feet if it falls flat to spin it again into something else. He is great with names and, in particular, name dropping where possible, and equally skilled at getting people excited.

Among the stories about him that have been passed down through Web Summit over the years is that he came into a meeting with a top-tier sponsor, wearing sunglasses and looking hungover. Almost immediately, he began rattling off the names of famous pop stars and tech industry figures he had recently been in the company of, who was fighting with who, and who was secretly in love. When the potential investor, apparently dazzled by the tale, left the room to get a more senior staffer to join, Daire turned to his colleagues and allegedly asked, 'Who are these guys again?'

Daire can also be extremely bitchy and catty. Some of those who worked with him recall that he frequently enjoyed laughing at or about other people. He is an older millennial gay who has had to keep himself in check over mocking words or phrases no longer deemed to be kosher. He can also be empathetic and knows the value of 'I'm sorry', when required.

In New York, where he has lived with his now-husband for over a decade, he currently divides his time between a brownstone in Brooklyn and a house in Connecticut. He has two dogs and hardly any wrinkles in his forehead.

The college relationship between Paddy and Daire was similar to that of a teacher and a student – Daire looked up to Paddy, saw he was going places and wanted to be along for the ride. He said Paddy was one of the first people he laid eyes on at college and that he 'wanted to follow in his footsteps'. In Daire, Paddy saw an admirer and an audience. A former classmate once described how it appeared they became friends after Paddy 'chose' Daire as his protégé of sorts.

David Kelly and Paddy's relationship goes back much farther – to secondary school in Glenstal Abbey, a private boarding school run by Benedictine monks. The exclusive all-boys institution in County Limerick, which currently costs nearly €22,000 a year, is located on the grounds of a building designed in the style of a twelfth-century castle, with stone-walled round towers greeting guests at the end of a long tree-lined driveway.

Students at the school studied Latin and Classics, attended mass on Sundays, and were required to have their identification details sown onto each item of clothing so the on-site laundry attendants knew who owned what. Older students were allowed to drink with the monks at monthly weekend socials, provided they had written parental permission, and had 'tuck lockers' opened with a key where they kept sweets and other belongings.

The line between bullying and friendly slagging can be very thin in all-boys boarding schools. David, who was called Dave in interviews and by those who worked with him, including Daire, was referred to by a variety of nicknames, 'Danger Dave' was one nickname that Paddy brought up in an interview during the company's early years, indicating it was because he was a cautious individual who would 'always question things'. Someone who knew Dave in school said he was 'tolerant' and appeared to be empathetic and self-deprecating. Paddy was a central part of his friend group, but the relationship was not described as one of equals.

Quiet and introverted, Dave has shied away from the limelight throughout his career, despite living in the shadow of two other men who frequently bathed in or around it. He has long wanted a simple life and has made that clear in his communications to Daire and Paddy over the years. 'I'm just happy working, I don't really want any public persona,' he told media in the past.

As a trained accountant who studied business in college, Dave, who came to Web Summit in 2010, was brought in to handle bigger-picture aspects of the enterprise in its early years. For a number of years, he and Paddy shared a house together on Manders Terrace, in the quiet upmarket south Dublin village of Ranelagh. Dave was unemployed at the time and by his own admission 'just hanging around'. 'I just kind of fell into doing what I'm doing with Paddy. I had no idea in school or even in college that I'd end up working with Paddy on the Web Summit,' he told RTÉ in 2013. 'And literally by chance, I wasn't doing much, kind of just hanging around. So I just basically came on board, and he was upstairs working on it. And we both kind of decided to start working from the living room,' he added.

While the three men are extremely different, they do have something in common, namely their ambition to be successful. Although they wanted it for different reasons, the unconventional trio all desired to create wealth while enjoying life as high-flying, international jet-setters. 'There was a lot of fake it till you make it with them,' one ex-employee said.

Chapter 3

IN THE BEGINNING, ~~GOD~~ PADDY CREATED ...

Every entrepreneur needs a good origin story and many will admit that it does not have to be true. It should impress and inspire, evoke feelings of serendipity or, at the very least, make the listener think the person regaling them with a visionary tale got lucky. Paddy has never shied away from talking about the less than rosy beginnings of his business career, but he's often left a few salient points out. As always, he tells the truth except for all the times he doesn't.

In late 2006, Paddy was trying to find ideas which could work outside of the close-knit world of college societies. He struck up a friendship with Hugh O'Regan, the high-profile publican, hotelier and developer. O'Regan, who died in 2012 at only 49, became a close confidant of Paddy's after the pair met in a coffee shop on Dawson Street. They struck up a conversation about the profitability of the Kilternan Hotel which the publican had recently purchased. Describing O'Regan as 'an incredibly colourful and wonderful entrepreneur' in a Trinity alumni magazine in 2013, Paddy has consistently spoken about the late businessman in glowing terms. In 2015, he told *Hot Press* that O'Regan was a 'magical character' and that the pair regularly went for long walks to chat about their ideas. 'Some people thought he was crazy but, if he was crazy, he was just the right sort of crazy,' Paddy said.

O'Regan gave Paddy advice, financial backing to the tune of €50,000, and, crucially, free office space at 15 St Stephen's Green. The building, which was owned by O'Regan, had been opened up to a number of social entrepreneurs over the years, including Gary McDarby, the scientist and inventor who has also praised O'Regan for sharing the spoils of his success with those trying new things. Unbeknown to many and under O'Regan's tenure as landlord, the building at 15 St Stephen's Green acted as an unofficial incubator of new ideas in early 2000s Ireland. For Paddy it would play host to 'Forge on 15', a networking event he set up with friends from Trinity which operated like a singles night because people were expected to work the room and make conversation.

Drink-fuelled chats sparked both fierce debates and more subdued monologues in soft-lit corners of the eighteenth-century Georgian townhouse. Those who attended recalled that they were asked to bring one friend with them, with the idea being to form a networking group for people to come up with interesting projects together.

It was an expansion of the Phil and a Web Summit precursor which relied heavily on pushing the idea that lasting connections could be 'forged' in just one evening. The initiative claimed to have been formed by 50 young leaders 'drawn from across the public, private and citizen sectors'. An invitation to a 'Forge on 15' event in February

2007 said it was about 'Connecting talented people and powerful ideas across generations.'

Lorcan Fox was among the attendees. A former classmate of O'Regan's son Stephen, Fox was then a wannabe filmmaker studying at the Dun Laoghaire Institute of Art, Design and Technology. With bright blond hair and a thick Dublin accent, he stood out among a group of recent Trinity graduates who were seeking to change the world, or at least get rich trying. Fox was linked to Paddy through friends who knew him from their student activism days in secondary school. 'I was just a working-class lad in fucking film school. You'd be walking around going these lads are all going to be running the country in about ten years.'

The 'Forge on 15' events were borne out of a desire to build something new by bringing people with big ideas together to chat. The gatherings bore many resemblances to what Paddy would go on to cultivate at Web Summit, especially those which occurred in F.ounders, its invite-only exclusive event, and the Forum, its networking area for high-profile attendees.

One of Paddy and Daire's first post-college endeavours was Rock the Vote, a voter mobilization campaign aiming to increase youth turnout in the 2007 Irish general election. The concept was modelled on an American organization which partnered with MTV in the 1990s and featured celebrities like Tom Cruise, Madonna, Whoopi Goldberg and Danny de Vito in its marketing over the years. Using a slogan 'good craic for a good cause', Ireland's Rock the Vote campaign toured more than a dozen third-level institutions across Ireland handing out merchandise in the form of T-shirts, wristbands, pins and lanyards. It also recruited bands to play gigs to help spread a 'get out and vote' message and garnered more than 500 people in a 'pledge to vote' drive.

Lorcan Fox knew Richard Cook in the Lisa Richards Agency through other work, and Cook agreed to send some of his biggest stars like comedian Dara Ó Briain and actor Cillian Murphy to perform in video clips. Colin Farrell, then just at the cusp of his *In Bruges* fame, also made an appearance in some of the clips. The camcorder videos, which were posted to Bebo, Myspace and YouTube, had all the hallmarks of a student project, with choppy editing and inconsistent audio. Irish celebrities including Neil Hannon and Rosanna Davidson would make 'rock n roll' hand gestures and stick out their tongue to the strum of an electric guitar. A green paint-splattered Rock the Vote logo would dance onscreen at the end. The content was cringey, but memorable and 'deeply ironic', according to Paddy, who later rebuffed criticism by claiming that the videos and hand gestures were just making fun of the American movement.

In one video, Ó Briain stands on the streets of Dublin telling the camera 'don't vote, it's a hassle, stay at home, and work on your Bebo pages and let old people run the country instead'. Des Bishop, Louis Walsh, Ryan Tubridy and Mario Rosenstock featured in other quickfire video segments. Emmet Kirwan was recruited to play 'Frazier Fraz', a tracksuit-wearing character fond of impromptu rhymes, hip-hop music and using cheesy phrases. Fraz even had his own Bebo page and was described in the following terms by Rock the Vote in a promotional release: 'Frazier is a pale-faced, flecky tracksuit wearing young guy from Tallaght who was plucked from obscurity by out of touch producers trying to find "the voice of a generation".'

Farrell and Amy Huberman, who Fox recalls attended the filming with her new boyfriend Brian O'Driscoll, made cameos in other videos. The videos took off on YouTube, racking up tens of thousands of views and bringing the channel into the top 75 most viewed in the weeks leading up to the election.

Daire was heavily involved in the campaign's PR and frequently made media appearances as a spokesman and defended it from allegations that it was superficial. Writing in the *Independent* in response to a column from Ian O'Doherty, who Daire described as a 'cranky hack', he said the campaign did not think it was 'cool' to lecture young people but had a 'subtle message' about awareness. He also used his entertainment contacts to recruit celebrity appearances.

Then a fledgling showman, Paddy was clearly enticed by his newfound fame and played to his age and his audience when describing how the Rock the Vote campaign came about. 'Eight months ago, it was nothing but an idea I had chatted about with mates over a pint,' he told the *Irish Examiner* in March 2007. 'If someone had told me back then that, in eight months, the campaign could count on the likes of Dara Ó Briain, Cillian Murphy and dozens of others as supporters I'd have just laughed.'

The conceived-at-the-end-of-a-pint analogy would be used in multiple Rock the Vote media interviews, and it would later be used to refer to how Web Summit was hatched. As an origin story trope, it's perfect for an aspiring Irish entrepreneur to showcase a sense of being relatable and casual, both qualities which do not come natural to Paddy's online and media persona. But at the same time, as many people who have known him in college and since have also noted, it's somewhat ironic because he rarely drinks, and certainly never in the form which would involve regularly staring at the end of pint glasses.

To accompany the in-person Rock the Vote campaign, it was decided that a website would be formed to host details of all the candidates running in the 2007 election. That website, called MyCandidate.ie, was never designed to make money, and it never did, but it achieved major success in showing what was possible in a very short time frame.

The MyCandidate.ie website was launched less than two months before the election on 24 May 2007. While the database was neutral, clear and mature, the 'About Us' section of MyCandidate.ie hinted that it was run by a bunch of kids fresh out of college. 'Which candidates support which issues? Which two brothers are running against each other for different parties? Which party leader lists "Getting laid" as one of his priorities? Find out all this and more!'

The answer to the last question was Pat Rabbitte, then leader of the Labour party, who took an opportunity to appeal to young people with a pledge to reduce the VAT on condoms under an all-caps headline GETTING LAID. 'Do I need to explain this anymore?' Rabbitte wrote in the section outlining his priorities.

The website was impressive for its time, featuring an interactive map of constituencies, a list of each politician running, and an 'interesting fact' about the person in question. For example, the website told voters that Taoiseach Enda Kenny was a fan of Bruce Springsteen, and Eamon Ryan, Green Party leader, created 'no logo day' to inform students about issues with marketing and world trade. A mish mash of fonts and grass-green-coloured splatters finished off the site, which boasted that candidates' profiles were viewed nearly 4 million times over a six-week period.

In the end, the 2007 general election bucked a 20-year trend, resulting in a 67 per cent turnout. Rock the Vote and MyCandidate.ie may have only been one small part of a changing electoral landscape, but the project was loud, fun and reinvigorated the idea that politics could be cool among young adults. Yes it was far from perfect, and dubbed a 'superficial pop culture campaign' in one analysis, but it was a positive initiative that occurred at a great time in Paddy and Daire's life.

For all the good times, the Rock the Vote period fills Paddy with some resentment in retrospect. When he got wind that I was looking into this part of his life, he messaged me out of the blue to tie it into his ongoing lawsuits. It appears that everything in his past is coloured by these fallouts. and it seems difficult for him to regard it as a truly successful, if superficial, endeavour.

In 2008, Paddy established the Undergraduate Awards along with Oisin Hanrahan, who knew Paddy from Trinity College. Hanrahan had experienced unusual early business success in the form of a property development company focused on Hungarian apartments. Historic buildings in the recent EU-entrant's capital were cheap and he quickly figured out that it would be lucrative to renovate and rent them out. 'There would be 20 feet of ceiling space with literally nothing but pigeon crap in them. You could build half a dozen new penthouses,' Hanrahan previously said about the venture. He would later go on to found a successful start-up called Handy, which matches home cleaners and handymen with those seeking these services, and be chief executive of Angi Homeservices, a Nasdaq-listed multi-billion-dollar company. Described as very awkward by some who knew him at the time, Hanrahan was well-liked, and brought a business-centred mindset to the project.

Often referred to as the 'junior Nobel prize', the Undergraduate Awards has been extremely successful and recognized thousands of students over the years under the patronage of Michael D Higgins, the President of Ireland, since 2012.

Paddy went on the Ryan Tubridy radio show on RTE One in October 2008 to promote the endeavour, then in its infancy. Harnessing the myth-making skills which he was already so fond of, Paddy opened the segment with the prompt 'Have you ever asked yourself what in the world happens to those thousands upon thousands of essays written by students every year? Where do they go, what happens to them?'

The idea of the Undergraduate Awards as a marketplace of ideas spurred the creation of a 'think-in' initiative held in late 2008 which sought to find solutions for the financial crash. Dubbed 'WhereNext.ie', it had some of the hallmarks of a Web Summit precursor in that speakers were invited to give talks on topical issues. The main event was held at 8 St Stephen's Green, another of O'Regan's properties.

As part of a drive to raise awareness of the initiative, Paddy told *Sunday Independent* journalist Niamh Horan, a contemporary of his, that he was sick of negative narratives focused on the past and that new ideas were needed. 'We're dwelling on the past, all the mistakes that have been made, the property bubble, and nobody is beginning to look forward,' he said.

While WhereNext.ie was collecting 'ideas for our future', Paddy remained keen to build on the achievements of Rock the Vote and the first iteration of MyCandidate.

MyCandidate.ie became the genesis for MiCandidate.eu but even before the latter launched in April 2009 it had overstated its potential. This was mainly due to it failing to deliver on promises that it would be linked to media companies like RTE, the *Irish Times*, Sky News and TV3. In reality, the company had a small number of contracts, including with RTBF, the Belgian state broadcaster.

In the months leading up to the creation of MiCandidate. eu in early 2009, Paddy and Oisin were mentored by a number of figures in the Dublin business community. Chief among these individuals was Aine Maria Mizzoni, a former president of the Dublin Chamber of Commerce and then managing director of Grafton Recruitment. A number of sources who were involved described Mizzoni as 'impressive' and a figure whose involvement lent a lot of credibility to the project. 'She seemed to really believe in him,' one person said about how Mizzoni regarded Paddy at the time.

The young founders were seen as having great potential and discussions ensued on how to turn their student campaign into a successful business. Help was recruited from Paul Healy, a tech project manager, who was brought on board by Mizzoni, his girlfriend at the time, to help get the website up and running.

The business model of MiCandidate.eu was that individual politicians would be charged to manage and expand their profile on the site. It also had a potential revenue stream from media outlets who could pay to embed the data on their site.

In a perfect illustration of what the internet really thinks of noble ideas, the company's old web address is, at the time of writing, hosting a porn site. Spelling with an 'i' instead of a 'y', MiCandidate was designed to be a database on politicians across Europe so voters could access information about those running for office while also enabling the politicians to recruit volunteers and accept donations. The selling point for politicians was that it would be hosted by media outlets so voters could potentially be just a click away from learning more about them.

With only a matter of months left before the European Elections in June 2009, the amount of work required on MiCandidate was colossal. Space was procured in Ballast House on Westmoreland Street, where Paddy, Oisin and a small team of people sought to make MiCandidate.eu a profitable endeavour.

At the end of February 2009, an email with the subject line 'Great Job, Great Pay' was sent by Paddy to a mailing list he had compiled: 'We've a series of positions available at MiCandidate, with great pay, starting immediately: €350–€650 p/week,' he wrote in the email.

There was considerable interest in the work given that many people, and in particular recent graduates, were desperate for paid work in the wake of the financial crash. The so-called Celtic Tiger years, a period of exuberant yet unsustainable wealth, were well and truly over. With that came the collapse of the housing market and an economic slowdown which quickly resulted in huge job losses and a steep rise in unemployment. By mid-2009, the OECD would report that more than one in four under-25s found themselves unemployed. So with the country on its knees, the lure of a start-up which had the potential to be, as former staff recalled Paddy claiming, 'the next Facebook' was too good to pass up.

The work involved researching candidates around Europe, inputting their details into a database, and getting politicians to pay for their profiles to be hosted on the site. In return, the site said it could help them recruit volunteers, accept donations and send out emails.

Candidates had the choice of a free basic package or a professional service for €239, MiCandidate Pro. Despite the steep price, they made over €41,000 from candidate subscriptions by September of that year. Politicians who purchased it said it was a 'big deal' that was pushed by a very persuasive sales team, but it failed to provide much use and was difficult to get rid of.

Within the MiCandidate office, young people buzzed with the hope that the company's dream of bringing democracy closer to people would also result in a commercial success. And despite its lack of meaningful income, Paddy became adept at selling a vision of the start-up that could be huge. He often referred to other new start-ups at the time which looked like they were heading for glory as comparators for MiCandidate's potential. This included Twitter which, in 2009, had just launched and was heading towards 50 million monthly active users. Other recent start-ups and the founders behind them, who Paddy claimed may have been sleeping on friend's couches when they first started out, were described to staff in reverential terms.

For some, the excitement of being a part of a company which was touted as having such incredible potential eased their financial woes, but the goodwill ran out among many before the website was launched. In early May 2009, staff were told that they would get 50 per cent of their April salaries and to submit their invoices, taking holiday/sick days into account.

The infrequency and insufficiency of the payments caused a gnawing gripe to grow among staff who felt they were misled when hired with the promise of set weekly wages. Some signed onto the dole to make ends meet on certain weeks. 'It was never really honest, we were always told that we would be paid, and we were part of this company and it was going to be great, and it was going to be such a success story,' one ex-staffer said. 'My lasting feeling was that everyone was used a bit, promised a lot of things that were never delivered,' they added.

A PR near-mishap was Paddy's attempt at illustrating how MiCandidate would allegedly render obsolete the concept of politicians needing to go door to door as part of their election canvassing. Former staffers recalled a plan to visualize this was to purchase a door and schedule a photo-call outside Leinster House where he had hoped to literally showcase his theory by burning down the door. The burning part was thankfully scrapped, and instead the door was knocked down with an axe. A surviving photo shows an axe-wielding Eoin Ryan, then a Fianna Fail MEP, appearing through a hacked open hole in a door. Captioned as Ryan 'illustrating the smashing down of information barriers' the photo was taken at MiCandidate's official launch of its website on 16 April 2009.

By late May of that year, the website boasted over 2,000 profiles and a partnership with the *Irish Independent* that allowed it to link in with the publisher's online offering as well as those of its 14 regional newspapers. But the venture was already in trouble after a report in the Irish edition of the *Sunday Times* said that promised links to outlets like

RTE had not materialized and candidates wanted their money back.

In many ways, MiCandidate acted as a trial run for what would develop into a Web Summit sales strategy: get a soft promise from one big name to buy (or in Web Summit's case, attend) and then trade off that until a series of clients have been snowballed. A verbal commitment can be developed into a written one, and in the meantime it can always be spun into something useful, was how someone at time described it.

Although many of the planned media partnerships failed to become ink and paper deals, an impressive feat of the MiCandidate project was the fact that they were seriously entertained at all. By the time the June 2009 European elections came around, MiCandidate had taken on a few unpaid interns. One of these interns recalled being invited on a lunchtime walk with Paddy ('he watched too many Aaron Sorkin movies') where an extremely vague idea for an event which would gather media representatives and tech founders in Dublin was discussed.

Paddy sought help from the intern in compiling a list of publicly available contact details for publicists and media representatives. The intern said Paddy was particularly keen on News Corp, Rupert Murdoch's media empire, which by then had acquired Myspace and was rumoured to have been interested in buying Bebo the year before. The former intern recalls repeatedly searching for 'How do you contact Rupert Murdoch' in Google for an afternoon. Other 'dream guests' included 'Tom from Myspace', referring to Tom Anderson, co-founder of the social network.

Despite being excited by his conference side project, Paddy was said to have been stressed about the company's finances. The liabilities were around €65,000 and included costs to a hosting company, a development company, a bank overdraft, a loan and nearly €25,000 in outstanding wages that went largely unpaid.

Both Paddy and Oisin wanted the chance to move on to greener pastures, but they were on the hook for the debt which was in both of their names. As a passionate believer in the potential of both Paddy and Oisin, Mizzoni wanted to ensure their careers could progress forward without the stain of a sinking start-up dragging them down. To achieve this, a deal was struck which involved her and Healy buying the debt of the company from Paddy and Oisin, in exchange for €1 for each young man.

On a cold winter's morning in January, I sat down with Paul Healy in a glass-walled extension of a house in Glenageary to chat about how Paddy and Oisin held the country to attention in 2009.

Healy, who at the time was crippled by his own debt arising from work that dried up after the crash, recalls needing to be convinced on the arrangement. 'I said, are you fucking mad?' he tells me. 'It was because I was in love with [Aine], and she's telling me this is what we're going to do … and in the end after twice round the garden I said, okay let's do it.'

The winter sun is falling on a corner of the garden behind us as Healy chats to me from the back of the home he's staying for the weekend, on dog sitting duties. Surrounded by mustard and navy-blue furniture, he squints through his glasses, as he pauses to reflect on what he describes as a foolish yet amazing venture.

Long before he had met Paddy or Oisin, or ran into business trouble during the crash, Healy had enjoyed considerable success during the early dotcom boom, making three-quarters of a million euros cashing out a small shareholding in JobFinder.ie. He then went on to amass a series of steady contracts as a self-employed internet project manager which earned him between €80k–100k a year. After this work dissipated when the crash came, his appetite for risk increased as a result and so the MiCandidate opportunity was seized with both hands.

Despite a business career marked by a series of gambles, some more and some less successful, Healy comes across as a very cautious individual. When I initially made contact with him prior to this meeting, he is reticent to speak and strictly stipulates the rules of engagement. But, like many of the voices in this book, he has a story to tell. So here we are, nine months later, sharing multiple cups of coffee in this house.

Healy is from Derry, but his accent has softened from years of living in Dublin. He has kind eyes and takes pride in the ambitious nature of MiCandidate, which strived to create and monetize a website in around three months.

'For me, hungry and looking for something to do, this had a lot of sense in it and in the bits that didn't have a lot of sense, like no money, no time, I was like, let's give it a go, what the hell,' he says. 'When we got into it, at end of January 2009, there was nothing, there was no office space, no people, just two mad young fellas with a crazy idea. So in that respect, as a piece of guerilla start-up, it was amazing, absolutely amazing.'

Healy is frank about the financial struggles, describing how when it all fell apart there were lists of creditors, many of them the young staffers who worked to get the venture off the ground. He says according to his memory it could have been up to a hundred people who came in to help after Paddy sent out mass emails looking for volunteers or interns. 'We filled that office with people, it was phenomenal,' he recalls. 'And out of that there was a small group, and I'm saying no more than fifteen, which had a payment relationship. It was small money, but not small money if you've got to pay your rent.'

To actually achieve what MiCandidate set out to do would have involved a minimum of 15 to 18 months, and in terms of selling it, Healy says they should have started a year out from the elections. 'The thought that a), you could build it was just bananas, in that time frame, and b), the thought you would sell profiles in it … and by the end of April, there's a website, that was … hickety,' he says. 'Technologically, it just wasn't good enough; it worked, but it wasn't good enough, and that's on me. Well, it's on me for being stupid enough to take it on and run with it in the time, but it just wasn't good enough and absolutely you could see why the *Irish Times* and RTE would go, we're not taking it.'

After he agreed to join Mizzoni in assuming the debt, the pair along with Paddy and Oisin sat around a table in October 2009, while the relevant documentation was exchanged. He recalls €2 in coins slid across the table toward the lads.

A few months later, Healy said he turned up to an early Web Summit event, which had been spun out of a MiCandidate conference that was originally called 'Digital Democracy' before switching to becoming the 'Dublin Web Summit'. It was June 2010, in the basement of the Chartered Accountants Ireland office on Pearse Street, and he says he was there to give Paddy, who was at a desk handing out lanyards, copies of some paperwork. But he had a bone to pick with his former business partner because he heard that Paddy had recently signed up as a consultant with Jolitics, a political social media site started by Michael Birch, the Bebo founder. To Healy, this was a potential breach of the non-compete clause in the contract Paddy signed when handing over the debt. Approaching the moment with 'righteous indignation' because he was now saddled with the company's debt, Healy questioned Paddy on the move.

'I said, you know Paddy, what the hell, you signed this agreement with a non-compete and I hear you're a consultant with Jolitics,' he says. 'And he looked me straight in the eye and said, sometimes you have to stab people in the back to get on.'

His next memory was standing there speechless. 'I looked at him and thought, fuck me, what am I dealing with here? What am I dealing with ... I have never met anyone like that in my business career who full frontal is telling you that you're scum to me, I'll just tread on you. And I was just that much of the story, like a little bit part, he might not even remember my name, but I just felt like wow ... I promised myself after that, not having said anything, that I would tell that story, again and again and again ... when you approached me, if that hadn't of happened, I would have said, nah, I'm not speaking with you, because all that stuff that went before, I'm proud of. It was foolish to get into it, but what we did was amazing, and what he did was amazing, and what Oisin did was amazing.'

With the debt handed over, Paddy and Oisin were free to forge new paths, with the latter moving to the USA shortly afterwards to begin an MBA at Harvard Business School before dropping out to found Handy, a wildly successful venture.

Both men would refer back to their departure from MiCandidate in ways which highlighted the serendipitous nature of the exit. Paddy tweeted in October 2009 that it was 'acquired in a management buyout' led by Healy. 'We exited MiCandidate for cash in a sale to one of its angel investors,' Oisin told the *Sunday Times* in 2014.

In a 2012 podcast, Paddy did acknowledge that those who took on MiCandidate were 'assuming all the debt that we had racked up'. 'So it wasn't in any way a good thing. People say failure is great; they're totally lying, that's absolute bullshit. Failure is probably the worst thing in the world,' Paddy said in a candid description of the experience.

Healy and Mizzoni ended up running most of the debt down by hanging on to a contract with RTBF, a Belgian broadcaster which found value in using MiCandidate to help demystify their complicated parliamentary system. The €15,000 deal was renewed for a few years before MiCandidate was eventually dissolved in 2018.

Looking back, Healy says the remarkable thing about his final encounter with Paddy was that it could have been so easily avoided. 'If he had said, ah shit, Paul I should have mentioned that, [but] it's only a social media site, there's no competition, you know, if he had justified it in some way … but the belittling that went on, I was like oh my god,' he says to me.

'What he has done is phenomenal, but there's just a certain side to him which is … not likeable.'

* * *

In the summer of 2009, Paddy travelled to the Aspect Hotel in Park West, 10 kilometres outside Dublin city. He was there to meet John Kennedy, then editor of Silicon Republic, an Irish tech news website, about the possibility of getting media coverage for an event he was planning to hold in the Autumn.

Kennedy was excited about the idea of well-known people in the tech world such as Jimmy Wales, founder of Wikipedia, coming to Ireland. He told Paddy to keep him posted on the plans and the pair parted ways after Paddy gave Kennedy a photocopy of an article on economics he had recently read in the *Guardian* newspaper.

A few weeks later, while sitting in his office, John recalls being summoned to the boardroom to find Paddy chatting with the publisher of Silicon Republic in what to him appeared to be a blatant attempt not to take a lukewarm promise as an answer.

Kennedy was unphased, chalking it up to generational differences, and what followed from these meetings was a working relationship between Silicon Republic and Web Summit events in the early years. In exchange for sharing content from the events online and promoting its work, Silicon Republic would get access to some of its high-profile speakers.

Paddy spent the next few months emailing and calling people in a scramble to firm up a list of speakers at a once-off event that October. Staged in the former Bewley's Hotel in Ballsbridge, now the Clayton, it was a one-day affair, lasting from 9 a.m. to 5 p.m., with content focused solely on how businesses can utilize the power of social media and 'online communication'. 'If you've ever wondered if you're getting the most from your online presence, or if you can do more, then why not join us?' its website stated.

A selling point of the event was that social media, and in particular Twitter, was still shrouded in a significant element of mystery for most people. Many of those who were online in Ireland all knew each other, and organized 'tweet-ups' to develop real-world relationships outside of the internet.

As his plans were coming together, Paddy had reached out to his old friend Daire Hickey, who at the time was working as a journalist with the *Irish Daily Mail*. He said 'the guys' he was organizing Dublin Web Summit with want someone to give Mark Little some 'sexy' questions.

'In short, make the 40-minute interviews punchy and exciting,' Paddy wrote on Google chat.

'Can't take time off to earn less ... you know how it is,' Daire replies.

'I'll just never understand it. You people and your jobs,' Paddy says. The pair then changed subjects to discuss a 'death mob' protest where 150 people collapsed simultaneously on South William Street.

'We should do one outside the Dail,' Paddy suggests.

Opening the conference was Eamon Ryan, TD and then Minister for Communications, with Anton Savage, managing director of the Communications Clinic, and Mark Little, then a journalist with RTE's *PrimeTime*, on MC-duties. Speakers included Alberto Nardelli, co-founder and CEO of Tweetminster, which began as a way for people to find MPs on Twitter. Sky News' Julian March, who had agreed to use MiCandidate earlier that year, attended as a speaker. So did Jimmy Leach, then online editorial director at Independent.co.uk and a head of digital communications at 10 Downing Street, working with prime ministers Tony Blair and Gordon Brown.

A few years prior Leach, while he was based in 10 Downing Street, had invited Paddy in after the pair connected with a shared interest in a voter outreach programme. Leach had been heavily involved in e-petitions, which allowed citizens to submit petitions to the prime minister's office. Leach describes it to me as a 'complaining device' which turned out to be 'quite successful' and became a 'poster child for digital democracy' around 2007.

'He had an endearing sheen ... there was almost like a religious fervency to the whole thing,' Leach says, reflecting on how he got to know Paddy.

When I ask if Paddy had got in touch to ask Leach for advice, he answers definitely not. After speaking at Web Summit that year, he says his interactions with Paddy tapered off over the years. 'I didn't think he thought I knew more than him,' he says, breaking into laughter. 'I never got that impression. I think it's typical, and I'm not bad mouthing him, there's a certain type of person who know and/or are convinced they're on the way up, and they will use people as part of that network, as part of that ladder.'

Paddy was said to be extremely tense before the first Web Summit event. When he walked out to chat with some attendees during a break in the day, someone there recalls him being proclaimed 'the nation's favorite intern' by Paul Hayes, a tech PR veteran, who would go on to play a big role in Web Summit's early years.

Although it was small and a relatively low-key affair that seemed to come together in a rush, the first Web Summit was successful in getting Paddy's name out among wider media and tech circles. It also showed that Dublin could be a place where people with power and influence would come to share their ideas, and that there was a way to do that without paying them a hefty speaking fee.

Jimmy Wales also made an appearance in Dublin later that year to become an honorary member of the Phil. Paddy got him to give a lecture in Trinity's Ed Burke Theatre, which became a regular stomping ground for early Web Summit events.

There was a momentum building behind these events and an emerging theme that the tech community in Ireland was not one to be overlooked. Whether by accident or design, by late 2009 Paddy was ready, armed with 270 Twitter followers and a bio that read 'Social Media Charlatan, Quack Economist, Chancer, Leg Puller', to spin himself out and big himself up to more of the world's most powerful people.

This time, the focus was the shiny buildings rising up from Dublin's docklands and tech bros thirsty for an excuse to travel to Ireland.

Paddy routinely discussed Web Summit's origin story in media interviews or onstage at events in the company's early years, but some details and dates changed with time. Part of this was because the early months and years of the company unfolded in ways that even his wildest ambitions could not have predicted. Each event was built on top of the momentum of the last event and in a way they all developed into what became the Web Summit brand.

For many years, the first-ever Web Summit was referred to by Paddy as being the one held in Dublin in 2010 which featured some of the industry's big heavy-hitters at the time, including Chad Hurley from YouTube, Jack Dorsey who co-founded Twitter, Michael Birch of Bebo, Niklas Zennstrom, co-founder of Skype, and Divyank Turakhia, co-founder of Directi. He drew this distinction because he was saying that Web Summit itself grew out of F.ounders, an exclusive invite only event the team also organized and which ran alongside the conference.

The 2010 event was undoubtedly the one which put Web Summit on the map and which drew huge media attention. It followed on from a year of hosting a collection of small events in tiny rooms as part of the 'Dublin Web Summit', which is what the Web Summit was known as in its infancy.

But there has also been more than a whisper of tension about when exactly the first ever Web Summit was held. In a 2012 marketing email which originated from his p@ websummit.net email address (he and many other staffers owned numerous Web Summit domain names for email addresses), Paddy said the company 'all started in 2010 when 600 tech folk showed up for a one-day event'.

The reference to 2010 being the first ever Web Summit was repeated throughout the early years of the company. In a February 2014 blog post on the company's website, it's stated that 2010 was the year the 'first ever Web Summit' was launched, yet the company's 'About Us' section of its current website states it began in 2009 with a 150-person conference.

Paddy would also refer to the 2010 Web Summit as the first one, in interviews and on social media for years after the company was founded, but has at various points become insistent that 2009 was the only accurate year of origin.

There is of course a PR angle to making 2009 the indisputably correct year of origin, in that it's more impressive to note that you started with only 150, as opposed to 600, attendees and have in more recent times attracted over 70,000.

And as Web Summit transitioned from its first event in a hotel ballroom into a behemoth of a conference machine, a tactical PR strategy was one of its most valuable assets.

Chapter 4

STACK 'EM HIGH, SELL 'EM CHEAP

Less than two weeks after the Dublin Web Summit in 2010, Paddy emailed Daire with an offer which would change the course of both men's lives forever.

'I think there is an opportunity to make a life changing amount of money, grow something quite remarkable, see the world, meet some incredible people and have a lot of fun doing it,' Paddy began in the email. With 'Call me to go through' in the subject line, the email contained details of how it was proposed that they would go into business together, including how much of a salary Daire would draw down and how much equity he would have a stake in.

The email followed on from discussions Paddy and Dave had been having in August of that year about their official foray into becoming business partners. At the time, Dave and Paddy were living together in a house on Manders Terrace, in Ranelagh, an affluent suburb south of Dublin city. In their discussions, Dave and Paddy hashed out the finer points about the business agreements they were planning to enter into. Dave outlined a number of conditions that could be attached to their agreement depending on whether the business was sold in the coming years or whether one of them walked away from it. He said he was confident he could bring value to both F.ounders and Dublin Web Summit 'but obviously it's your decision'.

'We really need to be as open and transparent at this stage,' Dave wrote to Paddy. 'Slight niggles can mushroom into massive issues.'

Paddy said he thought Dave's proposals were 'pretty damn fair and reasonable'. 'Now let's get rocking and rolling – and make some serious cash,' he added.

The Dublin Web Summit and F.ounders companies, the predecessor companies to what is now a company called Manders Terrace (named after the house where they lived), were incorporated later that year. Records filed in the Companies Registration Office (CRO) show that Dave was made a company director on 7 November 2010 and that Joseph Cosgrave, Paddy's brother, resigned as a director on the same day. Along with his brother Joe, Anna Cosgrave, Paddy's sister, was a big part of the work in establishing the early Web Summit events, especially those in 2010 and subsequent years. She would later go on to become a well-known figure in her own right as a result of her activism during the campaign to liberalize Ireland's abortion laws in 2018, including creating the wildly popular 'Repeal' jumpers.

In early 2010 Chris Newmark, founder of Craigslist, Matt Mullenweg, founder of WordPress, and Ben Hammersley, editor of *Wired*, spoke at Trinity College. The stand-alone event was marketed as the 'Dublin Web Summit 2.0' and for €90 attendees were told they could hear the men speak about important lessons they learned scaling their companies. Chris Horn, a well-known computer scientist and founder of IONA Technologies, a software company, also presented on the experiences for Irish entrepreneurs building companies at home. Unlike the first Web Summit event in 2009 which was focused exclusively on harnessing the power of social media, this event gathered multiple founders to discuss their experiences of establishing companies.

It was a content pivot for Paddy, who realized that having well-known speakers ruminate more broadly on their lives was better suited to attracting attendees, especially those in the tech sector. And although it was a relatively small affair in a lecture hall in Trinity College, the event secured a headline sponsor in DoneDeal as well as partnership deals with Enterprise Ireland and KPMG.

At the end of June 2010, another event was held with Michael Birch, founder of Bebo, Mike Butcher, editor of *Tech Crunch Europe*, and Ray Nolan, the co-founder of Hostelworld. This time the conference had moved to the Chartered Accountants House on Pearse Street which had officially opened the year before.

Dave Kelly, who was unemployed and living with Paddy in Manders Terrace, decided to help out. Shortly before the June event, Daire, who was working as a freelance journalist and writing for the *Mail on Sunday* at the time, messaged Paddy that he was going to write a piece about the event for the newspaper. 'Gimme a few worthy names,' he said.

Later that year, Paddy messaged Daire to ask if he would also help out with the event scheduled for the following month. 'I would like to hire your expert services for two days in the second week of October and for the entire last week of October,' Paddy said.

In a piece about how they made it all happen in 2012, VentureBeat said the three founders were 'a self-described failed entrepreneur, freelance journalist and unemployed asset manager'.

Daire said, at the time, he was 'chasing property developers around the place' for the newspaper when Paddy told him he had managed to convince the founders of YouTube, Skype and Twitter to come to Dublin. 'Paddy wanted people speaking on gaming and PHP [an open source programming language] and mobile, and I was meant to run all of this and I had no idea about any of these things,' Hickey says. 'But I did convince a lot of media to come to Dublin. There was one point where I turned to Paddy and said we are going to fuck up on a major scale in front of the world's media and they will all be there going, "What the fuck happened? How did we get here? This is the worst event ever!" We would be embarrassed for evermore.'

Along with being the biggest event so far, that year's Web Summit also managed to secure some of the most high-profile speakers in the tech industry worldwide. These included Jack Dorsey, founder of Twitter, Chad Hurley, founder of YouTube, and Niklas Zennstrom of Skype. The significance of founders like Hurley and Dorsey taking time out of their schedules to come to Dublin, which was still reeling from the financial crash, spoke volumes about the potential for Ireland to solidify itself as a location to do business.

Part of the October conference was dubbed a 'How to Summit' which offered masterclasses for start-ups, investors and developers for €250. 'Things are changing,' the company's website said. 'We're moving from a 3-hour event to a 12-hour event; from an average of 8 speakers to

50 speakers; from an event filled with inspiration to an event filled with incredibly hands on and incredibly practical masterclasses; from a single networking opportunity to multiple networking opportunities.'

Also running alongside the conference was the first-ever F.ounders, the exclusive invite only event marketed to the founders and other well-known figures in the tech world. That year, a drinks reception was held in the Westbury Hotel for the speakers and some leading figures in the Irish tech world. The crawl went up Grafton Street to Merrion Row and Baggot Street, stopping at well-known establishments like Toners and O'Donoghue's. The quality of the Guinness was touted to the celebrity guests, but Dorsey was not tempted, asking for a glass of tap water at each location and rarely cracking a smile with his tipsy pub crawl companions.

The city was buzzing with Web Summit events, and the chance to rub elbows with a Silicon Valley tech bro was an enticing possibility for young Irish people in tech. With only a few hundred attendees and events held at various venues around the city, it was also not outside the realm of possibilities that a techie without a ticket could weasel their way into the action.

Stephen O'Regan, son of Paddy's former mentor, was one of those looking for a chance to have his big break. He had co-founded Balcony TV, a platform for emerging artists to share videos (of them playing music on a Dublin balcony), around four years earlier and thought that if he could connect with someone like Hurley he could find a way to capitalize off YouTube's success. Google had bought YouTube in 2006 for $1.65 billion and Hurley continued to head up the platform since the sale.

O'Regan tells me over a phone call in mid-2023 that after arriving at Mansion House for an invite-only dinner hosted as part of F.ounders, he spotted a table plan with the various assigned seats for attendees. 'I saw where Chad was sitting and I decided to go up to the table and rearrange the names so I put myself sitting right next to Chad Hurley,' he recalls. 'Eventually I built up the confidence and I said to Chad wouldn't you just rather go to some Irish pubs and check out the nightlife in Dublin? And he said yeah, that is what I'd like to do.'

After a bar-crawl that ended with shots of tequila at 3 a.m. in the Workman's Club, O'Regan said he eventually exchanged email addresses with Hurley and woke up hungover but excited by the possibilities he had opened up for himself. 'I thought, wow, this is good, this is amazing! I'm going to email and we're gonna go for coffee, and I'm gonna take my little YouTube concept to the next level,' O'Regan says. Unfortunately for O'Regan, the news which broke that morning was that Hurley was stepping down as CEO of YouTube.

Even if they did not always end in a business partnership, these meetings were exactly the kinds of encounter that Web Summit wanted to promote to its attendees. It was a few years before Dorsey would become a billionaire when he brought Twitter public, but he and Hurley's status in the tech industry was still understood by many.

In simplifying it for viewers who may not have heard of a platform like Twitter, RTE's coverage stated: 'These big thinkers, all under forty years of age, are collectively worth hundreds of millions of dollars.'

After the two-day conference, Dorsey, Birch and Paddy appeared as guests on the *Late Late Show*, the most watched television chat show in Ireland. Paddy was asked about the concept of failing and said that in other parts of the world it was seen as a 'badge of honour'. 'In Ireland we don't just have a cultural issue and problem with it, and that also extends into the rest of Europe, we also have legislation that doesn't really help, bankruptcy laws which are incredibly punitive,' he told presenter Ryan Tubridy.

Why speakers like Jack Dorsey or Chad Hurley voluntarily chose to travel to Dublin for a small event that was largely unheard of has often been regarded as a bit of a mystery in Web Summit's history. But Paddy played the numbers game, emailing every famous founder he could find a contact for and organizing as many calls as possible. Crucially, he and Daire also relied on help from their friends in the Philosophical Society at Trinity to secure Dorsey and other early Web Summit guests.

In practice, this meant that a speaker like Dorsey was invited to receive some form of honorary award and speak at the Phil, tempted by its long legacy of great speakers. When a founder like Dorsey said yes to the Phil, Paddy or Daire would then be informed and promptly send out the Web Summit invitation. 'They'd be like, oh well, of course I'll speak at the technology conference because I happen to be in Ireland,' Daire described the bait and switch years later. 'If somebody had more than one reason to come then they are more likely to come.'

The method was simple, but it worked extremely well and this strategy ended up becoming the one which would radically change Dublin's reputation as a meeting point for the tech community. As the years went on, Daire and Paddy taught the team the skills they honed during their time as President of the Phil to convince people to come talk without paying them a dime.

Everyone, of course, has an angle. And there is both a business and pleasure case to be made for a trip to Ireland. For the star-studded 2010 conference there was a strong business case to be made to both Hurley and Dorsey. As chief of a platform owned by Google, a trip to Dublin could also act as a way for Hurley to visit the international HQ of his parent company. For Dorsey, the trip came shortly after he had been pushed out of his role as CEO of Twitter in 2008 and while he was working to build up his reputation as a well-known founder.

Although he rarely gave interviews after returning to Twitter as executive chairman in 2011, Dorsey did a big media push after his ousting in outlets like the *New York Times* and the *Los Angeles Times*. He was also on a PR tour to promote Square, a digital payments firm he founded in 2009. Less than a year after his Dublin visit, and following his return to the platform, Twitter opened its own international headquarters in the Irish capital. There was also a genealogical angle to exploit given that both founders have Irish heritage and Paddy hammed up a line about how Dorsey's surname was originally Darcy but the spelling was changed over time.

At a final dinner to mark the end of that year's F.ounders, Tariq Krim, founder of Jolicloud, reportedly stormed the stage to announce that it was 'the best event I've ever been to'. After a few years of failures and trying to find their way in the world, things finally looked like they were turning around for Paddy, Daire and Dave. Indeed, the company would grow and scale so rapidly after 2010 that it would outgrow two offices in around two years. That expansion brought responsibilities that all three men were unprepared for, and which exposed cracks in an already fragile foundation.

As Web Summit was becoming a 'stack 'em high, sell 'em cheap, get as many people in as possible' event, F.ounders was the company's way to 'bribe' high-rollers into coming. This was how one person who worked on events during the early years of the company explained it to me.

From exclusive receptions in parts of Trinity College Dublin that are not open to the public (and which the Americans loved to refer to as 'Hogwarts') to dinners in the crypt of Christchurch Cathedral, five-star hotel stays and scenic trips, F.ounders presented Dublin on a platter as a playground for the rich.

As it was discovering how to pack more lavish events into a two-day window, a spin-off event aimed at mocking the entire charade was born. 'Flounders', so-called because it was about celebrating failed founders, was the brainchild of Paul Hayes, Noel Toolan, the marketing genius behind Baileys and Tourism Ireland, Pat Phelan, a businessman best known for his Sisu chain of beauty clinics, and around half a dozen others. It began after a group of them were refused entry to an exclusive Web Summit dinner in Trinity and decided to walk across the street to drink copious amounts of wine in Dunne and Crescenzi, an intimate Italian restaurant on South Frederick Street. They were annoyed because a free dinner in exchange for help with the conference was expected, but their irritation was soon drowned out by Burrata, Chianti, and perfectly room temperature salami.

Hayes is probably the most affable man in Irish tech: his gift of the gab is delivered at lightning speed and topped off with a deep belly laugh that is quite contagious. The charm comes from being a mixture of disarmingly self-deprecating (he describes his body type as 'built by chefs') and astutely socially aware.

Under his leadership, although he maintains that it was a disorganized annual wine-fuelled escapade, Flounders quickly took on a life of its own. Along with becoming a calendar event at every year's Web Summit for a decade, it also introduced a new concept to business-themed get-togethers: being comfortable with failure. This was because the only rule it operated was that attendees must regale the room with a story of their own failure. Having skin thick enough to withstand Hayes roasting them in front of their peers was a bonus.

'The drunken evolution of it was, well, if we're not good enough for F.ounders, or whatever it was, we'd become Flounders,' Hayes tells me, sitting in the Dunne and Crescenzi dining room where it all began.

He recalls that they played tennis in the street outside the restaurant during one Flounders session. 'I'm not entirely sure, did we call it that that night or did we retrospectively decide it was the club for failed founders,' he adds. No-one involved can seem to recall the exact month and year of the first event, either, but they agree that they did play street tennis outside the restaurant at some point.

Wearing a paddy cap and coming from a busy morning of meetings, two of which took place in this restaurant, Hayes is in good spirits. He jokes that he went out to lunch the previous day at Montys of Kathmandu, a Nepalese restaurant in Temple Bar which has 'the best wine list in the country', according to the winos he dined with. It turned into a 'lunner', or 'when lunch becomes dinner' he explains when I look puzzled. 'I don't know my wine, but these guys know their wines, and I'm happy enough to go along for the ride.'

Along with stories of failure, the discussions also involved prompts like 'tell us the worst idea you've ever come up with' or 'bad start-up ideas', Hayes recalls. The latter prompt, he regretfully recalls, turned into a premonition.

'Jesus Christ, people were pitching things like, you know, Ring.com a year early, and then next year it was happening,' he says laughing. 'You know, *I think it should be a mobile bell that can follow you around*, and we'd all laugh at them, [then] it happens! I think it was like that cycle in Silicon Valley where it was like, "well that's what we're doing now". And so it became very lovely, let-off-steam, a nice mix. And we would sometimes declare people Flounders, but it was never really formal.'

The gatherings spawned spin-off events like 'Startup Wake' which Hayes says came about after the intervention of Declan Ryan, son of Ryanair founder Tony Ryan and managing partner of Irelandia Aviation. 'He came along and said, I love flounders, but you're all way too drunk and it's way too unstructured. There's actually something here … he said you should actually make it a wake, you should bury them, and so we did,' Hayes recalls.

The fun continued for many years and in many forms, including a party on a boat on the Liffey which Hayes recalls the group nearly sinking.

Paddy occasionally showed up to Flounders events where he was mocked by Hayes and other hosts. 'In fairness to him, I would take the absolute piss out of him and he would take it,' Hayes says. Those who attended said nothing was off limits and Paddy faced mocking for his hair, his clothes, his tweets and his general personality.

But the worst roasting was reserved for Mark Little, the former RTE *Prime Time* presenter who went on to found Storyful, a verification newswire service he sold to Rupert Murdoch's News Corp for €18 million. At a more recent Flounders event, Hayes was warming up the crowd with jokes about Ireland's recently announced €2 billion 'rainy day fund'. 'And Mark happened to walk in, and I said there it is, Ireland is now the Mark Little of Countries: keeps succeeding, has no idea how,' Hayes says, laughing uncontrollably. 'But I love him, he's a founder flounder ... he's very supportive as well, and just a lovely, lovely man, which they all aren't.'

Hayes has hired multiple former Web Summit staffers to work for Beachhut, his tech PR company, and he often jokes that his firm was 'a methadone stepdown clinic' for media professionals who worked for Paddy. 'It's like, okay, you've had your "tour of Nam", let's re-enter you into normal society. And they were great, they were so well versed ... and the last positive thing I'll say about Paddy, in fairness to him, all this stuff about, "oh, he left because he didn't get what he wanted whatever". He stayed here two years longer than he should have. He was building a Potemkin village down in the RDS every year!'

As much as the early years were a rollercoaster for the Web Summit founders and those in the Irish scene who could ride its coattails, things have turned sour between Hayes and Paddy in recent years. He said this began when Paddy began attacking long-time friends of his online. These included Pascal Donohoe, a Fine Gael TD and minister, who Paddy has repeatedly lambasted online.

Insults have included that he's a 'spoofer', a 'lapdog to vulture [funds]', 'a pushover', 'the little rascal', 'the clown emoji' and others. These occurred at various points over the years, including in January 2023 when Donohoe was under fire over €1,057 paid to a friend to erect election posters in 2016.

Hayes also found it hard to watch Paddy attacking Brian Caulfield, an entrepreneur and VC investor who is hugely well-respected in the Irish tech community. Caulfield, who was a judge at early Web Summit events, was accused by Paddy of having 'turned a blind eye' to illegal activity. This tweet appeared to come out of nowhere and only a couple of years prior Paddy was posting messages of support and admiration for the man he was now denouncing.

As an example of how his legal disputes have bled into nearly every relationship he had, the content related to Caulfield's refusal to cut ties with Paddy's co-founders and other enemies. It was met with dozens of tweets supporting Caulfield and denouncing Paddy. There is no suggestion of illegality on Caulfield's part.

For Hayes, the last few years have seen too many people 'caught in crossfires they don't need to be caught in'. He said it seemed like Paddy began attacking people for the sake of it, or to score points among his followers, with no regard for the hurt it was causing to those in the firing line. He said he could also not recognize the Ireland that Paddy regularly castigated online, saying the country had plenty of problems but was a far cry from 'downtown Beirut'.

'God forgive me to Beirut,' he said. '[He's] just a socialist, revolutionary, on the streets, corporate lover in the sheets, so it was like please just be consistent between the two.'

'Web Summit was made by him, and it was made in spite of him at the same time. Like, could it have been different? It's so sad, all the recriminations that are happening now. I'm just really saddened by it.'

When an extremely long box arrived at the Web Summit office in the summer of 2012, a few of the company's staff had a suspicion about what it contained. There was also a slight apprehension about what its contents would mean for productivity given that it arrived in the middle of one of the busiest and most important years for the fledgling conference company.

The team had only just moved from a tiny office in a Georgian building on Herbert Street into a series of converted office units in the Mount Pleasant Business Park in Ranelagh. And in an attempt to quickly scale up the business, the summer months were packed with meetings and staff were double or triple jobbing to prepare for Web Summit that year, which would scale up from around 1,500 to over 4,000 attendees.

Talks were underway ahead of the creation of Manders Terrace, the parent company for Web Summit, which would be officially incorporated in a few months' time. Daire, David and Paddy would also incorporate companies that year through which to hold their shares.

So in 2012, at least from the outside, things were looking positive even if the scrappy start-up was only finding its feet. The business was truly growing up: it had established itself as a brand and took on full-time staff who would become its earliest employees. As a result of this modest success, each of the founders increased their salaries and the company rebranded from the 'Dublin Web Summit' to the 'Web Summit', an indication that expanding beyond Ireland was already being floated. The profits for the company were also on an upwards trajectory and projected to rise steadily into low six-figure sums.

Paddy was in receipt of some glowing praise from well-known business figures, including from Mark Ryan, then managing director of Accenture, who told RTE radio's *Marian Finucane Show* in February of that year that the founder was 'a fantastic individual'.

'Paddy Cosgrave could easily have left this country and be doing things in other countries as we speak, but he has decided to stay here,' Ryan said.

Web Summit was also hitting its stride in terms of filling out the RDS for its second year there and Paddy told the *Irish Times* before the October 2012 event that a number of the Dublin 4 hotels were already booked out. Speakers that year included Stripe's Patrick Collison, Skype's Niklas Zennstrom and David Shing, then a senior marketing executive of AOL. 'People are coming because there's interesting speakers from all over the world,' Paddy said in an interview leading up to the event.

'If you're into Twitter, or Facebook, or Google, or YouTube and you're wondering, how can these technologies help your business, what's the next big opportunity, "what might I be missing?", then all of the key guys from all of those companies are here,' he added.

By all accounts it was clear skies ahead for the business. So why would the presence of an unusually shaped box in the office make a difference at all? The reason was because it contained a javelin, a two-and-a-half-metre spear thrown in track and field sporting events. Paddy had recently become obsessed with the hobby and chatted about purchasing one for a number of weeks. He told his colleagues that he intended to train to compete in the sport at the 2016 summer Olympics in Rio de Janeiro. The reason, he explained, was that he had researched the results of Irish athletes competing in throwing sports like the javelin and was confident he could beat them. Javelin has not been a sport for Team Ireland since the 1990s when Terence McHugh was competing in the Olympics, although he never made it to the final round.

Paddy thought becoming the nation's latest javelin-throwing success story was an open goal, and so he set about training as often as possible. Not content with keeping a hobby to himself, he decided to use his javelin practice sessions as a mentoring opportunity with the company's interns. A day trip was organized where Paddy took turns throwing the javelin and dishing out business advice to the recent graduates. The spear was occasionally retrieved by an obliging intern, who was rewarded with a book recommendation or an anecdote.

To the dismay of his colleagues, Paddy took to the sport and before long was 'actually pretty good' but his hopes of Olympic glory were not to be, as he quickly tired of the hobby. 'The thing about Paddy is that he is delusional, but he is also quite talented, so he was, at first, more than you would expect someone picking up the javelin, he was quite good at it,' a source said.

'And I think that's probably the story of Paddy's life, he picks up something, he is better than average, but then he puts it back down again, or whatever else ...' they added.

Despite what from the outside looked like a promising road ahead, the energy in the office at the time was intense and erratic. It wavered between being extremely positive about the company's future, to panicked and paranoid about whether plans would materialize. By this stage, there had been numerous blazing rows in the office, doors slammed by both Paddy and Dave (and in at least one instance, broken) and staplers thrown in anger.

Issues which caused particular stress were said to be table plans, which Paddy believed held the power to change the world, and people being Cc'd instead of Bcc'd on an email. A former staffer recalled that Paddy once played music on a speaker outside a room he was holding a private meeting in to drown out any potential sound getting out. They said they were asked by Paddy after if they were listening in.

Operating within an air of uncertainty and with the threat of failure positioned around every corner was not a place Dave Kelly was comfortable working in. In many ways his cautious approach to life and aversion to risk were part of what made the business partnership between him and Paddy work. But by 2012, cracks were beginning to show in that relationship which spelled early warning signs for the pair.

A May 2012 email sent by Dave to himself hints at some of the issues which were on his mind at the time. It began with the line 'Tr.igger.it', a reference to a ticketing platform that Web Summit launched that summer in private beta, meaning only a limited number of people could access it.

Including nine numbered points, it said, 'difficult for us to be massively motivated to run something whole, not have massive equity while you do something and make decisions that impact us'.

'You owe us something – two years and no massive financial gain. Sure we have made connections but we have facilitated your ascendency ... we all have strengths +

weaknesses ... let's be honest. I am not the best seller, can be grumpy, bad delegator ... own situation crap, lack of confidence, slightly socially awkward,' the email stated.

'Big weakness of business is everything goes through you and it's impossible to stay on top. We have to aspire for perfection ... Not here to point fingers. I think we all want the same thing. The business follows the following patterns crisis to crisis,' it added.

The details of the email are often cryptic and while they relate to issues on his mind at one isolated moment in time, many of the concerns, especially that Paddy strived for a level of perfection which others found unachievable, were repeated in years to come.

In his personal life, 2012 was also the year that Paddy got engaged to Faye Dinsmore, a young model from Donegal. Evidence of her star power at the time was demonstrated by the fact that it was her engagement the media reported on, with Paddy described only as her 'techy boyfriend'.

'Ireland's top model is officially off the market after Faye Dinsmore got engaged to her long-term boyfriend,' the *Evening Herald* reported. She reportedly celebrated by being 'whisked off to Milan for a photoshoot'.

Repped by the same agency as Gisele Bundchen and Kate Moss, Faye had already walked runways in New York and Paris, been the face of Galaxy chocolate, graced the pages of international magazines and was immortalized in fibreglass as a Rootstein mannequin, which appeared in fashion storefronts. She had also appeared dressed as a sexy bunny rabbit in the music video for Robbie Williams' 2009 single 'You Know Me', which featured her fellow dancers swinging on oversized carrots.

A former Assets model turned high-fashion aficionado, Faye was probably the closest thing Ireland had to a super-model at the time, and she knew it too. Throwing a few salty jibes at 'girls in bikinis at press launches', she told the *Irish Independent* a couple of years earlier that while pageants equal glamour, glamour does not equal fashion. 'It's just the way the world is,' she is quoted as saying, referring to Rosanna Davidson's career as a 'mixed blessing'.

'I never got to become an Irish promotion model but I still harbour ambitions to one day stand proudly at the top of Grafton Street, maybe in a sash if I am really lucky, as an icon for Irish women,' Faye said.

'Hopefully, for the sake of Irish women everywhere, with the help of the *Sunday Independent* or some other enlightened bastion of progressive change leading the charge ... we'll get to a bikini-less utopia. Until then, we're stuck in a bygone era long past in Britain, France and elsewhere.'

She was not the only model that Paddy dated in his youth – numerous sources said he went on a few dates with a woman who is now an Instagram influencer. And although she may be profoundly out of his league on a physical level, those who knew her said Faye was canny in her own way – and in a way that some felt was far less obvious than Paddy's attempts to ingratiate himself with the world.

'Most of Paddy's speeches he practises on me and all the taxi drivers in Dublin! So I know where he is coming from ... I really admire the way he takes a stand on so many issues,' she said in an interview years later.

Despite evidence of her success in endless magazine

covers, the one fact which was repeated in many media interviews at the time was that she was the 'most popular Irish person on Facebook'. This conclusion was reached because she had more Facebook followers than any other Irish person, with Jonathan Rhys Meyers, Ronan Keating and Pierce Brosnan among those she is cited as having conquered in popularity.

Her Facebook page was linked to a blog, set up with help from Paddy, which had a large banner on the homepage saying: 'Follow Faye on Facebook – Over 200,000 fans.' The rumour at the time, and which continues to be repeated to this day, was that Paddy had purchased the followers for Faye's dedicated 'fan page'. (This claim was made unprompted by a number of people over the course of researching this book despite them all acknowledging it was unsubstantiated.)

Her blog also had a cutout picture of her toy dog named Coco Rockman Papillon with a quote that the animal was 'famed for no fewer than three editorials during her time in Paris'. The origin story of how she got the toy dog, according to how she described it to the *Sunday Independent*'s 'Life' section, was that she purchased it from a homeless man in Paris in 2009. While in the French capital for modelling work, she 'became a muse of sorts for Sonia Rykiel', then a 79-year-old fashion designer. On her way home from a job, she saw a homeless man with three dogs at a metro station and 'bought one of the dogs'. Coco would later go on to live with Paddy's family in Wicklow. 'She has a wonderful life there,' Faye told the paper.

Her relationship with Paddy has been a source of curiosity for many years, especially since she went from being an extremely public figure to one that enjoyed the quiet life.

'I had my first job when I was 12 so I had never really been at home before. That shook me a bit, that feeling that you are not really doing anything, even though you are,' she said years later, when describing motherhood.

She seemed to slowly give up modelling in Web Summit's early years, and staffers recall her regularly appearing listlessly in the office on occasion.

'The Faye project' became code among early Web Summit staff for the various initiatives Paddy would seek to encourage on his new fiancée. Over the years, these were said to include language classes, Pilates lessons, and a stop smoking course.

Chapter 5

'ANYONE NOT ENVISIONING A LATE NIGHT SHOULD CHECK OUT PUBLICJOBS.IE'

Just a few weeks after Paddy and Faye's engagement in the late spring of 2012, F.ounders would host its first event in the USA with a series of invite-only events at Nasdaq's Market Site in Times Square. Paddy would then be on the road as Web Summit embarked on a tour of Europe as part of a 'tech crawl' across the continent which involved stops in Amsterdam, Paris, Brussels, Munich, Hamburg, Copenhagen and other cities.

The F.ounders pub crawl involved Paddy standing on some form of elevated surface in a European bar and saying a few words about Web Summit to a semi-tipsy, overwhelmingly male crowd. It began in London and abided by a brutal schedule of one city per night for two weeks, with around '100 interesting tech folk' invited to come join the company for a drink.

'The goal is to ditch the office in favour of a pint in the sun with a diverse selection of peers,' its now defunct website stated. 'We're also hoping to visit the offices of great start-ups, incubators and co-working spaces, using your WiFi as we please. No seriously, have you seen how much roaming costs?' it added.

Considering that they were planned on a shoestring budget, the trips gathered a modest crowd in each European city, but numbers were embarrassingly low for the Belfast event planned at the end of June. To rectify this, a minibus was rented to drive around a dozen Web Summit staff, interns included, to the Belfast event for the evening and then drive them back down that night.

During the pub crawl, Paddy was said to have been invited to visit his pal, Skype's Niklas Zennstrom, in his native Sweden. Zennstrom was becoming a regular feature of Web Summit events, including speaking earlier that year at the London Web Summit. The London Web Summit was done in conjunction with Mike Butcher, editor of Tech Crunch and another long-time friend of the conference and Paddy.

Butcher had attended the exclusive invite-only F.ounders event the previous year and had the time of his life, according to a blog he wrote in the days after the event. He met Bono, partied, in the Guinness Storehouse, attended a reception, drank until 8 a.m. and trashed someone's hotel room.

'Who said Tech wasn't the new Rock 'n' Roll?' Butcher wrote about his escapades.

Attendees at that F.ounders event were also given a signed copy of the Che Guevara pop-art image, created by Irish artist Jim Fitzpatrick, which was made from tiny pictures of Steve Jobs.

'The symbolism was not lost on the crowd of revolutionary technology entrepreneurs who were told by Fitzpatrick that they could only ever sell the print to other "revolutionaries",' Butcher said.

Standing about a foot shorter than Paddy but with even more boundless energy, Butcher and Paddy made for a visually interesting duo onstage together. As for Zennstrom, he is said to be quite soft spoken for a man who towers nearly 6 ft 6 tall. In 2012, along with hanging out with Paddy in Sweden, he would also bestow the Web Summit team with laptop cases made from the sails of his boat, speak at the London event, and then at the main event in Dublin that October where he was guided by a full-time 'handler'.

The one-day London event was held in the Brewery, a venue near the Barbican, and featured partners like Blackberry, maker of a mobile device then in its heyday with over 80 million subscribers. PayPal and Enterprise Ireland, the Irish government-backed venture capital fund, were also partners of the event.

Paddy was also proudly wearing the green jersey throughout the 2012 events. Speaking to Bank of Ireland's All About Business team for a YouTube segment, he said he knew there were people out there who were critical of Enterprise Ireland, but he had first-hand insight into both the agency and similar ones around the world. 'I can honestly say there is no organization that I have come across in the world that is better than Enterprise Ireland in supporting start-ups,' he said that year. By contrast, years later he would describe the relationship between Web Summit and Enterprise Ireland as a 'cold war' in which he was spurned because he publicly criticized the agency.

* * *

Back in the office after the pub crawl around Europe, tensions were rising as the date of that year's Web Summit approached. An event in Miami had been in the works, but despite extensive planning it never materialized.

Throughout the summer, the days began to melt into an exhausting mix of early mornings and late nights.

On 17 July, at 1.50 a.m., Paddy sent an email to the entire office saying that for the second night in a row he and Tony Ennis, then the chief technology officer, were 'hustling' late into the night.

'I'll be up again before 7 a.m. working on some emails, posts and more. And Tony might not even sleep tonight,' the email, with 'IMPORTANT: It's 1.50 a.m.' in the subject line, stated. It went on to name-drop staffers Paddy said had been working similar hours, including one developer who 'shouldn't even be answering my emails and working on updates at midnight, but he is'.

'You can work like most people until the day you retire for the sake of an unremarkable career marked only by a middling impact on your company, never mind the world; alternatively, you can work your socks off to build something that defines a generation and that leaves an incredible impact,' Paddy said in the late-night missive.

'That takes an extra mile. It takes drive. And I know everyone in this office has that drive, applied at the right time. Now, by the way, is the right time. I wouldn't have spent all those weeks reading CVs, ringing references, doing endless interviews, debating and pondering, if I wasn't certain. If I wasn't certain of the ability of each and every one of you to do incredible things as individuals and as part of a team not because you are obliged to, but because you want to. See you tomorrow.'

Waking up to the email was overwhelming for some staff, especially those who were not named as being among the select group of hard workers. It was also difficult not to regard the practice of sending late-night emails as some sort of test; an attempt to highlight that there were people going above and beyond in ways which had not been previously anticipated.

The choice of whether to respond to them or not was one which plagued more than a handful of Web Summit staffers over the years. For those who did, the praise that arrived in the immediate aftermath was addictive, but moments in the glory of Paddy's good books can be fleeting. As a result, those who threw themselves into their roles, as many did, found that their confidence was directly linked to their position in the workplace pecking order.

This was not a trait exclusive to Paddy either: a number of other long-serving staff said that being within a close radius of any of the founders could be a recipe for disaster.

'Fly too close to the sun and you'll get burned,' was how one person phrased it. And over the years, there were many scorched wings.

In many ways this was par for the course for new entrants in many industries, but what made Web Summit unique was that the line between founder and staffer felt very thin. By 2012, the concept of the annual conference had been around for three years, but the company was only beginning to regularize itself legally and financially.

Considering that all of the staff at this time were millennials who had left college at the cusp of a financial recession, hard work and graft were expected in order to command a full-time salary. It was also clear that while many of their peers went into big tech companies, marketing agencies or financial firms, choosing to get a start at Web Summit was about more than just earning a tidy wage. A number of staff in the early years believed in the company and its potential as much if not more than the founders. And even those who didn't, because some did think it would burn bright and fade out fast, were still motivated by the passion of their colleagues.

But passion and energy can only take a person so far, especially when they are acutely aware that the company and its future is not under their direct control.

The following weeks and months leading up to Web Summit 2012 were full of mounting stressors. Then in September things came to a head when a casual email from the office manager to staff said: 'If anyone is envisioning a late night could they let me know and I'll order some food for them.'

A few hours later a reply from Paddy, which was cc'd to the whole office, followed: 'If anyone is not envisioning a late night they should check out publicjobs.ie.' When some staff questioned the email and its tone, it was said to have been passed off by Paddy as a joke.

The concept of not being up to scratch to work at Web Summit and therefore more suited to the civil service is one which Paddy would refer to again in the years to follow.

The 2012 Web Summit kicked off at the RDS on a cloudy day in October 2012 with David Shing, an AOL executive known for having long black hair which sticks out in multiple directions, delivering a speech that year.

Stripe's Patrick Collison also took to the stage and discussed his company's journey to becoming a leading fintech platform. While the fintech company was already a major player in the market despite employing only a few dozen people, its success soared in later years. Stripe is now valued at around $50 billion and the Collison brothers are the most successful businessmen to emerge from Ireland in the last decade.

Another famous attendee at that year's Web Summit was Titan the Robot, a 2.2 metre tall robot which sang and danced for attendees on the floor of the RDS. Bono also returned for his second year leading a pub crawl as part of the F.ounders event.

That year's event also scaled up to over 250 start-ups from around the world exhibiting their wares. Taking home the top €100,000 prize as part of the Electric Ireland Spark of Genius award was Smart Things, a home automation company acquired by Samsung for €200 million only two years later.

Also at that year's event was Marcy Simon, a well-known tech advisor and public relations guru. Simon is a founder of Agent of Change, a company which specializes in helping businesses develop media and PR campaigns. She had also appeared in the US media more than a couple of times over her relationship with Eric Schmidt, then Google's executive chairman and its CEO for a decade. As her Twitter handle @teflonblondie indicates, Simon does not fear the scrutiny that comes with being in the spotlight, even if her job requires her to often stay in the sidelines.

The 2012 event was not her first time at Web Summit (she had attended previous events including the main conference in Dublin the year before) but her attendance that year capped off a huge year of growth. And as a connector of famous tech founders and C-suite executives,

Simon was a valuable asset for a fledgling Web Summit. She opened a lot of doors, including to some of the most famous companies in New York and San Francisco such as Google, Facebook and Apple.

When the company went to New York City for its first F.ounders event in June 2012, Simon worked closely with the team when it secured space on Times Square. She introduced Paddy to Nasdaq, which sponsored the event and their use of Times Square billboard space. Simon even arranged for one of the billboards to feature a congratulatory message to Paddy on his engagement to Faye at the time.

The relationship between Paddy and Simon was foundational – Nasdaq continued to be a sponsor of the conference in later years – and it allowed the company to make history in Ireland by bringing the bell to Dublin and ringing it onstage with political leaders.

At Web Summit 2012, she was filmed in an interview with RTE *News Now* showing off her yarn-spinning skills to describe her journey toward becoming a trusted tech advisor. Her speech, while dotted with corporate slogans like having a 'global context', is extremely polished, free of filler phrases or pauses.

'I come from nothing, and one of my first jobs was driving a yellow bus, a yellow school bus, and with that license you had to stop, look, and listen ... and that is something that has really helped me advance,' she said in the segment.

'I was really fortunate in that I started out in television, in broadcast journalism, and then I helped companies make news, corporations make news, and work with C-suite executives, to help them understand how to deliver the news, and it just evolved in terms of being able to look at whatever needs to be done, and it's sort of like I know where lightning hits,' she added.

Simon was a master PR-exec and one who would act as a mentor to both Paddy and Daire in helping them to leverage their contacts in later years. From an early stage, she could spot that Web Summit had the makings of a major success story. After noticing that the first few events were extremely male affairs, she was part of developing a campaign to encourage more women in technology, including speaking at a 'Leaders Lunch'.

While she was visiting Dublin, a photoshoot was arranged in a reception room of the Shelbourne Hotel, where Simon was staying. The pictures and an interview were meant to run in 'The Gloss' magazine, the monthly supplement from the *Irish Times*, but they never did.

Simon was also instrumental in helping Web Summit realize that in order to sell the conference as a place where big deals got over the line, it needed a library of success stories and the skills to sell those stories in public. Given how many times she came up in conversation with Web Summit staffers, and how often I saw her name mentioned, I chased Simon for months to talk about her experience.

When she finally got in touch in August 2024, she reflected on meeting Paddy in the summer of 2011, at a start-up event in London. Simon said he told her about Web Summit, and how he wanted more visibility for the events and to work with her on strategic communications. She said he promised her 2.5 per cent equity in the company behind F.ounders, and she accepted this in December 2011.

'I worked for Web Summit for nearly six years and never took a salary from the company,' Simon said.

'I approached Paddy on many occasions to paper our agreed equity and he always asked me to just trust him – he was working on it and he would take care of me when he had a sale, acquisition or investment,' she added.

Simon said she introduced Paddy to tech investors, founders, CEOs and other high-profile companies and brands in the tech world, including Nasdaq, which went on to be a big sponsor of the event for a number of years.

'I brought Paddy into my community and my world, and I trusted him on his word. I feel Paddy became larger than life in his own mind,' she said.

'He loved creating an illusion that it was only him who created and owned Web Summit and F.ounders, forgetting about the people that helped him start and build the company, and to whom he gave equity in the company,' she added.

Simon said she was still considering her options in relation to enforcing the equity she alleged she was promised.

It was through Shervin Pishevar, who Simon knew through her work in the USA, that the company would facilitate what it would claim as its most significant success story in years to come. As legend has it, it was over a pint in Bruxelles pub in Dublin that investor Shervin Pishevar wooed Uber founder Travis Kalanick. A term sheet was reported to have been signed that night in the Shelbourne Hotel and a $26.5 million investment followed.

Depending on which version was told, sometimes the signature occurred on the back of a napkin, and other times the businessmen were described as having enjoyed a chance encounter in Dublin. Regardless, it was a perfect tale for Web Summit to capitalize on because it helped bolster the idea that the conference was more than just a piss-up: that real, meaningful business was being done at it. This idea was crucial to the company in the early years as it was being sold on this basis to both start-ups and investors spending thousands on tickets.

As one former staffer noted, Paddy was extremely good at 'weaponizing gossip' so he ensured the story lived on in the hearts and minds of attendees. He frequently referenced it onstage, including at one Web Summit conference where he stated that it was 'at the end of a pint' of Guinness that Pishevar decided to invest in Uber.

There have been numerous articles in Irish media describing the Uber deal in similar terms, and sales staff at Web Summit described it to potential attendees as an example of the types of big breaks that can happen at the conference.

The story is true: Pishevar and Kalanick did sign the term sheets in Dublin in October 2011. But the investment process between Uber and Menlo Ventures, which Pishevar had recently joined that year, had been underway for a number of weeks before the pair met at Web Summit. Pishevar hinted at this when he said on stage at Web Summit 2013 how he flew to Ireland 'in a rush' to meet Kalanick when the offer presented itself.

'Ireland has actually changed my life,' he said. 'I have a lot to be thankful for and grateful for both for this nation and also for Paddy and the F.ounders conference and the Web Summit,' he added.

At the time of the investment, Uber was only operational in a handful of cities but it had already been the subject of an $12 million funding round by Benchmark Capital, an early investor which led a Series A funding round.

(Benchmark would later sue Kalanick for fraud and try to force him off Uber's board; the suit was dropped in 2018.)

For an established VC like Pishevar, Uber was a well-known company, and according to *Super Pumped: The Battle for Uber* by Mike Isaac, the chance to invest in the ride-sharing firm was one which Pishevar worked on for quite some time. 'He eventually convinced Kalanick to let Pishevar's firm, Menlo Ventures, invest in Uber. One of Pishevar's partners, Shawn Carolan, did much of the work to make the deal happen,' Issac wrote in the 2022 book.

'But Pishevar managed to take most of the public-facing credit for it; at one point, Pishevar shaved the word 'UBER' into the hair on the back of his head, an attempt to prove his devotion to Kalanick's company,' he added.

There is no mention of Dublin, Ireland, or the Web Summit anywhere in the 384-page book which was sourced from hundreds of interviews with Uber staff.

A 2019 TechCrunch article, which centred on an interview with Shawn Carolan, Pishevar's former colleague at Menlo, looked at the details of how the Uber investment was secured. Like the Isaac book, the article paints Pishevar as being more focused on style over substance. 'While Pishevar, described to TechCrunch as "overpowering" and "self-promotional", developed a lasting relationship with Uber co-founder and former chief executive officer Travis Kalanick crucial to the deal, Carolan, a reserved Midwesterner, crunched the numbers and worked to convince his firm that Uber, a young startup with a hot-headed leader, was worth their time and money,' the piece stated.

Despite occurring in 2011, and being referenced onstage at the 2013 event, the notorious Uber story did not make headlines in Ireland until 3 November 2014, coinciding with the first day of that year's Web Summit. The piece, which appeared on the front page of the *Irish Times*, featured quotes from Pishevar ahead of him speaking at that year's conference and described the deal signed that fateful night as being worth $26.5 million.

Menlo Ventures did invest $20 million in Uber in 2011, but it was after the initial financing when the firm bought stock from insiders which brought it up to the $26.5 million figure.

The story was able to land on the front page of the *Irish Times* after Web Summit connected the journalist, who had been chasing the interview for nearly a year, with Pishevar. Daire made the introduction and Sherpa Ventures, the VC firm that Pishevar had set up after leaving Menlo, set up the call. The result was a story that became Web Summit folklore.

But there were plenty of other stories that Daire and the rest of the media team shopped around in the early years. These included that SmartThings, which won its start-up competition in 2012, met Josh Elman, a partner at Greylock, a California VC firm, at the conference because he was a judge on the panel.

Daire also told journalists that a number of companies came to Ireland 'directly due to Web Summit' including Smartling, Wonga, Qualtrics, Quantcast and Nordeous. He also said that Paddy introduced Ruchi Sanghvi, then VP of operations at Dropbox, to Ireland and talked the team through their move here.

To further stoke the increasingly positive narrative around the Web Summit, the firm recruited the help of Laurie Mannix of MKC Communications to focus its efforts to land stories, especially in the Irish media.

Mannix worked with Web Summit between 2011 and 2014, winning an award for the work in 2012. She was initially introduced to the company after her contract with Google led to her shadowing Chad Hurley when he was over to speak at the 2010 Web Summit. Paddy had a lot of respect for Mannix and the help she offered Daire's internal media team in the early years. But ahead of the 2014 Web Summit their working relationship was ended when Paddy had her fired after she told him he could not organize a press conference to call Ireland out as a tax haven. This occurred after a meeting at the Web Summit offices where Paddy became angry at Mannix for her stance and for allegedly being what he regarded as too cozy with the types of people he was looking to lambast. Daire, instructed to make the call to fire Mannix, gave her a heads-up text that Paddy was listening in.

After the 2012 Web Summit event, the company lost some key staff, but work in building an even bigger Web Summit the following year began almost immediately.

Getting the message out there about the company, its success and that it was run by three Irishmen was part of the PR drive in early 2013. In February of that year, Dave, Daire and Paddy went into the RTE studios to appear on *The Business* with George Lee to talk 'friendship, fearlessness and failure'. It is one of the only times that all three men, who were introduced as 'the founders' of Web Summit, ever appeared on radio together. In the segment, Paddy heaps praise on Dave as a friend and business partner.

'I think both myself and Dave certainly would always balance each other's ideas by challenging each other and probably challenging each other because we know each other for so long,' he said.

'He's meticulous, and he plans and he thinks ahead, whereas a lot of young guys are completely headless,' Paddy added.

The interview makes for difficult listening when viewed through the perspective that only eight years later all three men would speak only through lawyers. Regardless of what may have been going on behind the scenes, the nine-minute interview does not indicate any obvious strife between them at the time.

Echoing an idea he would repeat in legal filings, Daire said that he looked up to Paddy as a first-year college student while he was President of the Phil. 'That's exactly where I'd like to be,' he said on the programme.

Friends in life and friends in business was the takeaway from the interview, but this illusion would be shattered in countless ways in the years to come.

Chapter 6

ELON MUSK SAMPLES SOME IRISH HOSPITALITY

It was Halloween 2013, and Elon Musk was back in Ireland for the first time since he was seven years old because he was promised a party. The CEO of Tesla and Space X, which were already worth over a billion dollars each, smiled nervously from the stage of Web Summit that day while confessing that the real reason he travelled 5,000 miles was for a rager.

'I understand there's going to be a great party tonight,' he told the crowd when asked how he found the time to travel to a small island in Europe for a tech conference.

While he was a few years away from being crowned the world's richest man and becoming the controversial celebrity figure he is today, Musk was, even then, the most high-profile guest to grace the Web Summit stage. Wearing a jacket with fabric sleeves and black leather on the vest, he was fresh faced and subdued, a far cry from the anti 'woke' crusader, 'free speech absolutist', Twitter owner that he has become today. But even back then the confidence he exuded was palpable as he sat, still, at the very edge of his armchair, leaning forward for nearly the entire

40-minute interview, and gesturing with steepled fingers like a politician or a cartoon villain.

Along with getting a boost from Musk's presence, that year was a milestone for the Web Summit because it had more than doubled its attendees, going from 4,000 in 2012 to over 10,000 in 2013.

Musk was an ideal guest for the time because, while slightly niche to the general public, he had a rock star quality for tech bros and aspiring digital entrepreneurs. 'It gave a very real legitimacy to the whole event,' one ex-staffer recalled. 'Like if anything's good enough for Elon Musk, it's good enough for hardcore entrepreneurs which meant that we could start leveraging his name to get more interesting entrepreneurs there.'

For many in the tech industry, 2013 was the year that put Web Summit, as a company and a concept, on the map. The audience was also full of its fair share of tech celebrities, including Patrick Collison, co-founder of Stripe, who sat up front for the interview and was said to have been rapt with the discussion.

For some of those in attendance, that year's event was the first time that Dublin was establishing itself as a destination for tech, investment, digital innovation and enterprise. It made people want to work for the company. 'I got to see a lot of people I would have idolized in tech at the time, it felt cool, like being in a little club,' one individual said.

It may have been surprising that Musk found time to travel to Dublin, but to the man sitting directly beside him it was an unbelievable sales opportunity. Grinning from ear to ear, Enda Kenny, then Taoiseach and leader of Fine Gael, could hardly contain the excitement he felt at being in proximity to such a rich and powerful businessman. Wearing a microphone headset and appearing later from a cloudy mist of dry ice, Kenny was doing his best to look the part of a cool prime minister. Earlier, he had been driven into the RDS in a Tesla with Musk behind the wheel to the sound of the James Bond theme tune.

Over the course of their 30 minutes onstage, Kenny would pitch Musk on all the possibilities that Ireland held for him, such as a young and educated workforce. The unspoken reason was the country's low rate of corporation tax, which was a factor that had enticed an increasing number of tech behemoths like Google, Facebook and LinkedIn to Irish shores.

At some points the conversation became such a shameless plug for Irish industry and enterprise that the crowd laughed at Kenny's wink-and-finger-point diplomacy.

'Henry Ford started off his motoring business in Cork, at the turn of the last century, and it was here for 60 years,' Kenny said, turning to face Musk directly.

'So if you're looking for a good base, we'll certainly give you an opportunity. Seriously, I've been saying this to you, if you're going to come to Europe, with Tesla, we will compete with the best, so if you want to do that, you give us a chance, we'll give you a fair hearing and our workers will not you down, believe you me,' he added.

Kenny's decision to focus on Ireland's potential as a manufacturing hub was a relief to some of those in attendance who recall him describing how Irish rain was good for a person's complexion only the evening before.

Also onstage was Shervin Pishevar, one of the biggest players in the VC world, with the Uber deal one of biggest successes of his career. Around four years later, in 2017, he would go on to be accused by multiple women of sexual harassment and assault. He has denied the claims and maintained they were part of a 'smear campaign'. But at that year's Web Summit he was flying high, holding an afterparty at his room in the Shelbourne Hotel, and according to Emily Chang's *Brotopia*, ended up alone with one woman on a couch there. 'Pishevar, she said, was holding a phone – it's unclear who it belonged to – and was smiling as he was showing her photos of genitalia of women they claimed to have slept with,' Chang reported in the 2018 book.

Onstage during the interview earlier that day, Kenny leans over with one hand cupped behind his ear when the billionaire is asked what he would do if he was Taoiseach. Musk replies by comparing early and medium-stage companies to 'a little sapling growing in a redwood forest'.

With Kenny nodding beside him in agreement, Musk speaks in a small voice while explaining his theory.

'You've got giant companies and if you don't get a little bit of sunlight and nutrition, it's game over,' he says.

While Musk would not go on to open a company in Ireland, the possibility that he might even consider it was thrilling in the context of where Ireland was positioned globally at the time. In 2013 *Forbes* magazine crowned Ireland 'best country for business' because of what it said was an extremely 'pro business' environment which attracted investment from some of the world's biggest companies.

IDA Ireland, the agency responsible for bringing foreign investment into the country, also marked a record year after it said employment at its client companies was at the highest ever.

The post-2008 banking crash appeared to be finally easing, tech companies were expanding their presence in Dublin's so-called Silicon Docks, and unemployment was almost back at pre-recession levels. Put simply, the idea that a billionaire who wants to go to Mars would set up shop in Cork was not as outlandish as it may sound today.

If there was a clear message from the 2013 Web Summit, it was that despite all the hardship, bank bailouts and International Monetary Fund loans, Ireland could still dream of bringing its economy to a rolling boil.

That year's Web Summit was capitalizing on everything that Ireland could be, and doing so in the most kitsch way possible. On entering the RDS for that year's two-day conference, three little people dressed as leprechauns offered guests the chance to win a 'pot of gold' in the form of a free pint of Guinness at a nearby pub.

Silicon Valley-based attendees, many in Ireland for the first time, were bedazzled by the scenes on display at the RDS, lapping up performances of so-called Irishness like they were wandering around a theme park. Kenny himself even dubbed the country 'the new digital capital of the planet' to the tech bro turned plastic-Paddy crowd.

Web Summit said tickets for that year's event had sold out by the time it got underway, fuelled by celebrity speakers such as Musk and Tony Hawk, the professional skateboarder. Hawk was there to discuss how he used social media to promote his video game franchise. He spoke about his charitable foundation and his video game franchise, telling the conference it was difficult watching his avatar die. 'It's tough watching yourself fall, watching your character blow out his knee repeatedly, that's the one I can't bring myself to look,' he is quoted as saying in the

Irish Examiner the following day. After the event, he went to the opening of the Bushy Park skatepark, meeting fans and young skateboarders there.

The company was also preparing to try out a re-brand by calling itself 'The Summit' in certain marketing material. *The Peak*, a newsletter given to attendees that year, contained some of the earliest forms of Web Summit's origin story, as it was devised then.

'Dublin Web Summit – home to the eponymous European tech conference and F.ounders – is not really an events company but a product company. The product is an experience,' it stated.

Alongside headshots of the trio of founders taken by renowned Irish photographer Kevin Abosch, it described how the famous Manders Terrace sofa 'where the whole thing started' had been moved into the RDS for that year's conference. 'A monument to how far the founders and their team have travelled and how big things have become. They're only going to get bigger,' it said.

That year's event also featured its first-ever 'Food Summit' which showcased Irish food and was the result of a remarkable effort by producers from all over the country in an extremely short period of time. Chef and founder of Ballymaloe Cooking School, Darina Allen, wrote about the mammoth task of helping to feed 10,000 people from a tent in Herbert Park in a blog post shortly afterwards. She said Paddy had contacted Margaret Jeffares, founder of Good Food Ireland, less than two weeks before the event asking if she would take on the job and work contacting suppliers got underway.

It may have been an entirely chaotic and exhausting experience, but it was a testament to how valuable Web

Summit's attendees were regarded that producers jumped at the chance to get involved. Jeffares said the experience was 'unbelievably inspirational'.

'Hard bloody work for everybody, nightmare work, but we thrived off it,' she told me, noting that everyone was paid on time for the enterprise.

The company would later scrap the practice of offering food to delegates, saying that the food bill for their event the following year topped €1 million. A text message exhibited as part of the legal cases with his co-founders would later reveal that Paddy had opposed Food Summit because it made 'no commercial sense'.

That year's conference also introduced the company's first in-house app development, which allowed people to find attendees to connect with. The website that year also had a fully built-out API, which the company credited to Tony Ennis, its CTO at the time.

On the morning of the first day of Web Summit 2013, Paddy narrowly avoided a radio grilling on how the ongoing water shortage would be negatively impacting on all the high-value attendees. The *Morning Ireland* feed died just as Brian Dobson was asking him about selling out hotels to techies who couldn't have a shower past 8 p.m. When it resumed after a nearly three-minute break, the subject turned to why less than 10 per cent of the 300 speakers were women, which Paddy said was a reflection of the broader industry.

'What do you get out of all of this?' Dobson asked.

'Well … I get to have a great time, and three years ago I was sitting in my student house with two of my friends, David Kelly and Daire Hickey, and I don't think we ever thought for one moment that we would get off that couch into any other office and we've been through two to three offices and now there's 50 wonderful Irish people working for us,' Paddy replied.

That night, after an exclusive dinner in Christchurch Cathedral where he sat near Bono, Musk would get the party he was promised. The night out consisted of a trip to Copper Face Jacks, a three-floored nightclub known for being the go-to place when in Dublin and hammered. The venue, which still boasts on its homepage that Musk popped in for a 'boogie', was packed full of people in fancy dress who were out celebrating Halloween night.

Coppers is chaotic at the best of times but that night it was complete bedlam. Musk wanted champagne bottle service and a VIP area, but he got the offer of a gin and tonic and an area slightly separated from the inebriated crowd. Although he loved socializing, Musk is remembered as a man of relatively few words, despite his rock star status among those in the know. As it was Halloween night, the club was full of people dressed as witches, vampires, comic book characters and in generic 1970s- or 1980s-themed attire. A woman dressed as a mermaid was said to have caught Musk's eye and he was spotted chatting to her alone, although it became clear to some in attendance that she had no idea who he was.

As Musk mingled, Paddy, who was having a drink in the Shelbourne with Bono, got a call that he should probably make his way over to Coppers.

The details of the night would have filled endless gossip columns, but Founders operated under Chatham House Rules in an effort to ensure tech bros felt they could let loose. For this reason even Musk's presence in Coppers was not reported until over a week later when the *Sunday*

Independent ran a piece headlined 'Billionaire Musk samples some Irish hospitality – in Coppers'.

The presence of a billionaire like Musk in Coppers, a nightclub popular with nurses and gardaí, has remained one of Web Summit's greatest stories. It is still talked about among staffers current and former as well as by those in the tech sector when reflecting on the more entertaining early days of the company.

The piece about Musk's presence in Coppers incited panic within Web Summit because it contained references to him chatting up a woman and spurred Daire and Paddy to pressure the journalists involved to have it changed.

The original piece had a quote from Tom Millett, a co-founder of Balcony TV, as saying that Musk had been 'talking to a very attractive lady' and engaged in conversation for 'some time' with 'one woman'.

'After he left, I heard someone told her, "Do you know who you have just let slip through your fingers?"'

Curiously, this quote, and all references to a 'woman', were scrubbed from the online article shortly after it was published. The only evidence that they existed at all is in the physical print copy of the newspaper from 10 November 2013, which also featured a blurry selfie of Millett posing wide-eyed next to Musk.

The print edition of the newspaper landed in shops late on Saturday, 9 November. Its reference to Musk ensured that the article secured a spot on the front page of that week's paper, and when Daire spotted this, he contacted Nick Webb, then editor of the newspaper's business section.

On Monday, Daire contacted Webb again to argue his case for why he thought the story was inappropriate. Along with being annoyed that Chatham House rules had been broken, there was concern that Musk's own PR team would panic as the billionaire had only recently remarried Talulah Riley, the English actress whom he previously married and split from, twice.

In order to exert extra pressure, Webb was told that potentially damaging the company's relationship with Musk would not be good for business. He floated the possibility that Musk could be involved in an important foreign direct investment (FDI) project, and how it would not be a good look for Ireland if Musk felt unfairly treated by its media.

Stephen O'Regan, co-founder of Balcony TV who was living in New York at the time, claimed he got a phone call that week from Paddy in which he was asked to intervene in the situation. He said this involved asking for a retraction to be made, which he declined to do.

After enormous pressure, the *Sunday Independent* relented by editing out the offending references from the online piece.

Normally edits take place because there is a glaring inaccuracy, and even those are typically met with resistance from editors who, it may surprise no one to hear, are typically opposed to admitting they are wrong. The fact that multiple edits were made on an entirely accurate story is evidence of how, by 2013, Paddy had become a powerful force within Irish media and business circles.

'The funny thing about Paddy's whole thing about corruption in the Irish media, which he's obsessed with, was that they got a really easy ride from the Irish media, I felt, for a long time,' a former staffed said. 'Prior to them busting out of Dublin they could pretty much get any story they wanted, it seemed like. There were a few who were more critical but most years it was like, look at the triumph of the Web Summit.'

The episode did not tarnish Paddy's relationship with Tom Lyons, the journalist who wrote the story, or Nick Webb. In fact both men would continue to have professional and friendly relationships with him for many years to come.

Paddy was developing a remarkable skill at manipulating the media to get Web Summit in the spotlight, even if the rhetoric propelling that was derisory and contentious. Part of this occurred via his own research, as revealed by book reviews he wrote and distributed to select staffers. In a review for *Contagious: How to Build Word of Mouth in the Digital Age*, which was published in January 2014, Paddy remarked on how word association in the media can translate into real life results.

'Mars bars have above average sales when planet Mars is in the news. Why? Mars is top of mind. Can we make Ireland, Web Summit or other relevant things top of mind?' the review stated.

An attempt at making this happen occurred in May 2014 when Paddy claimed he would consider hiring people with a 2.1 degree from Trinity College Dublin, but only a first-class honours degree from any other Irish university. The comments followed on from a PR pitch when the company told media at the start of the month that they were trying to hire 40 more people but were having trouble identifying 'high quality graduates' for the job. A referral fee of up to €10,000 was floated for those who suggested someone who was ultimately hired.

When questioned about why there was a stipulation regarding the degree held by interns at the company,

Paddy, who at the time sat on the board of the Higher Education Authority (HEA), a state body that provides policy advice, doubled down. He said, 'a 2.1 in one university would not equate to a 2.1 in another university' and that Trinity operated four-year degree cycles which he said made a 'huge difference'.

The comments were extremely controversial, and led to the HEA distancing itself from him in a statement released later that month which said it did not agree with his remarks.

A statement characterizing his stance as 'deeply upsetting' for students who have chosen to study at colleges other than the ones Paddy named was released by the National College of Ireland.

Paddy quickly moved to clarify that the comments related to internships and not the 40 positions it had open at the time. He responded to the backlash with a lengthy blog post entitled 'we even hire pirates' which defended the position and updated that post a few days later to bat even harder for his stance. He also engaged in a multi-tweet thread snarkily responding to a post from Ruadhán Mac Cormaic, of the *Irish Times*, who noted that the current editor of the *New York Times* never graduated from college and 'wouldn't get a look in at the Dublin Web Summit'.

'Correct, for the intern role he would not. Nor would Zuck or Genghis Khan,' Paddy, who was not tagged in the post, responded a few hours later. A series of additional argumentative tweets from Paddy followed.

Years later he would characterize this ordeal as another example of him playing the media at its own game, saying it fed into the uncertainty that sold Web Summit tickets.

'It's like Formula One. People will tune into a race where there's some degree of conflict, or there's uncertainty. Is the track going to be ready? Part of it is the drama that people want,' he told me.

But if this is how he regards the comments reflecting back from the present day, it appears at odds with how much he fought to argue his point at the time and with how seriously those in the company regarded his claims. He discussed his position with staffers who were hired in the wake of the controversy and remained steadfast in his reasons for thinking this way. But he also rejoiced in the media attention that his comments had garnered.

I have heard numerous stories over the course of reporting this book about how Paddy would say or do something only to claim as soon as the following day that he was joking or it was part of a running joke. In some instances, people told me he would not overtly state that it had been a joke, but he would make jokes about it, and the substance of the remark would be discarded.

In two separate instances, he was said to have lost his temper at a staffer and then, without addressing the incident, approached them in a cordial manner a few days later or ignored it entirely.

His appetite for reading books on the tech world and business management was voracious and staff felt that he was regularly experimenting with what he learned in the workplace. Part of this involved refusing to speak first in contentious meetings, which is something numerous former staffers have recounted as occurring to them personally.

'It was a tactic,' a former staffer recalled, saying it also involved him 'staring someone out of it'. In one example, when an employee was meeting with him after handing in their notice, he walked out of the room after Paddy refused to speak.

'It was such a brazen interviewing 101 tactic of "if I say nothing, they will have to fill the silence". I went into that meeting to hear him out because he asked me to. He knew why I was leaving, so I had nothing else to say. So when he just sat there, I decided to leave,' the former employee said.

The 2.1 débâcle occurred amidst rising tensions between the three Web Summit founders as emails and messages exhibited in the legal row reveal. The correspondence shows significant cracks had already formed in the relationships they had with each other.

In a Google chat exchange the month before, Paddy tells Daire, 'When you're ready let me know you've got so much more to give ... Too many people are surprised you are a shareholder and a very substantial one. I want leadership ... I am going to beat and prod you until you realize you can do 20/30/50x what you achieve.'

Daire pushed back in his responses, telling Paddy at one stage that if he kept pushing him he was 'done'.

'Seriously about to lose it. You have no appreciation,' Daire adds.

Both Paddy and Dave at the time appeared to regard Daire as not working hard enough and meeting the targets expected of him in his role as a manager. By then Daire had moved to New York, where he worked remotely for the company.

Paddy wrote to Dave that summer. 'Jaysus, Daire has no idea what is going on. The company is passing him by.' Dave would later tell Paddy that 'Daire moving to NY is a waste of time'.

In September, Paddy wrote to Dave saying that he had talked to Daire and that there was 'no talking to him unfortunately'. 'He just doesn't work,' Paddy said in the message at the time.

A conversation between Daire and his partner was also exhibited by Paddy in the lawsuits which showed the pair discussing a 'demotion'.

'Well, I'm saying … sure, I'll do what you want but let's not call this a demotion,' Daire tells his partner.

'This is like the Palestine-Israel conflict. If you accept the two-state solution (the new structure) you are crystalizing your lower position. I think you need to explicitly say you're an equal partner to Dave and you need to be positioned in the exact same way as him. But remember, you're lovely and amazing and you shouldn't be punished for being valuable at your role while Dave is rewarded for being a pointless manager,' Daire's partner and now husband wrote.

'In reality it's about two things for me. Money and peace of mind,' Daire says.

At the start of a conversation the day before, Daire tells his partner that Paddy was 'being a knob again'.

'Ah sure, listen, he probably doesn't like that you're getting lots of attention,' he said in reply.

Paddy has repeatedly denied that his growing dislike of Daire had anything to do with his rising public profile at the time, stating that it was solely related to his performance and conduct. But people who worked around both men said it was clear that Paddy disapproved of Daire's lifestyle. In an affidavit filed for the lawsuits, Paddy refers to Daire's 'excessive socializing'.

Following the discussion about the 'demotion', Daire would also chat to Gearoid O'Rourke, his long-time friend who had been previously involved in the Rock the Vote campaign. Daire told O'Rourke, 'I think it's over.'

'In that case start making an exit plan and pull the trigger first, document everything,' O'Rourke told his friend, adding that he should 'play up the crazy Paddy angle' and 'paint the picture for when you have to sue him'.

When Paddy retrieved this conversation years later as part of a data scouring exercise, he would place it in his grounding affidavit as evidence of an allegedly long-term plan to litigate their issues. He would also cite a message he sent to Dave around that time about how he noticed that Daire was 'trying to draw me into putting stuff in writing constantly'.

'This would later prove a prescient observation, as these proceedings confirm,' Paddy says.

His implication in this comment is that Daire's plan all along was to fight Paddy in court. If this was a concern in Paddy's mind, he does not state whether it was also something he himself was preparing for.

A number of ex-staff, particularly those from the early years, remarked to me during the course of reporting this book that they were entirely unsurprised that the founders and former friends would end up involved in such contentious litigation. This was not, they said, because of the practical dispute over equity, especially that which is divided unevenly, but rather because as the years went on a perceived animosity between them seemed unsustainable.

Interestingly, despite exhibiting a litany of messages and emails which clearly display an intense dissatisfaction with the other from 2014 onwards, both Paddy and Daire would deny being motivated by a hatred of the other.

In correspondence with Paddy throughout 2014, Dave would also complain about Daire allegedly not pulling his weight and indicate he would support Paddy in proposals to remove his responsibilities.

As for his role in the company, Dave was becoming increasingly unsure where to direct focus or how to navigate the rising celebrity enjoyed by his co-founders. 'I look after most of the operations, the sales teams, and sponsorship. I used to be involved in the event management planning but not so much anymore. I love putting on events but I'm more focused on sales,' he said in an interview conducted as part of research for the book *Silicon Docks: The Rise of Dublin as a Global Tech Hub*.

As evidenced by the controversial recruitment drive, Paddy was on a mission to staff up Web Summit with mature professionals. He engaged extensively with Marcus Segal, who had worked in senior roles with a number of Silicon Valley enterprises, and who would later become a partner at Y Combinator, a California-headquartered start-up accelerator. Segal relocated from San Francisco and spent nearly two months living with Paddy in Dublin helping to identify key management hires. Among those was Aaron Steinberger, who previously worked under Segal at Zynga, a video game development company. Full of corporate jargon, Steinberger was said to have been effectively hired to be Paddy's bad cop, and whip what he regarded as a young and not fully committed workforce into shape.

Also joining the team that year as VP of Engineering was JD Fitzgerald, who had previously led development for Hostelworld. JD was a key hire and he set to work helping to redesign the website and worked with Tito, a ticketing software platform that Web Summit had been using and which Paddy would later issue an apology to after taking credit for building it.

Web Summit also contracted out work on redeveloping a new mobile app to withstand the spikes in traffic needed for a conference-based product. And to top it all off, his team often worked with the data science team, Paddy's pet project in the company, on whatever idea he would conjure up at 1 a.m.

Paddy was hungry for Web Summit to be seen as more than an events company, telling media that it was 'much more' and developing software to improve how events were run. A central tenet of that plan was having a strong group of software engineers, and by ensuring he sat near this department in the office he appeared to almost fancy himself part of the team.

By comparison, Daire's media team was segmented in a completely different building when the office was located in Ranelagh. 'I think he was very keen to get people into his domain, nearly completely separate, physically, not just a wall in the way like, just a completely different building,' a former staffer recalled. 'I think that was intentional because there was space for them in the other building, we weren't short on space.'

For Paddy, who had a life-long obsession with queues, being in proximity to the teams making decisions about future modelling and growth plans for the company was thrilling. Ideas like installing Go-Pros inside boxes on the ceiling of the RDS to model how people moved through the space were allowed to become reality thanks to a cherry picker the team hired. Paddy also had the team pour over papers published by Disney on lessons learned from its queuing system and interns would be dispatched at events to test the time it took to get through a line.

At 34, JD was among the older employees working for Web Summit at the time and his maturity was apparent in a company which was still very green. With dark hair and a thick beard, he stood out in a team of baby-faced engineers. When it was announced that he was joining the team, the company released a blog post that said he was the 50th employee and that he would bring both technical and management expertise and experience to the team.

Along with being a talented developer, JD also knew how to manage Paddy by telling him when he had gone too far or been unfair in his dealings with staff. A number of staff who worked under him said he 'sheltered' the team from a lot of the demands that Paddy would have directed at his various managers.

One ex-staffer said the atmosphere in the office in 2014 was 'volatile' and that 'blow-up fights' were a fairly regular occurrence. 'Live events are crazy, and I don't think Web Summit is unique in that, but everything has to be delivered on time, it just adds so much tension,' they added, noting this meant teams in charge of tech and engineering worked under added pressure.

Another ex-staffer said about JD, 'You may have rarely needed to talk to him, but you knew he just knew everything.'

Another big hire for Web Summit at that time was Sinead Murphy, who joined as head of production, overseeing the most unpredictable side of its business: the live part. Joining from MCD Productions, a well-known event management company in Dublin, Murphy was a no-nonsense leader who brought a refreshing dose of realism to Paddy's cohort of lofty dreamers. Her résumé included a few years at Live Nation in England, as well as organizing festivals like Oxegen closer to home, and events in Slane Castle and Croke Park.

Fond of styling her hair in a high bun, Murphy and her predominantly female team were said to often move around the office together, exuding confidence. One staffer recalled that they were all seen as 'scary but efficient'.

'She didn't take any bullshit, she was like we're doing this and this is how we're doing it,' they said.

Speaking that year on RTE radio, Murphy was asked about whether there was a lot of pressure on her to get everything right. 'Emm,' she said, laughing nervously. 'Yeah, I mean it's a big challenge, I welcome a challenge myself,' she added.

Another person brought on board at this time was Eamon Leonard, then a developer and well-known figure in the Dublin tech scene. In a Web Summit blog post he penned shortly after being hired as 'chief community officer and entrepreneur in residence' he claimed to have once told Paddy he was 'full of shit' and that he did not care about those working in Irish tech. But, as Leonard outlined in the post, Paddy won him over.

'I was impressed by how he responded to my line of interrogation, and over the course of the next 20 minutes he laid out for me what his vision was for the Dublin Web Summit, and the impact it would have on the tech land-scape, never mind "community", in Dublin and Ireland. I had to hand it to him, he was saying all the right things,' Leonard wrote.

In the end, working in the company was not for him as Leonard would leave six months later. Although multiple staffers from the time said they regarded his departure as not occurring on good terms, he and Paddy remain friendly to this day, and he is regarded as a loyal supporter of the company.

A final key hire that year was Mike Sexton, who joined the data science team and became known as 'Doctor Mike' by colleagues. Sexton, who has a PhD in physics, was announced as a new recruit in a blog post penned by Paddy where he cited numerous examples of his new employee's 'outstanding work' in college.

'Dr Michael Sexton finished first in his class in physics and computer simulation in Trinity College Dublin, one of the top 30 physics departments in the world,' Paddy wrote. 'His primary research interests include complex network theory, statistical analysis and mathematical modelling of complex systems, and the physics of economics,' he added.

The team was essentially charged with using data to help boost sales and improve the conference experience. It was also behind a lot of the mass marketing initiatives and data harvesting projects: pushing the boundaries of what was possible before the General Data Protection Regulation (GDPR) put a stop to much of it.

During the summer of 2014, while Web Summit was recruiting some key staff members, it was also facing a lawsuit from an American entrepreneur named Elliot Bisnow.

Bisnow, who founded the 'Summit Series' in 2008, accused Paddy of deceptive business practices and unfair competition by infringing on his trademark. He subsequently launched a $6 million lawsuit against Web Summit in the USA over the use of the name 'The Summit' which the company had re-branded to as of 2014.

There are a number of similarities between Bisnow and Paddy, including similar career paths, unparalleled levels of confidence and an ability to sell their conferences as pseudo-religious experiences.

Bisnow purchased Powder Mountain in Utah to build a community of like-minded innovators or, as the *Guardian* described it, a 'mecca for altruistically minded members of the global elite'. In the same article, Bisnow is quoted as saying the goal was 'to be a beacon of inspiration and a light in the world'.

The details of the lawsuit, which was filed in the United States District Court for the District of Nevada, makes for entertaining reading given that it sheds light on the inner workings of the conference world as well as the egos of Paddy and Bisnow.

For his journey to the conference world, Bisnow claimed he had an 'epiphany' to create an invitation-only networking event for high-profile entrepreneurs to get together. 'And that is exactly what he did, inviting other successful young entrepreneurs for a ski trip to Utah,' the lawsuit stated. 'Mr Bisnow did not have the capital to finance the initial event, so he paid for his first attendees with credit cards,' it added, noting that it was a 'smash hit'.

Bisnow claimed that he had invited Paddy to participate in the Summit Series in 2009 and that in January 2010, following his exit from MiCandidate, they spent several days together in Montana. He further alleged that Paddy was impressed with the following and brand recognition that Bisnow's company had garnered and 'indicated he was interested in partnering with Summit to conduct Summit Series events in Europe'.

'He claimed to have significant connections in Europe

and offered to exploit those connections to help the plaintiff further develop the Summit Series brand in Europe,' it said.

After exchanging a series of emails discussing a potential partnership, the lawsuit alleged the pair decided not to go into business together and Paddy would go on to start his own company in Dublin.

In the lawsuit, filed in May 2014, Bisnow indicates that it was earlier that year when Web Summit rebranded as 'The Summit' and registered www.thesummit.co that he became angered by the similarities. He alleged that Paddy was 'choosing a domain name that is practically indistinguishable from the plaintiff's www.summit.co domain name for a website offering competing services' and that this rebrand coincided with Web Summit's first North American conference in Las Vegas, Nevada. Bisnow claimed that he had received 'at least 50 emails from confused customers' inquiring whether Web Summit was related to his company.

Paddy denied all the allegations made in the lawsuit at the time and said through a spokeswoman that the company was changing its name back to 'Web Summit' because 'The Summit' was too generic. 'The stages are being expanded to include music, a sport stage as well as a food summit. We had changed the name to The Summit to reflect this wider focus. However, it has become clear that the "Web Summit" has a very strong legacy and branding,' according to a statement reported by the *Irish Times*.

'We've also found that, at a most basic level, "The Summit" is so generic a term that on search engines it can be hard to find us,' the statement added.

The lawsuit was covered extensively in the *Irish Times* on 16 August 2014 and that day Paddy rang Mark Paul, the business journalist who penned the story, to complain about inaccuracies within the piece. Three days later, on 19 August, an email was sent by Daire to Mark Paul with the title 'URGENT Correction needed' which began with a line that he was 'quite shocked and disappointed' by the piece. Referring to the event as the 'Dublin Web Summit Series' and the 'Summit', Daire listed out 'a number of inaccuracies' that he wanted changed.

'To be frank I feel you took little time to ask specific questions or to lay out the facts as you saw them in order for us,' Daire stated in the email.

'I'd like these updates made immediately before any further damage is done ... Feel free to call with me to discuss, otherwise I'll take it for granted that the inaccuracies will be rectified by close of business,' it added.

The first point of contention was the date of Web Summit's foundation, with Daire highlighting that it was 2009 and not 2010 by linking to a report in Silicon Republic which covered the first event.

'A cursory glance at the internet would have verified this fact,' Daire said.

Another issue was that Paul had incorrectly stated that Paddy spent a month in Montana with Bisnow when in fact the lawsuit stated it was 'several days'.

'Paddy Cosgrave only spent 2 days with Mr Bisnow in the USA in 2010. This line maligns Mr Cosgrave's character as he did not spend a month with Mr Bisnow,' he added.

On 19 August 2014, the *Irish Times* amended the online article it had published only a few days prior which stated that the Web Summit was launched in 2010. The correction made the year 2009. Mark Paul emailed Daire to add that 'it might also be an idea' for Paddy to remove the 2010 reference on his LinkedIn account so that others don't make the same mistake.

Web Summit repeatedly denied at the time that rolling back on the re-brand had anything to do with the lawsuit, but during the spring of 2014 getting the name to catch on was actively pursued.

Only a few months before the *Irish Times* story, Paddy appeared in a two-page interview spread in the internal comms magazine of Mason Hayes & Curran, the law firm, called 'Times'. The piece, which referred exclusively to Web Summit as 'The Summit', said the firm was focusing on expanding into the USA with its first-ever North American conference in Vegas that May. Collision, the company's sister event, would be held in Las Vegas for two years before moving to New Orleans and then Toronto, where it remains to this day under a multi-year deal with the city.

His first line of the interview with Philip Nolan, head of MHC's technology team, was: 'When we started The Summit back in 2010 ...'

Chapter 7

'YOU WILL ALL BE SEEN, YOU WILL ALL BE HEARD'

A camera pans through the overwhelmingly male crowd, illuminated by blue-tinted light, a shade reminiscent of a toddler's plastic toy.

Attendees react by smiling, waving and using their phones to film the camera which in turn films them. An excited gentleman stands to direct his wave toward the camera while another next to him punches the air with two fists.

It is Web Summit 2014, inside Dublin's RDS. The event that year scaled up to accommodate 22,000 people, up from just under 10,000 the previous year, and the surge meant that the Dublin venue was bursting at the proverbial seams.

Wearing a T-shirt featuring his Twitter handle, Paddy had earlier asked for a show of hands on who was having problems with the WiFi system in the RDS. After a large number of hands shoot up at once, he remarks 'that is unbelievable' from the stage, his voice dripping with incredulity.

'Hold on a second keep your hands really, really high,' he instructs as he takes his phone out to snap a photo of the crowd.

'So the RDS have told me they have solved the situation, and they've asked me to thank them from the stage for resolving the WiFi issues for everybody. So a huge thank you to the RDS for resolving the WiFi issues,' Paddy says, initiating a mocking clap.

The 2014 event was another star-studded affair with U2 frontman Bono, once again, and actress Eva Longoria among the celebrities speaking that year. It also included an appearance from a relatively unknown writer from Belfast named Lyra McKee who would go on to become one of the most successful young Irish journalists before being shot dead six years later while observing rioting in Derry. McKee spoke on a side stage at the conference, on the subject of the media and its future.

Tech industry heavyweights such as Drew Houston, the founder of Dropbox, Phil Libin, then CEO of Evernote, Tony Conrad, founding partner of True Ventures, and Tim Armstrong, CEO of AOL, were more the focus of the main stage.

Ahead of the conference, Paddy had invited these men to his house for a soiree but the evening was interrupted by a fire and the group had to be evacuated. Daire, who arrived at the house after the fire had started, eventually took the men to a bar where Houston sang 'Wonderwall' by Oasis.

Walking onstage, Eva Longoria receives rapturous applause from a largely male audience. Jemima Khan, then European editor at large for *Vanity Fair* interviewing Longoria, remarks at one stage about how she could 'barely see a female face in here'. A cheer of voices erupts from the back of the room.

'Apparently there's 85 per cent men in this audience,' Khan adds.

'There's a few,' Longoria replies.

When asked the question that was on everyone's minds, why was she at a Web Summit event, Longoria tells the packed crowd that she has never been to Ireland.

'They invited me to come and speak about my philanthropy and how it's tied with technology,' she adds.

Later, Paddy takes to the stage for another poll on the state of the WiFi in the RDS. Smiling unnerved, he repeats similarly sarcastic lines such as 'that's quite incredible' and 'the RDS have assured us that the WiFi is actually working'.

Although it would be another year before the decision was announced to move Web Summit to Lisbon, Portugal, this was the beginning of the end of Web Summit's time in Dublin. Paddy would warn attendees on the third day of the 2014 event that the conference may leave Ireland unless the RDS could resolve the WiFi issues, which he said had persisted for two years until that point. He also referred to the 'old dudes' who ran the RDS as symptoms of a wider problem whereby Ireland was being held back from its true potential.

Raising the issue at a press conference, in post-mortem interviews and repeatedly from the stage, Paddy left little of the row with the RDS to the imagination. The dispute would spill out into national headlines the following year when he decided to release a series of emails with the government urging it to sort out the problems. Along with the connectivity issue, there were also legitimate concerns regarding planning, transport and other areas where Dublin's infrastructure fell considerably short.

But in 2014, as is often the case with Paddy, the manner in which he chose to relay his complaints betrayed a certain petulance.

The Royal Dublin Society (RDS), which was founded in 1731, was clearly ill-equipped for thousands of techies expecting uninterrupted access to the internet. 'The stately Royal Dublin Society is more used to hosting equine events than cutting-edge technology shows,' Vincent Boland, then the *Financial Times* Dublin-based correspondent wrote in 2015.

When highlighting from the stage in 2014 how he wanted Cisco or Vodafone to run WiFi for the Web Summit, Paddy put on the type of voice an American would use if they were impersonating a leprechaun to mock Michael Duffy, then CEO of the RDS, and Matt Dempsey, then its chairman.

'Ah sure, what would that say about us, giving away the WiFi to these big companies,' Paddy said, crouching down slightly in what appeared to be an attempt to showcase that the men were shorter than him. Tempering his insults with remarks about how Duffy and Dempsey were 'patriots and gentlemen' who have 'done so much for this country', Paddy told attendees that they were 'gentlemen from a different generation'.

'The only way likely to persuade them, due to a lack of usage of email, is a letter-writing campaign,' he added.

In case anyone missed the point or perhaps to hammer it home because he regretted attempting to be polite, Paddy said on the last day that 'old dudes' who ran the RDS 'hold this country back'.

'I just hope to God next year is a little bit better than this year ... or else we won't be in this country very much longer,' he warned.

Clearly bruised by Paddy's comments but maintaining a 'working forward' stance, Duffy went on RTE's *Morning*

Ireland programme the Friday after the conference to address how the problem related to the 'very high density' of mobile devices. He said the issues experienced were 'not particular to the RDS' and happened at events where large quantities of people were connected to devices.

'You have to recognize the fact that this is a really, really technically challenging environment,' Duffy told the radio programme.

If the techies in the audience at that year's event were annoyed about a lack of access to WiFi, they kept it light for the cameras on Day 1 as their faces were flashed onto a screen in Manhattan's Times Square.

The 2014 Web Summit event marked the second year in a row where the Nasdaq bell was rung from the event as it remotely opened the New York-based stock exchange.

As evidenced by his disparaging remarks about RDS management, Paddy was irate by his techie guests not being able to access WiFi, and for good reason, given that start-ups depended on an internet connection to demonstrate their wares. It was also bad PR for Web Summit generally, both in terms of guests viewing the conference as not up to scratch and the company missing out on free social media marketing.

According to an ex-staffer who worked during the 2014 Web Summit, the problem struck at the core friction in a company simultaneously trying to be both event and technology focused. This is because multiplying your users by a hundred times overnight is both a stressful and necessary venture for a firm trying to straddle both industries.

The issue also hit a nerve for Paddy because his recent hiring push was part of a pivot to turn Web Summit from a purely conference-focused company into an engineering company which sold conferences. The conferences should be seen as the product, as opposed to the purpose, was how he pitched it to staff at the time.

That year the conference gathered more than 2,000 start-ups, and with each paying around €1,500 to attend, this cohort was bringing in approximately over €3 million.

Although the company put a lot of emphasis on the senior managerial roles it was recruiting, the start-up team were doing some of the heavy lifting at the time. The team was headed up by Paddy Griffith or 'PG' as he is known, from the summer of 2014.

PG, who has worked for Web Summit for nearly a decade, was described by some of his former colleagues as 'a machine'. He loved nothing more than making sales and motivated the team with chants, gags, and an endless stream of puns. 'He ate, slept, and breathed Web Summit. Like Paddy [Cosgrave], PG could also work 24 hours a day. I think that drove the fact that we were meant to work insane hours because of Paddy and him, it wasn't like they were asking us to do stuff they wouldn't do themselves,' one said.

A scratch map was placed on the wall and every time the team recruited a start-up from a new country they would scratch that country off the map. If the week had been a success, someone may have been told to run to the shop to buy a bottle of whiskey or vodka so the team could do shots.

A real mark of success was when the team secured a few start-ups in the highest bracket of value, meaning they already had the backing of a well-known celebrity or VC. If a couple of those companies had been secured by the week's end, PG was said to mark the occasion by lifting up a bottle of cologne he kept on his desk and spray himself while saying, 'If you're selling well, you're smelling well.'

Although slightly socially awkward, PG had amazing skill on the phone and a razor-sharp memory for some of the finer details about Web Summit start-ups. He was full of energy and always thinking of ways for the team to expand and grow. Like a lot of people who went through start-ups, he moved into partnerships as the company put more focus on SMEs and large corporates in later years.

The team put an immense amount of hard work into convincing start-ups to attend but the graft was as much a numbers game as it was an exercise in skilful persuasion. Workdays were occupied almost exclusively by 15-minute calls with start-ups that had applied for tickets. If a staffer's calendar was not already full with start-up calls, ones would be added so the section of the office in which the team would later base itself sounded and looked like a call-centre.

It was repetitive work that involved asking a series of questions, presenting a short pitch about Web Summit, and often finishing with a roundup of the companies' success stories. The decision on whether to accept or reject the start-up was made on the call and processed afterwards. If it was a yes and they accepted, they would be passed to another team which handled the company from that point onwards.

While a number of former start-up team staffers said the bar to entry was lower than the company let on publicly, they did reject companies they believed would not get any value from the conference because they were too young. Another former start-up staffer disagreed with this characterization and said the motto at some point was 'if it's tech, it can come'.

Start-ups were so much of Web Summit's bread and butter during this period that every new hire was required to do a week of start-up calls. Even non-Web Summit staffers like Jamie Heaslip, the professional rugby player, and Faye, Paddy's wife, came into the office to make some calls with the team. In this way, everyone in the company, and even some of those outside of it, knew what was being sold.

Unsurprisingly, given its prominent role in the company's business model, Paddy was also fond of the start-up team and sought to mentor some of its staff. The content of the mentoring varied, with some saying he dished out detailed sales tips while others recall an online autism test being a suggested distraction for an hour.

The start-up team worked hard and played hard, with after-hours drinks on a Friday frequently resulting in late nights out in Dublin or house parties. As many staffers were young and single, numerous romances blossomed over the years, and while some are still together others ended in tears. Tinder was also a popular dating app, but certain staff learned the hard way that swiping with your colleagues can result in very awkward moments when someone you're sitting with pops up.

'I found out about Tinder at Web Summit … people would Airplay their Tinders up, while others would say no, swipe left, [or] swipe right,' a former staffer recalled.

A number of women who worked at Web Summit during these years before the move to Lisbon described a 'tech bro' culture in the workplace which they found difficult to navigate. Male managers, they said, often invited male employees for lunch and rewarded male staffers more often than female staffers. Numerous sources said that women did most of the legwork in making things happen during Web Summit's early years, but received limited credit.

'A lot of women didn't get credit for things that happened at Web Summit,' one said, describing how this was despite the fact that so many were 'solid on logistics' and 'got shit done'.

'The boys did a lot of flying around and talking big and pretending to be in the film *Wall Street*. It's interesting how limited the credit was spread around,' they added.

A less direct tactic which some staffers said Paddy was fond of consisted of playing people off each other based on how well they were doing performance-wise. This could involve passing remarks or it could involve a more public comment on performance metrics, as some of these were visible on dashboards.

According to one female staffer, there was a unifying aspect to working for the company at this time because people worked hard even if they did not always know how to advocate for themselves.

A running theme which emerged from many women who worked there was that they regretted not standing up for themselves more. But in spite of the stress, the contribution from the majority of staff was significant and led to the company rapidly scaling and expanding. 'Everyone worked really hard, went hugely above and beyond, and it wasn't just that pressure from him [Paddy], you know, it was like you actually wanted to create these things, and you did have autonomy and you got responsibility and there was something incredibly energizing about it,' one woman said.

Another person who said they did not have a good experience at the time acknowledged that this was due to their own dissatisfaction with the work. 'Part of it was that I wasn't able to hit the targets they were setting, but if you can see a chance to move up in your career, this is your line of work, and you know how to fight your corner, Web Summit can be a very good place to be,' they added.

The company's rapid expansion in 2014 resulted in its staff numbers going from 37 to 66, although staff from this period referred to a 'churn' and said many people came into the company only to depart less than a year later.

A tidy cash pile was also being accumulated by the firm, reaching €2.5 million in 2014, which it would use in the months ahead as further expansion plans materialized. It did its first ever US conference in mid-2014 and brought 1,500 people to Las Vegas, Nevada, for Collision. A second one was set to be held the following year that targeted 10,000 attendees and the company was already ready to branch out into Asia with its RISE event launching in Hong Kong the following year.

But back at the RDS in 2014, it was all about keeping Ireland as the 'digital capital' of the world. Holding a red clipboard, broadcaster Pat Kenny walked onstage and welcomed the crowd. A suspenseful string soundtrack played in the background as he kept things upbeat, saying the moment that lay ahead was a 'very auspicious occasion'.

'In 18 minutes time, we will be ringing the bell which will launch activities on the stock exchange in New York,' Kenny tells the crowd. This marked the second time the Nasdaq bell was rung as part of a Web Summit event in Dublin, having been utilized the previous year to unleash a spending frenzy thousands of miles away.

In a true display of his showmanship and ability to kill a lengthy 18 minutes, Kenny hypes the crowd by telling them 'you will all be seen, you will all be heard'. Images of the RDS crowd were set to be live-streamed to Times Square, with the event coinciding with the mid-term elections dominating headlines and screens in the USA.

'So bear in mind that your brother-in-law, your cousin, your aunt, your uncle, in Times Square, will be watching you on the big screen,' Kenny remarks.

Taoiseach Enda Kenny then appears onstage, accompanied by Adam Kostyál, senior vice president of Nasdaq, and Paddy. The Taoiseach gushes with praise, saying what Paddy has done is 'quite incredible'.

When pressed by Pat Kenny to give a nod to the Irish living abroad, such as people from Mayo (the taoiseach's home county) who may be watching from New York, he happily obliges.

'It's so important that they can see that through all of the turmoil that we had for a number of years, there's now a rising confidence, and brighter days ahead,' he says.

Chapter 8

'REALLY, REALLY, REALLY, FUCKING BAD'

'In the last three quarters, we've terminated four people,' Paddy told Web Summit staff in a town hall meeting on 23 January 2015. 'I could list many of the reasons why you could be terminated by making a large booboo,' he explains, discussing how there are 'two buckets': people fired for company-driven decisions and people fired for their actions.

The atmosphere was tense, angry and anxious. Staff morale was low following recent departures which some felt were not conducted fairly. Pay was becoming an increasingly big issue and a number of people would leave the company in the coming weeks and months over issues about their wages and what they perceived as a lack of transparency in assessing an employee's value.

Many Web Summit staff felt underpaid, with some describing salaries hovering in the mid-€20,000 a year range, despite often working what they said were twelve-hour days and bringing in many multiples of that in revenue for the company. The commission for those involved in certain sales was patchy and there had been rows with management when it didn't materialize. Those who had been at the company longer and held more senior roles made more, but considering the staffing levels had increased from 37 to 66 in the previous two years, many staff were not long-serving at the time.

Interns were paid around €15,000 a year, and also worked around the clock while struggling to pay rent in Dublin. By 2015, the company had made a few senior hires, but the majority of staff was mid-twenties and the office culture often felt like an extension of college culture. Along with a youthful cohort of staff, including many recent graduates, the new office in the leafy Dublin suburb of Dartry featured a breakfast bar, free pizza and beer on Fridays and homemade or cheaply purchased décor lining the walls.

Inside the three-steepled converted Tramway House, some employees felt chronically overworked, and concerned that complaining seemed to result in accusations of being ungrateful or selfish. In a bid to prove themselves, most poured themselves into their roles while spending hours each week contributing to the workplace generally through participation in various committees.

A few months prior to this momentous town hall meeting, staff had spent their weekend working to decorate the new HQ. As the name suggests, Tramway House housed trams that ran from College Green to Dartry from 1872 until it closed down in 1948. Converted into an office around 40 years ago, its status as a protected building means that its structure has remained largely unchanged. As a consequence, the interior is reminiscent of a summer camp gymnasium with bright lighting, white walls and popcorn ceiling. It spreads over two floors, with two cutout squares on the second landing that allow for a view onto the first floor.

The openings are surrounded by a three-foot wall that is trimmed with wood and acts as a railing. Like any good tech start-up office, the second floor features a corner kitchen with large tubs of breakfast cereal and a stage made from wooden pallets.

For many years, the décor in the office consisted solely of what the employees had purchased during a weekend shopping excursion that was marketed as bonding exercise. Armed with a few hundred euros' budget, they were tasked with going to charity or craft shops to purchase items which would turn plain office suites into themed rooms. The 'games room', the 'map room', the 'cloud room', the 'cinema room', the 'garden room' and the 'granny room' were some examples, with the latter being where soon-to-be-sacked staff were said to have been taken before their imminent departure. It also featured mismatched pieces of furniture.

Astroturf lined the floor of the garden room, a factor which resulted in various office dogs deciding to relieve themselves on what they thought was grass. As a result, the room earned the nickname 'the toxoplasmosis room' among certain staff and the astroturf was eventually removed.

To incentivize employees, a number of perks were put in place such as subsidized meals. Down the Sofa was a delivery company Web Summit used to offer staff subsidized lunches. The company would pay €5 toward the cost of lunch or €10 toward the cost of dinner if the food was ordered through this service.

A group known as the 'Kinara crew' would also pre-order food at Kinara Kitchen in Ranelagh and car-pool there to get out of the office, and Dartry, for an hour once a week. The restaurant became so popular that at some point there were around 30 people making the weekly pilgrimage for Beef Korma or Chicken Bhuna. In what some interpreted as an attempt to stop the mass lunch exodus, Kinara was added to the Down the Sofa list of delivery options.

As events drew nearer and longer hours were expected, free dinner would often be provided at the office, although the time it was served would often become later and later into the evening.

The status of the office as a dog-friendly space was also intended to encourage people to stay there longer. Regular canine appearances included a Pug, a Burmese mountain dog, and 'Fluffy', Paddy's tiny sandy-coloured mutt who has been described as 'having a noticeable underbite'.

'Quite aggressive, really yappy. Paddy is so tall and he would walk in with this tiny bichon-frise type dog following him around. Fluffy knew she was the boss's dog,' one employee said.

'Someone was always saying 'who's handling Fluffy?" another said.

'It was a mid-aughts tech space, with a "hey it's like a big creche and you can just chill out here" kind of vibe as opposed to "it's an office where you do a professional job and you're compensated appropriately,"' was how another staffer put it.

A dog-friendly office was not without its mishaps, as those who found themselves cleaning the astroturf room soon discovered. A small Pomeranian was also described as once falling through a skylight separating the ground and first floors. 'He was fine. He lived to see another day.'

Other perks like rent reductions were also introduced. These included rent discounts depending on the proximity to which a staffer lived to the office. Additional discounts were also applied if a person lived with work colleagues who were not on their same direct team. From a company perspective, it was great value as it ensured those living close had fewer reasons to be late and were more inclined to work long hours since they had less distance to travel to get home.

Travel opportunities were also a big factor in recruiting and retaining staff. By early 2015, Web Summit had hosted events in London and Las Vegas, with Hong Kong and New Orleans on the agenda that year.

By January 2015, some of these perks were still relatively new and staff were clever enough to know the motive behind them was for productivity. So to counter any idea of a less than diligent work ethic, to compete with colleagues and stave off criticism, they produced considerably for the company. And regardless of whether the beer fridge had a lock on it or not, or whether a subsidized dinner was on the cards, living on a few hundred euro a week was not easy in Dublin.

After Web Summit 2014, a number of those who had been brought in that year were let go, and recent performance reviews had not gone as well as some hoped, meaning the prospect of a pay boost in the near future was looking increasingly unlikely. As a result, many people felt aggrieved and the atmosphere in the office swirled with 'toxic feelings' at that time, according to a characterization from one ex-staffer. Similar remarks were made by a number of others.

To add salt to an already festering wound, a mishap like no other occurred. An email was mistakenly sent out to a wide group of people which revealed the starting salary details of a new cohort of full-time employees. The details showed that some of these new staffers were being brought in at higher salaries than those who were more established in the company and it caused widespread discord.

Those who had worked hard for the company for a year felt they were misled when told that their pay couldn't be increased because the company had to stay lean. Why were brand new people, who had previously been interns, making more than them?

The catastrophic fuck-up was on everyone's minds and many had attended the infamous town hall meeting to see it be addressed. Anonymous questions were put into a system which allowed management to answer them, but the email débâcle had yet to come up.

Aaron Steinberger, the chief operating officer, hinted at the elephant in the room when he said he was getting 'more and more' questions about compensation and, ultimately, 'the more value someone brings, the more value you put into them'.

At one stage he said, 'The best thing you can do for yourselves and your co-workers and everything is put the company first.'

Steinberger, who moved to Dublin after years in San Francisco, had the unenviable job of trying to revamp the company's operating systems. He was fond of pausing for dramatic effect and punctuating the end of his sentences with 'right?'. He was brought in by Paddy to institute a more regimented corporate culture within the office and was said to have been well paid to do so.

Numerous ex-staffers said they found him difficult to deal with. At the town hall meeting, Steinberger wavered between attempting to convey empathy toward staff concerns and becoming irritable when his explanations were not accepted.

Then, one staffer stood up to mention the email. 'I'm just going to ask it because I know everyone's thinking it,' they said.

While he was in the middle of explaining how the incident had made staff feel, especially those who had been there for a year or more, Steinberger interrupted with an 'okay, thanks for asking'. He had clearly been expecting this to come up and strode into crisis management mode by asking for a show of hands to see how many people had heard about the email.

'So there was a small group of people who were moving from one salary to the next, they were a group of interns, I think it was definitely an error that it was sent out to a group of people because that was confusing, it wasn't a company policy,' he said.

'We did move a few people's salaries at once, we moved a bunch of salaries at the end of the year, and in doing that, in the scrappiness of moving things forward we sent a communication across which looked like it was a public service announcement, but it fucking wasn't a public service announcement and I'm sorry for any confusion that that caused … frankly, people aren't all going to make the same wage … ultimately people will make different amounts, that's just how it works,' he added.

A heated and emotional debate about meritocracy, transparency and trust ensued. Steinberger put forward a dichotomy of either accepting that everyone has different salaries for reasons which cannot be appreciated by non-managers, or agree to be paid the same as everyone else.

'You can do this, this is what the army does, this is what bureaucracies do, and that's okay, especially if you have some kind of nationalized service which is not really that competitive, and you want to amass a large army, but ultimately we need to have as much value as we can in the organization.'

A back and forth debate ensued between him and various staffers, and requests were put forward to have formal appraisal systems and clearly outlined performance expectations.

Steinberger said he thought the stress people were feeling was natural because the organization had scaled very quickly.

One woman said it was not about the salary number 'because we are working for something much bigger than just revenue'. When she said it was actually about the unfairness inherent in two people doing the same job for different money, she elicited a remark from Paddy who spoke up to note that 'we don't disagree'. But a few minutes later, when the same woman made references to this being an important issue because of transparency, open discussion and maintaining trust, she drew the ire of her boss.

The room fell silent as Paddy raised his voice to announce, 'You don't know, have people been let go for sexual harassment, have people been let go for stealing company information, you don't know at all, we don't disclose any of that stuff, and like on the same level you just don't know the performance of other people.'

Allegations of theft and sexual harassment would be ones Paddy would level at ex-staff in the years to come as well, but there is nothing to suggest that any of those who had been let go at the time were as a result of these issues.

The unusual specificity of the claims was not remarked on by staffers during the meeting. As a consistent fan of saying something dramatic to cut through tension, Paddy was known to occasionally come out with statements which appear foreboding.

After more prolonged back and forth between staffers and Steinberger, Paddy intervened again with a monologue that featured him answering questions he posed to the audience, such as 'Is there a possibility that in any human organization or structure there will be error, a margin for error?'

In years to come, he would repeatedly deploy this strategy of answering a quick-fire succession of his own questions, conveying an impression of 'it happens' to multifaceted and complicated issues like staff wages and employee turnover. The skill comes from his ability to impart a feeling that the list of questions he poses is exhaustive, as opposed to selective.

'Mistakes can happen, so the email that was sent was an entire mistake,' Paddy told the room that day. He said it was not in his interest to 'hoodwink' people or have a culture that does not reward meritocracy. 'I'm sorry to all of those who have been kind of sidelined, that have been hurt, it's been a pretty unique week I have to say in the kind of context of the company, definitely, it's been pretty incredible in fact ... bad,' he said to some muffled laughter.

'Really, really, really, fucking bad,' he added.

Interestingly, on the same day that the town hall meeting was held, Paddy had also text Daire, who was in New York, about his shareholding.

Daire would later allege in legal filings that these messages were an attempt to 'coerce' him out of one per cent of his seven per cent shareholding. The messages advised that, for tax purposes, Daire could be shafting himself out of 'incredible amounts of money' if he ended up being classified as a US resident.

Paddy denied that the messages were any attempt to pressure him out of a portion of his shareholding and say that the tax advice 'arose entirely out of the fact that Mr Hickey had chosen to reside in the US'. In any event, Paddy would say in court documents, 'the tone is reasonable and the reasoning clear'.

It was during 2015 that Daire would claim as part of his legal case that it became clear to him that Paddy's objective was to push him out of the company.

'He moved executive meetings to early in the morning in Dublin so that I could not participate while in New York, whereas previously they had always taken place in the afternoon,' Daire claimed in his grounding affidavit as part of his lawsuit. 'I received no financial information regarding the Company, other than the draft annual financial statements.'

'There was no such motivation,' Paddy would contend. 'Rather the impression that we had in Dublin was that Mr Hickey was entirely uninterested in the affairs of Web Summit and that he was following a personal agenda much of the time.'

A number of staffers who worked for the company at the time said that while Daire was rarely seen in the office by early 2015, it was clear when he did attend that there was tension between him and Paddy.

From Daire's perspective, the environment was stressful because of how he was treated by Paddy, whereas from

Paddy's perspective it was 'a question of his performance in the company rather than anything personal'.

While relations between the founders continued to sour, Paddy had very real issues to face in the Dublin office: namely the anger festering among staff following the town hall meeting on the third Friday in January.

Paddy's patience with managing the message around salary discrepancies was wearing thin, as evidenced by his behaviour at the following week's town hall gathering. He made remarks about people being unable to find a job elsewhere, according to multiple people in attendance. Numerous ex-staff recall him making comments about how they were not well-read, had not travelled, and had not lived enough to fairly assess the business of the company. He is also alleged to have said that certain people were spending all their money on runners, which was interpreted as a dig at someone who recently had packages delivered to the office. Many of these claims are supported by messages I have seen where staff discussed the 30 January town hall meeting after it was over and mocked Paddy for his speech. A number wondered whether Paddy was angry because they had yet to read the books he assigned to them.

A reason why the issue of pay exploded in the manner it did was because more and more people began to feel that while the company was prospering like never before, this was not being reflected in their remuneration. Start-up staff expect to be paid pennies at the beginning, and even embrace this as a badge of honour, but if the social contract is broken whereby those at the bottom don't feel lifted up by newfound wealth, goodwill can quickly erode.

Although every single ex-staffer spoken to during this period raised pay as being one of the most pressing issues, it's hard to imagine a company where pay would not be a major issue for a lot of the workforce. And even though many felt wronged by the way pay issues were dealt with in early 2015, the idea, vocalized during the 23 January town hall meeting, that 'something much bigger than revenue' was being pursued, goes to the heart of how the company wanted employees to internalize its brand.

The word 'cult' has been bandied about by numerous ex-staff when describing what Web Summit was like to work at, and a pervasive feeling that being liked depended on having an unfettered devotion to the company. Even Paddy himself once described the Web Summit event as a 'quasi-religious experience' for the average attendee. He also compared the design of the event's main stage to St Peter's Basilica in the way it was laid out and in the 'transcendent' experience it attempted to evoke.

As recently as July 2023, Web Summit's website home-page cites that the *New York Times* once called the conference 'a grand conclave of the tech industry's high priests'. The quote came from an opinion piece about the value of self-doubt by Mark O'Connell, the award-winning Irish writer, which was published in the newspaper's magazine in December 2013.

O'Connell used the conference as a starting point from which to compare the stratospheric levels of confidence exuded by Web Summit's so-called 'high priests' to the self-doubt which plagues creative minds. In the piece, he wrote about how he wandered through crowds of the conference, jotting things down in a notebook under the auspices of potentially writing something about the Irish tech start-up scene for *Wired*.

'After sufficient exposure to this stuff – to 20-minute multimedia presentations, "fireside chats" with victorious founders, public pitches to panels of venture capitalists – my perception of these entrepreneurial people began to blur to the point where they converged, all of them, into one breezily self-assured dude with a cordless head mic and an overinvestment in the concept of disruption,' O'Connell wrote.

O'Connell's observations can be taken as a critique of tech bro types who exude extreme self-confidence from their pores, but his proposed solution was to find some sort of middle ground. Or to know when to listen to nagging self-doubt and when to ignore it.

The nuance in the piece, or the fact that it highlights the value of 'graceful intercession' of self-doubt, is irrelevant to understanding why Paddy loves the quote. He loves it because, as a stand-alone line, it invokes a pseudo-spiritual yet academic performance he seeks to embody.

It's easy to sell tickets to an event as a once-off excuse for people to let their hair down; have a few headliners and throw a party is the premise to every festival in the world. But if you can sell them on the idea that they will be changed as a result, even if only a minority truly believe it, you can recruit attendees that go the extra mile.

This sales strategy capitalizes on what has been a long-running search for meaning with the American tech community, and one which has spurned hundreds of essays and countless hours of in-house mindfulness classes. For example, journalist turned HubSpot staffer Dan Lyons described his colleagues in *Disrupted* as 'people who listen to Tony Robbins audiobooks on their way to work and dream of unleashing the power within themselves'.

Even previous content given to start-ups selected for the 'Alpha' track, which was a €1,500 non-refundable ticket package designed for early-stage start-up attendees, utilized somewhat mythical language. It said the programme offered start-ups the opportunity to present their businesses to a global audience alongside the 'titans' of the tech world.

As Web Summit developed more bespoke events, and especially those which centred on exclusivity, the desire to have people speak on subjects other than tech took on a renewed focus.

Subjects like migration, race relations, discrimination, climate change, women's rights, philanthropy, whistle-blowing and even morality have been an increasing focus of speaker discussions as the company has evolved.

Newsworthy topics coupled with celebrity appearances are a vital way to ensure that the company can make the headlines and feed an insatiable internet content machine. A perusal of the videos on Web Summit's YouTube account is reminiscent of a collection of Ted Talks, but these discussions are only a small part of what it sets out to provide.

For much of the company's early years, getting the right people in a room together centred on two clear groups: start-ups and investors. The former need the latter's money to grow; the latter need to feel like they know how to throw their money around on the right company, at the right time.

By 2016, Paddy wanted ways to get more powerful people into a room together to build clout for the brand and to draw in a more diverse audience. It had been trading off success stories like the Uber investment deal for years and it wanted to offer spaces other than the Web

Summit stage where world leaders, diplomats, Hollywood actors, rappers and sports stars could meet each other.

This was what inspired the creation of 'The Forum', which was designed to be a mini-Davos style event. The Forum was a notable success, recruiting well-known and respected figures on the world stage, including representatives from the White Helmets – volunteers who rescued civilians during Syria's civil war.

It followed on from 'Series 150', which featured at the Collision festival in New Orleans earlier, and sought to target 'C-suite' leaders, i.e. those in the top levels of a company's management with the word 'chief' in their role title.

The idea behind both was to introduce another ticket category with a hefty price tag, but also to establish relationships with large companies in order to make it easier to get a CEO onstage.

The relevance of the number 150 was because of its connection to a theory from Robin Dunbar, a British anthropologist who became convinced that there was a limit to the number of meaningful relationships a human could maintain. If a human exceeds 150, the network is unlikely to last or work well together. For Web Summit, harnessing this theory gave the company valuable talking points when selling it to potential attendees because they were told that if a person can only sustain 150 relationships, then these 150 people were the ones to know.

It also involved a new style of selling since C-suite executives rarely responded to cold emails from strangers, and connections had to be forged with the marketing departments that helped call the shots on what events made it into a boss's calendar.

The only problem was that limiting an event to 150 tickets was restrictive from a financial point of view and so the number was quickly dropped.

The team tasked with making it all happen were taught, by both Paddy and Daire, how to harness fame and influence to make money.

A list of those behind companies a VC firm like Andreessen Horowitz invested in was used as a starting point to find high-value attendees. Email invitations for sought-after attendees to other exclusive events like Founders were framed to be drafted and sent directly by Paddy, with a single line stating they were invited and 'are you in?'

Some wrote back confused, asking who or what was inviting them where.

'He [Paddy] was adamant that was how we had to reach out to people because it was the secret to the elusive, exclusive, VIP element of the party,' someone told me.

Getting celebrities who wanted to promote their new start-up or tech charity was a win-win for the actors and Web Summit. And it was solely because of this two-way street that their attendance was guaranteed. As someone who worked with the company around this time described it, there was 'always a case to be made' to people by selling them on their own interests and on the attendance, real or otherwise, of others.

If more politicians were desired, then more big business heads needed to be here, and if more business leaders were wanted, then sell them on hot shot founders; hot shot founders like hot women, and intergovernmental figures want to chat to prime ministers, and so on.

'You tell them that the next person is coming, and then use that as the basis for them being interested and if you can close the loop fast enough before someone figures out that you're lying to them then you will get a lot of powerful people in the room who probably otherwise shouldn't really come to this random tech conference,' someone described the process.

It was a unique kind of hustle, and one which not many were suited to, especially when it often involved attempting to live in a world of high-rollers while earning around €25,000 a year.

Part of the work involved making things up as there was no formula for convincing a famous person to attend. The model was also at constant risk of collapsing if promises made to secure attendance fell through. Some of these problems arose on a small scale in early years, with start-ups being unhappy about the placement of their booths, as well as what was and was not available to them with their ticket packages.

It also emerged in companies and attendees being annoyed about WiFi issues, food options and marketing opportunities, but receiving complaints for on-the-day issues is part and parcel of work in the live events industry.

Staff who were assigned to work on the floor during the conference were carefully instructed on how to deal with complaints in a handbook provided to them ahead of an event. In one of these, a section entitled 'staff information and welfare' stated that if an employee received a complaint 'be polite and helpful'.

'Do not argue or offer an opinion,' it said. 'Apologize, not because you have done anything wrong but because they are having a bad time and not enjoying themselves or they are having a problem,' it added.

Handbooks were also provided to start-ups exhibiting at the event and these featured a list of 'Do's' and 'Don'ts'. The former featured advice such as 'Use your team effectively. Be everywhere! Have one teammate work the crowd, bringing people to your stand while you pitch and demo.' The list of Don'ts included 'Don't dwell on rejection. Consider it a learning experience!' and 'Don't expect success to walk up and offer itself to you.'

'Aside from promotional material and business cards, start-ups are welcome to bring freebies, prizes or their company mascot,' a list of frequently asked questions provided to the Alpha track of start-ups stated.

'Booth-babes are strictly forbidden,' it added.

A number of staff who worked on the floor of the main event said there were often complaints to field from start-ups who felt they were not getting their money's worth. Other more pressing issues were those which threatened to become PR nightmares. A former staffer recalls having to manage an aggrieved company who claimed to have scraped the Web Summit app and complained that the number of people registered was far less than the number of attendees promised. The incident was a real-life manifestation of the low-level paranoia which lived within many staffers' minds: that an event would kick off and it would be glaringly obvious that there weren't as many people as promised in attendance.

While the company has packed out conference centres for many years now, many staff recall the days when this was not the case. Enterconf, the company's first and last attempt at an enterprise conference in Belfast, was plagued by low turnout and Web Summit staff were told to sit in the audience to help bulk out the attendees.

Aside from the genuinely held fears of not being able to deliver, there were also some ex-staffers who believed the company traded off attendance numbers inflated by free tickets for media, students, partner companies and the free tickets that every Web Summit staff member is entitled to.

A number of staff have described how the numbers were regularly set at extremely ambitious or vague targets. A well-placed source even said it was their understanding that the headline attendance figure was calculated by using a combination of total ticket sales and the average number of days each ticket holder will attend.

Fluffing the numbers is a regular facet of the marketing world where millions of impressions are sold as containing real-world value, even if they only result in more modest sales, subscriptions or conversions. And this is not a tech-specific issue either, as anyone who works in media can attest to.

Some ex-staff said the fear of being caught out on attendance numbers was always a part of work in the live events sector, while others said it was because Web Summit went to such lengths to push a 'sold out' experience.

'There was a major cultish vibe that everyone talks about, where if you're not sipping the Kool-Aid, then you're not cool,' one ex-staffer recalled.

The Kool-Aid came to mean a variety of things as the company evolved, but it primarily revolved around loyalty. The company revelled in promoting its success as a direct result of the astutely clever and hard-working staff it employed.

Marketing that idea as a recruitment strategy was relatively easy given that it was far from spin, and while the face of the company was becoming an increasingly controversial boss, dozens of talented staff kept the wheels turning behind the scenes.

Among those who have remained are people who could have easily risen through the ranks at much larger companies, but instead honed their skills at a small Irish start-up. And these loyal employees have been duly compensated, with some of the longest serving commanding significant six-figure salaries in the present day. Live events is also not a notoriously well-paid industry, so those who have excelled at Web Summit are likely making more than they would in another Irish company.

The best workers were smart, but more importantly ambitious. 'Doing more requires building our technology, operations, live events, sales and communications teams. I'm sure our greatest accomplishments are still to come – have you got what it takes?' Paddy is quoted as saying in a series of recruitment slides in 2016.

A former long-serving staffer said it was very easy to stay despite feeling undervalued. 'The culture is built around making great memories and friends, and that's why it's hard to leave Web Summit. People think if I leave I'm not part of that craic anymore, the events, the social events … there are so many social events, the whole interview process, the hard work in the early days, it's almost like a fraternity or sorority pledges,' they said.

Another said their years at Web Summit were spent expending their productive energy, and the rhythm of constantly running up a hill, then celebrating that you made it, was addictive but exhausting. 'It should have been a dream job, it should be a dream company, but it's just people who frankly were insufficiently emotionally mature for leadership, and raised in a toxic environment of what it means to be a leader or a business owner and ruining it for everybody including themselves,' they added.

The general interview process by 2015 consisted of seven stages and featured a specific 'culture fit' segment where potential staff would be evaluated by how well they were likely to assimilate with the company. It was said to be indiscreetly disarming, with caveats like 'We're just here to chat' and questions like 'What was the biggest fuck up in your life?'

One ex-staffer said a cultural fit interview helped the company scope out whether a potential employee was robust enough for the stress of the job as well as up for becoming extremely close, occasionally in the physical sense, to their work colleagues.

The culture fit segment was not the only usual aspect of the interview process, which one source said featured a question like 'How would you describe the colour blue to a blind person?'

Another unusual aspect of the company's practices was that it operated a system where staff would share hotel rooms while on trips to international conferences. 'It was awkward, and weird, and gross, it was bizarrely uncomfortable and close,' they added.

Partying was a big part of the company's early days in Tramway House and numerous staff described how many Friday evenings turned into 'effective lock-ins' inside the Dartry office, with employees getting absolutely trashed on craft beer or whatever free booze was in the fridge. The emphasis on unwinding among your work colleagues was a big plus for many staff, but it was also a huge liability. Not only did the lines blur between work and pleasure, they also heavily blurred between colleague, friend and romantic partner.

As was to be expected in a company staffed by so many young, single people, numerous couples formed from within the ranks of the firm. There were also more fleeting romances and some which resulted in tense working conditions if the tryst was between people of varying power levels in the company.

Before the company officially moved into Tramway House, staff had a 'warehouse rave' there and spray-painted the walls with graffiti. After the rave one staffer was said to be irate to notice that someone had spray-painted over artwork he had decorated the walls with.

Drugs like cocaine and ecstasy were popular with staff on work nights out, and tales of taking drugs at after-work gatherings have become war stories among long-serving and former employees. According to one that has been passed around for many years, a Web Summit employee took drugs with Snoop Dogg at a separate event during the Collision conference in 2016.

Part of the interest in a party-heavy lifestyle was because the staff were young, but it was also because the behaviour of the high-flying investors the company engaged with was contagious.

As a relatively sober person, and one who has never had much time for exploring the effects of psychoactive substances, Paddy did not partake in any sessions of this kind. Instead, he was said to occasionally purchase a few cinema tickets on a Friday and invite the office to come watch a film with him over the weekend.

He also liked dining out. At an after work gathering for food at the Market Bar on Dublin's Fade Street, Paddy was alleged by one former staffer to have shown up unexpectedly, ordered a significant number of dishes and 'disappeared' before the bill came to meet someone.

'We didn't make the interns pay for it,' they added.

Chapter 9

'OUR ABSOLUTE PREFERENCE IS TO STAY IN IRELAND'

While the company was walking a fine line between containing upheaval over pay and maturing a cohort of young adults into working professionals, a number of battles brewing in the background would soon spill out into the public domain.

Most notable among these was the company's decision to move Web Summit to Lisbon, Portugal in 2016. The government there was offering Web Summit €1.4 million upfront to base the conference there, calculating that it would hoover up many multiples of this in tourism and business revenue. Although this was less than what other cities were pitching as an 'event fee', or base price to buy the conference location, Lisbon was regarded as being 'up and coming' – a factor which would go on to be a prerequisite in determining which future cities would shell out.

Other issues such as Ireland's lack of large-scale conference facilities and the persistent problem with WiFi within its current home in the RDS were also very much high on the minds of those involved in talks to relocate the conference. The company had undoubtedly outgrown Dublin in many respects. Internet aside, the infrastructure in the RDS was old and spread out, requiring attendees to cross roads or move through the space in a disjointed manner.

Some key staff were informed ahead of the announcement in September that the move had been decided. Paddy consulted with some of his trusted advisors at the time about whether he should release a trove of emails with the Irish government over issues around WiFi, transport options and hotel prices.

The answer was a resounding no, but in typical Paddy form, he did it anyway.

Among his key advisors was Mike Harvey, a former features editor at the *Times* and an ex-Google communications director who was a big hire for Web Summit, from both a PR angle as well as a financial one, since he was brought in as one of the more higher-paid employees. Harvey's claim to fame was that he 'brought Sudoku to the masses', as one employee who worked under him recalled. He talked about this accomplishment so often, another likened it to the 'greatest achievement of his life'. Indeed, the veteran journalist was behind the move to have the Japanese number puzzle published in the *Times* in late 2004, making it the first British newspaper to ever do so.

After the *Times* published it, the *Telegraph*, *Independent*, *Guardian*, *Mail* and *Express* all followed suit. Harvey praised it as an international phenomenon. 'It's the combination of its simplicity and its addictiveness. The rules are so straightforward – you just fill in one to nine horizontally, vertically and in the box,' he told the *Guardian* back in 2005. 'Obviously, the strength of ours is that it's the first. I believe strongly that it's the best. Some of the others have been impossible to solve or have had multiple solutions. That has never happened with the *Times*,' he added.

Paddy regularly bragged about Mike, discussing his past work rubbing elbows with powerful politicians and contributing to pieces about well-known figures. As someone who has long been and continues to be fascinated by the Fourth Estate, Paddy loved talking to Mike about the inner workings of the media business. It was not uncommon for the pair to gather together in a back room of the Web Summit offices three to five times a day.

In this way Mike was his right-hand man for many years and staff described how he 'schmoozed' his boss with his experience which occasionally sheltered him from being picked on by Paddy. He was also one of the oldest employees and in a very senior role during his time there, which staff said gave him a unique perspective. 'He was a real British geezer, funny but difficult, and usually spinning way too many plates,' a person who worked with him said.

He lived in a nearby house rented by Web Summit, known as 'the Web Summit House', during the week and travelled to London to see his family on weekends.

Mike also absorbed a lot of Paddy's anger if press coverage did not work out as planned, and staff recall him frequently being on edge about falling on the wrong side of his boss.

He would later experience a fall from grace in Paddy's eyes, which would eventually lead to him being stripped from certain reporting lines and culminate in his resignation. Despite this, the pair are currently on good terms and have a working relationship, with Mike advising Paddy on high-level communication strategies to this day.

But in 2015 he was focused on putting out fires and managing the message around Web Summit's departure from Dublin. Part of managing that message was, for Mike, putting a dampener on unnecessary drama and being pragmatic. For Paddy, it was, as it often is, about putting others on the defensive and creating a spectacle.

Even if the overarching goal of constructing a narrative around the separation did not work in his favour within Irish media, it cannot be said to have failed from a big picture perspective given that the model of having cities bid on hosting the event has been extremely profitable.

And so began the PR push, driven by Paddy, which built up a sense of FOMO and implied Ireland was losing out because it was run by lazy civil servants – a section of society Paddy held considerable disdain for.

But first, it's important to recognize that there was more than an ounce of truth in the criticisms detailed in over 30 pages of emails released by Paddy to the media over his spat with RDS. Numerous ex-staff, as well as those working in the tech and media industry at the time, agreed with Paddy's outlook. The RDS was not an ideal venue for the conference, and it was reluctant to change its way of doing business to suit the company. It was, as it usually is, Paddy's delivery that they had a problem with. There was also a gnawing feeling, backed up by what some said were real life exchanges, that the RDS regarded Web Summit with hostility and sought to retaliate after Paddy mocked it the year before.

The commercial aspects of moving toward a city-bid model were obvious: it was guaranteed income in a sector which is often plagued by insecurity and unpredictability.

Interestingly for many people, especially those outside of the tech world, this public row was their first exposure to

Paddy, and it's not hard to imagine how someone would come across as extremely disagreeable when they start making noise about not getting their way.

The spat that played out in the Irish media did not paint a flattering portrait of a businessman making a rational business decision, which the Lisbon move had all the hallmarks of. Instead it portrayed Paddy as a petulant and bitter child who, not satisfied with leaving quietly, had to make it a lesson-learning exercise for his former pals in government.

'Our absolute preference is to stay in Ireland,' Paddy told Nick Reddy, private secretary to Taoiseach Enda Kenny, on 21 August 2015.

'We haven't heard from you since last week. We believe it's essential to keep communications open and constant and would be open to a call or meeting at any point,' he wrote in a follow-up on 24 August.

'Without even a basic plan for Web Summit 2016, the company will be forced out of Dublin in the coming weeks. We don't want a penny, we just want a plan for public transport, traffic flow management, WiFi and hotels,' he added in another on 1 September.

The emails increased in length as the weeks went on, with an email sent on 3 September from Paddy stretching to over 1,350 words. The message was very clear: other governments and other politicians are running circles around Ireland in terms of how much attention they show Web Summit.

Paddy lambasted Irish politicians, painting them as lazy, attention-seeking individuals who were ill-equipped for their jobs and incapable of even organizing a meeting.

'Are you aware of Prince Charles' involvement, or No

10 Downing Street, or the Chairman of the Conservative Party? I've detailed it privately over and over again, but it seems not to resonate,' Paddy said.

'How can you be outplayed by the British government in your own backyard? Or by the Dutch, the French, the Danes. It's surreal.'

The condescending tone and sense of desperate urgency also increases as the weeks go on and, despite a decision having already been all but made, Paddy dangles the possibility that 'in these last days' the response he seeks will be delivered.

'This is a great country, filled with great people, who have and will continue to achieve great things. But doing great things requires careful planning, coordination and the desire to do things differently and better. And that's all we're ultimately asking for,' he said.

It had all the hallmarks of a parent or a boss using the 'I'm just disappointed in you' line to coerce a child into behaving differently.

Staff who worked closely with Paddy said this was him applying leadership tactics he had honed over the years, but the problem was that the setting was wrong. He couldn't control the direction of the narrative or deflect criticism and so his handling of the episode from start to finish was scrutinized from afar. Paddy had anticipated that the public and the media would naturally side with a business owner over the government in a battle like this, but he let his temper get in the way.

In a separate email to John Callinan, then assistant secretary general at the Department of the Taoiseach, Paddy hits out at the one-page draft framework sent to him a few hours earlier.

'It's a plan to have an indicative plan. And represents no material change since we started this process all those years ago. Finally, we've stressed repeatedly that without a plan for 2016 we need to make a decision on 23 September. Web Summit is now so large is requires far more than a single year's planning. We have yet to be presented with even a plan.'

That email was sent at 7.20 p.m. on 22 September 2015. By 9.30 a.m. the following morning Paddy announced the Lisbon move online.

Callinan would note in a later reply that by the time Paddy had sent his email the civil servant had already been informed of the decision to move to Lisbon and that he would be announcing it the following morning.

'While I am naturally disappointed with your decision to go to Lisbon next year, I wish you and your colleagues well with this next phase of the Web Summit,' he added.

This could have been the end of the squabbling but it was actually only the beginning. In a blog post announcing the release of the emails, which Paddy claimed were going to be unveiled via a Freedom of Information request, he said he hoped the correspondence 'starts a real debate' about how to make Ireland a 'conference destination'.

According to much of the commentary at the time, the court of public opinion was on Paddy's side in regarding the government's claim about being a business-friendly jurisdiction with scepticism. Having a successful company depart for the reasons outlined in the emails was not, by any assessment, a ringing endorsement of Ireland as a business destination.

A few days after the Lisbon announcement, Dave, who was cc'd on email exchanges with the senior civil servants

153

and described by Paddy as 'leading' on the issue, messaged Daire.

'Paddy is relentless,' he said. 'Just with work … he does not stop.'

'Well, you also have a tonne on your plate,' Daire replied.

'I am just not programmed like that … I'd like to be a VC', Dave noted.

'Defo. Be a VC. Genuinely,' Daire said.

'Management is a cunt,' Dave added.

The story of the row remained in the news cycle for days. As the emails included criticism of the hotel industry for alleged 'price gouging', Dublin city council and state agencies, each of these in turn came out to rebut the claims.

Paddy had some of those in power on the back foot, rushing to defend themselves against what they regarded as baseless claims. But these defences, which contained blanket denials of his claims, only provoked Paddy. He wanted a *mea culpa* from those in power and regarded anything less as a lie.

In his mind, the emails were proof that he was in the right and there was no other takeaway possible. Unless, as he would go on to accuse many who refute his claims in later years, those involved were being dishonest.

In a very real way, this strikes at a fatal flaw which continues to plague him to this day: that he is an arbiter of truth and a courier of retribution. His binary view of morality was on full display.

It has been suggested by numerous people as part of the reporting for this book that Paddy manufactured the row with the government as a publicity stunt. They noted that he did appear to instigate it by releasing the correspondence, which garnered him endless headlines, and may have contributed to a stronger hand in future bidding negotiations. But how he responded when he did not get the reaction he was hoping for after releasing the emails implies that much of the motivation was impulsive anger.

A few weeks after the emails were released, Paddy appeared in a *Morning Ireland* interview sounding absolutely incensed.

The conference was off to a great start but the rage in his voice was palpable from the outset. He referred to the around €750,000 given to Web Summit by the IDA and Enterprise Ireland as 'hush money' and said the government inflamed the fight to distract from issues like homelessness and the health crisis. 'The way it's played out and the way it's been spun and lies told by the government are a useful and practical distraction from the day to day beating that they take at the hands of the Irish media,' he told Brian Dobson, who sounded slightly bewildered in his questioning.

Then that evening, Paddy pulled out of an interview with Sharon Ní Bheoláin on the *Six One* news, leaving Daire to take on what has gone down in Irish television history as one of the most awkward business interviews in recent memory.

Ní Bheoláin questioned him on why Web Summit did not front up the cash to pay for its demands and why the company contacted the Taoisearch about issues with hotel prices. The exchange features Daire going to bat for Paddy with a line that described him as 'an entrepreneur who cares incredibly about his product' and the experience of attendees. The uncomfortable interview ended with Daire audibly pulling the microphone off his shirt and walking away.

'That poor fucker', was what one national newspaper editor watching it live remarked in his office at the conclusion.

A few days later Paddy would pull out of a planned appearance on the *Late Late Show*. Then on Saturday the *Irish Independent* ran a lengthy profile under the headline 'Spoofer turned prophet: the enigma of Paddy Cosgrave' which featured an anonymous ex-staffer saying, 'Paddy has lost the plot.'

On the front page of the *Sunday Independent* the following morning, Brendan O'Connor's tongue-in-cheek editorial said Paddy 'wondered why he, whose only crime is to try to make the world a better place, should be subjected to questioning by ingrates on old media'.

'We were prepared to feel a bit sad about losing the Web Summit. But by the end of the week we were feeling sorry for the poor bastards in Portugal who have to deal with this petulance for the next few years,' it added.

Paddy was fuming at the fallout, that staff were briefing against him to the newspapers, and that what he believed were eye-opening revelations about government inaction in the emails were not appreciated.

The stage had clearly been set for what developed into years of a tumultuous back and forth between Paddy, the media and the government. How these events unfolded also made its way into the legal dispute, with Daire referencing Paddy's tirade on *Morning Ireland* as an example of a media engagement which he and Dave found to be 'gratuitous, destructive and unnecessary'. It was among a series of examples which he alleged damaged Web Summit's brand.

'What Mr Cosgrave said was needlessly controversial,' he says in his affidavit.

Although he does not state the decision to relocate was purely financial, Paddy addresses these allegations in his legal filings by claiming that 'the simple fact' was that Web Summit received a 'much stronger offer' from Portugal than it did from Ireland. 'This is why we moved Web Summit to Lisbon in 2016. The event has been enormously successful ever since, which has justified that decision,' Paddy states in his affidavit.

Later that year, the Department of the Taoiseach would release its own trove of correspondence, spanning nearly 250 pages and covering a year-long period from 2014 to 2015. The correspondence showed that a Dublin City Council representative met with Paddy in the spring of 2015 and agreed to convene a cross-department/agency meeting to consider his company's 'asks'. These included road closures, dedicated shuttle buses, temporary Dublin bike stations, suspended parking permission in places, complimentary rental of council-owned venues, city-centre branding for Web Summit in the weeks before and during the event, garda escort services and travel cards, among other measures. (The government had proposed discounted travel cards for Web Summit 2016.)

Paddy, writing from Singapore airport on his way to China, said in an email the real issue was not that the government had let Web Summit down, it was that it had let down 'Irish businesses and the State'.

'You missed the elephant in the room. In fact you completely sidestepped the real issue in my email ... At no meeting I've had elsewhere in Europe has a government once said: "Can you come with your list of asks" to a meeting. Instead, they clearly outline what they want for their indigenous businesses and their state, and then what they can offer in return. They say: "This is what we want and this is what we can do for you."'

Signing off, Paddy added, 'I'm sorry if this comes across quite blunt but we are really up against it and I've tried the softly softly approach for four years. Flight is taking off.'

A senior agency source said they were never offended by Paddy's denouncements ahead of and after Web Summit's departure because 'at the end of the day, Paddy has to make it sound right for Paddy', describing him as someone who 'shoots from the hip'.

'I think Portugal were prepared to pay significantly more and then Paddy wanted to make sure everybody didn't think it was just money that drove him,' they said.

The email débâcle was only one of two Web Summit-related spats to play out publicly in the space of a month that year. Another, which occurred at exactly the same time, bruised Web Summit staff much more than a PR war with the government.

Jason Calacanis, a well-known American entrepreneur, tweeted at the end of September 2015 that F.ounders had informed him that Web Summit was charging start-ups $10,000 to meet angel investors.

'Not cool, not worth it,' Calacanis said in a now deleted tweet.

In reality, the figure of $10,000 was based on the price that Web Summit told start-ups their packages were worth, but those chosen to attend received a 'code' which reduced the price down to around $1,500.

A few days later a scathing opinion piece was published by Neil Murray, a writer and investor, on Tech.eu entitled: 'Why I'm not going to Web Summit – in Dublin, Lisbon or anywhere else'.

Murray complained about Web Summit's alleged 'spam' marketing tactics and history of asking companies to 'host' drink or dinner receptions for its events. Citing Calacanis's tweet, he said his biggest issue was charging start-ups thousands to attend and get the chance to meet investors. 'This is where I have my biggest problem with Web Summit: start-ups should not be where you make your money from at an event. This is harmful to them, and to the wider community,' he wrote.

The piece ignited a war of words online which resulted in back and forth statements and responses from Paddy and Tech.eu.

In a blog post on Web Summit's site, which had originally been titled 'Is Web Summit a Scam? – Setting the Record Straight' but has since dropped the first part of that headline, Paddy hit back. Hinting that some of the criticism was coming on the back of competitors taking notice of Web Summit's rapid growth, he said, 'some incumbents have gone on the marketing attack' and alleged his company was 'hoodwinking' start-ups all over the world.

'They claim that Web Summit charges startups $10k to meet angel investors. They also say we are a "pay to pitch" or "pay to be accepted" organization. None of this is true,' he added.

Paddy's blog post resulted in an article being penned by Robin Wauters, editor of Tech.eu, who claimed that since Murray had written his initial piece they had received 'heaps of emails, direct messages, Skype and Facebook IMs thanking us for "exposing Web Summit"'.

'Most are afraid, for whatever reason, to have their opinions out in public,' he wrote.

The Tech.eu row seemed to throw the kitchen sink at Web Summit, hitting out at 'deceptive' marketing practices which used targeted ads that it alleged contained inflated numbers.

In pointing out that the company focused on hiring data scientists and engineers, something that Paddy had proudly proclaimed numerous times in interviews or blog posts, Tech.eu said this was 'the core of the problem'.

'The advertisements they run, and a large part of the emails that they send, are straight-up deceptive, to say the least. That's worse than spam, and Web Summit has demonstrated that it's prepared to take things up a notch with every event,' the piece added.

Facebook advertisements that specifically targeted a user's location were an extremely effective part of Web Summit's marketing strategy during this period. It also experimented with other novel ideas, such as targeted ads based on a user's friend group or wider connections across multiple platforms. It was a part of the business that was helping to bring in huge revenue, which made what felt like an unfair assault sting even more.

One ex-staffer described the ordeal as a 'smear campaign' in communicating how much of an upheaval it felt like in the office and how the firm felt 'under threat'. He said other conferences around the world operated similar business models and the timing of the criticism levelled at Web Summit indicated it was related to the firm branching more into North America.

The social media posts which followed in the wake of the Tech.eu piece included additional accusations of scammy behaviour and alleged false marketing practices. Taking heat from Wauters was exceptionally difficult for the company to withstand given that he had a large following in the European tech community and had attended Web Summit events in the past.

He was far from the first or last famous person to hit out at Web Summit online. Jay Rayner, the *Observer's* food critic, had also criticized the company in social media posts over 2014 and 2015. 'That @WebSummitHQ are a weird (ill mannered) lot. Twice they've asked me via email to speak at a Dublin event. I've explained they'll have to pay cos [sic] I'm not Bono or CEO of a tech company. Twice they simply haven't bothered to reply,' he said in a series of posts.

The onslaught of online criticism weighed heavily on many Web Summit staffers, and the team, especially those who had been there for a couple of years, felt extremely under threat. 'It felt like these well-connected people were slinging barbs at us,' one staffer recalled. Such was the level of passion and belief that some Web Summit staffers regarded their work that having the company criticized in public felt like a personal attack.

The negative attention also threatened to upset one of its biggest revenue stream, and so it was taken seriously by those in charge.

Around the height of the mudslinging, the company rented out the MV Cill Airne, a boat docked in Dublin's River Liffey, for a planned staff party. The entire company gathered on the boat to eat, drink and mingle, but the controversy that had been circling seemed to be on everyone's minds.

A senior staffer got up to make a speech but while attempting to rally the troops became so emotional that he was said to have cried.

In a counteroffensive, and to add another bizarre twist to the story, an anonymous account with the handle @ startupjustice began responding to those tweeting critically about Web Summit.

'Web Summit has created immense value and opportunities for 1000's of startups. This is a fact! Only the bitter and jealous are complaining,' the account, which was deleted soon after it was established, noted.

After Wauters repeatedly floated that it was someone in Web Summit, Mike Harvey shot down the idea by replying on Twitter: 'Not us. I know you are trying to do your job as you see fit.'

As if the drama of the emails and the departure news were not enough for the company, that year's Web Summit would also be cursed with negative publicity from poor WiFi and allegedly overpriced food.

As 2015 was the first year that the Web Summit took control of the WiFi, hiring Signal Share to manage the system, this greatly reduced the amount of public shade that Paddy could throw on the RDS. So to keep attention on the good news, and to showcase the scale of delivering uninterrupted WiFi to 40,000 people, he instead tweeted: 'We've flown past 1 terabyte of data downloaded on WiFi before lunch today.'

Another change from 2014 was that Web Summit no longer offered attendees free food, claiming that this cost it €1.2 million and now that it had doubled in size again this was not economically viable. Photos of a burger and a bottle of water were shared by some attendees with the claim that this was what the conference offered as a €20 lunch.

Mike Harvey fielded media queries on both the WiFi and the food issues, saying of the former that there had been 'former blips' and that people using hotspots got in the way of the service.

He referred to complaints about the food as misinformed. 'What you get for your €20 now is a meal, drink, coffee, snack and a dessert. People focused in on the fact that it was a meal and a drink,' Harvey told Joe.ie.

In the wake of Web Summit's departure from Dublin, Harvey would find himself involved in another fire, this time involving an allegation of hacking a competitor.

The Dublin Tech Summit was established as a company in February 2016 and as its first CEO it hired Noelle O'Reilly, an ex-Web Summit staffer.

Following this, Paddy and other senior Web Summit staff became concerned that O'Reilly had taken company data with her on her departure and IT were instructed to trawl through her de-activated company email address. According to how he characterized it in legal filings, Paddy said this review led to the discovery that a company database had been allegedly downloaded by O'Reilly. 'I confronted the competitor with this information and a confidential agreement was reached whereby the database was returned/deleted,' he said.

In Daire's version of events, after the company became concerned that Dublin Tech Summit may have access to Web Summit data, legal advice was take on the best way forward. He claimed that while the issue was under consideration the company received a letter sent on behalf of

Dublin Tech Summit alleging that their files had been hacked.

'Mr Cosgrave then admitted to colleagues, including myself, that he was responsible for hacking the email of Dublin Tech Summit in order to identify the extent of Company data which they possessed,' Daire said.

Mike Harvey was extremely nervous about the issue being reported on in the media because he knew people would not have trouble believing Paddy would go to such an extent. In a confidential internal memo, he described how the issue would be 'irresistible to the media' given Paddy's 'history of outspoken behaviour'.

Harvey suggested that they could bury the alleged hacking breach in the drama or 'go after' O'Reilly but 'do we want to be seen to be going after a single mother etc?' He also provided advice on how to deal with the public relations fallout which would arise if this information became widely known.

Paddy had decided that it was better to be proactive on a potentially embarrassing issue rather than waiting to be on the defensive. 'I think we need to write up a very detailed 1,500-word hacking the hackers post ready to press live if that day ever comes,' he text Daire at the time.

'The banter letter that we send needs to be a piece in that piece if we ever need to publish it. Just so everything ties together. As much as I like a good fight this is so minor and such an unnecessary distraction that we just need to move on,' he added.

In an email chain with an external solicitor who provided legal advice to Web Summit, Daire said his concern about going legal over the issue was 'not so much our reputation' but rather that it would involve a High Court battle with

Denis O'Brien, the telecoms mogul who was believed to be funding DTS.

'It's a massive distraction of time, money, and resources and although we're entirely right, it's not a good use of any of our efforts,' Daire wrote.

O'Reilly would not remain at the Dublin Tech Summit for long and she would move abroad a year later where she took up work as personal assistant to FKA Twigs, the singer whose real name is Tahliah Debrett Barnett.

Her name would end up featuring repeatedly in a lawsuit taken out by Barnett against Shia LaBeouf, the actor, over allegations that she improperly provided him with private and confidential information about the singer.

It also accused O'Reilly of stealing Barnett's designer clothes and committing identity theft in order to recommend herself for membership of Soho House.

Chapter 10

LISBOA

Inside Lisbon's Panteão Nacional, a seventeenth-century baroque monument on the site of a desecrated church, rows of picnic tables extend out like spokes from a wheel-shaped centre.

The light from dozens of candelabras flickers on the marbled floor, which radiates toward a rust and navy-coloured flower design positioned directly underneath the building's dome.

It is a sombre post-dinner scene as the low hum of chatter is drowned out by choral singing in the background. The tables are metres away from a tomb dedicated to Vasco de Gama, the Portuguese explorer, as well as the burial sites of some of the country's presidents and national heroes such as the footballer Eusebio and the writer Almeida Garrett.

Web Summit staff potter around the room, waiting for a chance to break free from what could be mistaken for a subdued wedding and head out to enjoy themselves after a long day.

This is the 2017 edition of F.ounders, the company's exclusive invite-only event for people it deems interesting and who are rich enough to pay over €4,000 for a ticket. The ticket fee can be waived for some of the more rich and powerful attendees.

Earlier, Werner Vogels, the CTO of Amazon, arrived at the Four Seasons flanked by staff and talking rapidly on the phone. Vogels was a big coup for the team but there was concern up to the eleventh hour that he may be too busy to attend.

The F.ounders dinner had been a roaring success, until Portuguese politicians and diplomats expressed their disgust that such a revered location was chosen as the site of an exclusive dinner. Pictures circulated on social media were described as making the monument resemble a 'cult'.

Antonio Costa, the Portuguese prime minister, said in a statement that hosting a dinner in this space was disrespectful to the memory of those who were honoured there. Costa, who was not at the dinner, pledged to change the law to ensure the situation was not repeated in 'violating history, collective memory and national symbols'. He said the decision which sanctioned the event had been made by a previous government.

As some commentators pointed out, the Web Summit dinner was not the first time that this monument had been rented out for a private venue. And if it was cult-like occasions which were angering the Portuguese leaders, a publishing house had rented the space for a Harry Potter book launch in 2003.

The minor diplomatic emergency was addressed by Paddy, who said the company 'apologized for any offence caused'.

'Culturally, the Irish celebrate death and in the past the most important dinner at F.ounders has taken place at

Christ Church Cathedral in Dublin, in the largest crypt in the UK and Ireland,' he said.

'I love this country as a second home and would never seek to offend the great heroes of Portugal's past,' he added.

This was Web Summit's second year in Lisbon after an eventful 2016 which included numerous conferences in New Orleans, Hong Kong and Bangalore. Each was not without its fair share of mishaps, especially the Surge event in Bangalore. The company announced it would return the following year but never did.

Mistakes and regrets aside, the scrappy Irish start-up was becoming increasingly adept at bringing its technology jamboree on tour. It was also continuing its trend of having a star-studded line-up at the flagship event, with Lisbon 2016 drawing the likes of actor Joseph Gordon-Levitt, model Lily Cole, rapper Tinie Tempah and R&B musician Ne-Yo.

American businessman Billy McFarland also appeared at the inaugural Lisbon Web Summit, speaking at a side stage just six months shy of his 'Fyre Festival' fraud in the Bahamas. He was introduced onstage by the rapper Ja Rule as his 'partner in crime'. McFarland would later plead guilty to wire fraud and spend nearly four years in prison.

As it was the first time the company had shipped its flagship Web Summit conference over to Portugal following a public spat with the Irish government, there was immense pressure to make everything perfect.

In so many ways, Lisbon and its officials had rolled out the red carpet for Web Summit. It was authorized to set up pre-registration tables at Lisbon airport so that visitors from over 160 countries could access information as soon as they flew in. The company was also able to negotiate a special transport ticket for delegates to use the city's metro or bus system for a flat fee.

Most importantly, the MEO arena, as the venue was then known, worked closely with the country's telecom agency and Cisco to provide uninterrupted and reliable WiFi. The company had heavily staffed-up the arena, with its own IT experts and there was a separate dedicated team in an upstairs control room. A large communication cable ran through the length of the arena and a dedicated pop-up cell tower was installed in a space between the main arena and a separate hall.

'To give you a sense of the scale of our network in Lisbon, we laid enough fibre optic cable to reach the peak of Mount Everest eight times – that's 80,000 kilometres,' one of its engineers would recount in a blog post after the event.

As all of this demonstrates, a widespread effort went into ensuring that the tech infrastructure at Web Summit 2016 did not fail and for the most part it withstood the pressure of 50,000 people and their respective devices.

But it was not enough for Paddy to have things go off without a major glitch; he wanted to try something new to show off just how much better things were in Lisbon compared to Dublin. And he wanted to do this live, onstage, in front of over 15,000 people in the audience and an additional 3,000 more watching from outside the arena.

During his remarks welcoming a packed arena of attendees, he told the crowd that his wife Faye could not be at the event because she had recently given birth to Cloud, their first child. He said he wanted them all to go live on Facebook.

This moment has been burned into the brains of some of the Web Summit staffers watching it unfold from a few hundred metres away. They knew full well that trying to have the system withstand an attempt to have thousands of people simultaneously go on Facebook live was risky and likely to fail.

Panic descends on the troops. As Paddy scrolls through his phone, his notifications appearing in a drop-down window at the top of the screen, he states 'Let's see if 4G and WiFi holds up, it would be pretty incredible, a first in the world of this scale.'

'Uh oh, is the WiFi working? Fingers crossed ... here we go,' he says, staring at a blank window while a spinning wheel turns on the screen behind him.

'I don't think it's working, ok, we'll try this again later, let's, let's not worry,' he adds.

Although he was furious at it not working out, he came out later that evening to state that he was going to do something that he 'really shouldn't risk again'. He said in the previous attempt he had been connected to a 'Dutch mobile network' and now he was connected to a Portuguese WiFi signal. Most notably, he did not ask the audience to join him.

'Is it going to work, grimacing, oh my god, I think it's actually working, oh it's working, wow. Ok, I would like to thank Portugal Telecom for making the WiFi work,' he said.

The episode garnered headlines back in Ireland about the company's 'WiFi woes' and sent social media users into a frenzy with comparisons to the conference's time in the RDS.

At a press conference Paddy fielded queries from Irish media on the issue, saying Web Summit was 'never perfect'.

'But if we find something wrong, we fix it,' he added.

Lisbon 2016 and the years ahead were a commercial hit for the company. The nearly €1.5 million it received to hold the Web Summit event there for the first few years turned into €11 million per year until 2028. That deal, inked in 2018, contained a €3 billion 'buyout clause' should another city try to woo the company before the time was up. It was a mutually beneficial arrangement as Portugal wanted to be seen as a European hub of technology and innovation while Web Summit wanted financial stability.

The Portuguese government at that time said it believed that the event generated €300 million for the capital city during the week it takes place every November. It even honoured the deal during the Covid-19 pandemic amid criticism that the income the event brought into the local economy had been destroyed by the lockdown.

But even as far back as its first year in the Portuguese capital, Web Summit was welcomed with open arms by politicians and business figures. Opening the conference in 2016, Prime Minister Costa said he wanted people who attended to 'remember Portugal as a dynamic, progressive, and open to business country'.

The first year of the Lisbon conference was one of the most significant years for Web Summit and for the three founders in their personal lives, having started families and accumulated wealth. But as the lawsuits have revealed, even if it was smiles for the cameras, there was a deep misery taking root among the three men. The most striking example of this is Dave messaging Paddy at 7 p.m. on the opening night, just before he walked onstage to do his failed Facebook live attempt, to say that he 'just can't do this unfortunately'.

The year started off with bang for Daire, who became one of only two Irish people named on the Forbes 30 Under-30 list in January. The other was Hollywood actress Saoirse Ronan, then known for her role in the film *Brooklyn*.

'Hickey takes care of top-tier partners, like Google and Facebook, and holds the keys to F.ounders, an invite-only event for top tech founders,' it noted.

Making the list was a huge ego boost to start the year with and he had spent much of his time during this period travelling around the world. A couple of months before the 2016 event in Lisbon he boasted that he had clocked up around 700,000 airmiles in the last three years.

Daire, who was based in New York at the time, was regarded by a number of staffers as distant and aloof when he appeared in the Dublin office. Some said he appeared to be so unphased by unfamiliar faces in the company's Darty HQ that it seemed like he was waiting to see if they stayed longer than six months before learning their name.

Yet even if he was too preoccupied with big-picture ideas to fully engage with newer staff, he was all guns blazing in his promotion of Web Summit. In a Creator Lab podcast recorded a couple of months before the 2016 Web Summit, Daire provides what is to date one of the most in-depth interviews he has ever done during his time with the company.

It paints the picture of a man at the top of his game and he heaps praise on Paddy at numerous points throughout, telling host Bilal Zaidi that he would happily do another company at some stage in his life, but that Web Summit was 'super, super exciting' for the time being.

'It's growing like crazy. I'm happy to do this for another few years and then, you know, see how it goes,' he said.

But less than eight months later, Daire would resign as an employee in circumstances which are hotly contested in the lawsuits.

Daire would claim that his resignation was to 'pursue other interests' and occurred as a result of being unhappy with how Paddy had treated him. He alleged that from 2015 on it became clear to him that Paddy's objective was to push him out of the company.

Paddy denied this and alleged instead that it was issues with Daire's performance and revelations that he was being paid for side work which caused their relationship to deteriorate.

A striking aspect of the entire fallout was the speed at which Daire and Paddy's relationship, which had continued for more than 12 years at this point, fell apart after the 2016 Web Summit. In some ways it is extremely believable that a mounting list of stressors could finally implode any shred of goodwill left between the men. But in other ways this does not stand up to scrutiny as Daire would have by then been well-versed in Paddy's ways of doing business.

Even by his own admission in the podcast recording, Daire said he had no intention of leaving 'for another few years' and he spoke extremely candidly about his history of clashing with Paddy in the preceding years.

Part of the answer can be found in some of the documents exhibited as part of the lawsuit, which depict a regular stream of angry messages between Paddy and Dave about their other founder in the months preceding Web Summit 2016 as well as in the months afterwards.

As early as 2014 the pair talked about their apparent frustration with Daire. The feeling among them at the time was that they were working hard to grow the business in Dublin while Daire was living it up in New York.

Dave referred to the move as a 'waste of time' that summer and the discussions about the 'demotion', as previously described, occurred shortly afterwards.

By February 2015, the tone became more pointed, with Dave telling Paddy that he could not stand Daire's attitude.

'I feel like we've been taken advantage of,' Dave said.

The issue came to a head in June 2015 when Paddy contacted Daire by telephone. The call, which was recounted by Daire in his legal filings, consisted of Paddy 'aggressively' telling him that he had 'ruined everything' and to 'stay away' from that year's RISE conference.

On 22 June 2015 Daire emailed both his co-founders to described the allegations made in the call as 'unexpected and out of the blue'.

The following day, Paddy messaged Dave to say that he was asking Daire to finish up.

'He needs to go off and figure out his life ... he has repeatedly fucked teams. I have carried him and cleaned up his mess at least since 2011. We all have. No process. No records.'

Although he does not address the phone call from the day before in his replying affidavit, Paddy describes being unhappy with Daire's performance in the company at this time and refers to the matter as 'behavioural issues'.

A couple of days after sending this email, Daire had a conversation with Dave where he was 'persuaded' to remain with the company but to take two to three months off. Daire agreed to this proposal. Shortly after, Dave told Paddy that Daire was going to take three months off and come back for the week of Web Summit that year. 'Fair play on achieving that. That's really great,' Paddy replied.

Despite this heated exchange and Daire's few months off, it was business as usual when the company's last event in Dublin kicked off that year.

As already described, Daire's role at that year's event included going on the national evening news, defending Paddy, and taking an extended grilling on live television. Mike Harvey praised Daire's performance on the evening news, saying after that he 'acquitted himself very well'.

The infighting over alleged behavioural and performance issues would only be the tip of the iceberg to emerge as an alleged catalyst to the fallouts described in the legal documents of all three men.

A sexual harassment complaint made by a staffer against Daire in 2016 has become one of the most contentious issues in their commercial lawsuits. It would emerge repeatedly in the legal documents, related to claims about how the men alleged it was handled or used as a threat.

I am not going to attempt to litigate the details or significance being attached to this, especially having regard to the fact that there is a person at the centre who has indicated they do not want to speak to me about it.

In addressing it in his legal documents, Daire states that he had been aware of a complaint made against him by a staff member and was 'told at the time that it had been resolved via an informal process to the satisfaction of the staff member concerned'.

'As such I was never asked or given the opportunity to respond to the complaint. I was given to understand by Mr

Cosgrave at that time that he did not consider it a serious matter, and it was never mentioned to me again,' Daire said in legal filings.

A few weeks after making the complaint, the employee would resign. A number of staff I spoke with over the course of reporting this book said they had been aware of the complaint at the time because it had been discussed among people in the office. All of them said they regretted that it was widely known.

The issue would go on to become one in which Paddy and Dave sharply diverged in their respective characterizations years later.

Paddy would allege that Dave mishandled the complaint and incorrectly told him that the staffer had withdrawn it. Dave would allege that Paddy 'grossly misused' the complaint as a vehicle through which to further his 'campaign of coercion and intimidation'.

But the focus of Dave and Paddy's ire during Web Summit 2016 concerned what they alleged was Daire selling access to the company and its speakers.

The issue, Paddy claimed, came to light because Deirdre Foley, the businesswoman who purchased the Clerys department store in 2015, was 'secretly' added to the list of guests at a dinner being held by the Portuguese prime minister during the first Lisbon Web Summit.

The 2015 purchase of Clery's department store by Natrium, a company Foley was involved with, was extremely controversial because it involved 460 people being unceremoniously fired from their jobs. Foley would later face criminal charges over the redundancies, but these would later be dropped at the Dublin district court due to delays in disclosure of evidence.

At the time, Foley was regularly in the news over job losses and it was widely reported that the Workplace Relations Commission (WRC) was investigating the lawfulness of collective redundancies.

Along with being annoyed at Foley being allegedly invited, Paddy separately alleged that he became aware that the IDA was hosting an 'unsanctioned event' during Web Summit that year which he suspected Daire 'had a hand in'.

On 6 November 2016, the day before the Lisbon event got underway, Paddy wrote a short but curt email titled 'Rule Breaking' to Foley and Martin Shanahan, then CEO of the IDA.

'I am straight down the line. But when you break the rules there are consequences. I'd advise both of you as close friends to reflect. I have absolutely no time for cronyism, favours, or the old ways of doing things in Ireland,' he said.

The email did not address any of the specifics of what he was angry with both Foley and Shanahan about, but in his affidavit, where he exhibits this email, he states 'it is no exaggeration to say that I was furious with the IDA for hosting an event in Lisbon at the same time as the Web Summit conference' and describing the event as a 'Web Summit event'.

If his interview with *Morning Ireland* the year before marked a turn in Web Summit's relationship with the IDA, this email did nothing to improve matters.

The allegations regarding a business relationship with Foley would anger Dave as well. Shortly after Web Summit 2016, Dave messaged Paddy: 'I want to smash Daire up.' A month after, in December 2016, Dave would write: 'I am a little shocked by Daire … it does feel like a betrayal of trust and friendship.' He also proposed a way to 'get rid of Daire by buying him out cheaply'.

'I tell him I am leaving and selling for X, then I change my mind. That way I am on his side, but I am not.'

According to multiple well-placed sources, Dave would later confront Daire in person about the claims related to his work with Foley.

Daire resigned as an employee of Web Summit in April 2017. And in what was regarded as a literal representation of his divergence from the company, he was seen at Dublin airport boarding a flight to New York as a cohort of Web Summit staff were travelling to New Orleans for Collision.

This would be far from the end of the matter as Paddy would allege that he asked Dave to initiate an 'investigation' the following year regarding Daire's alleged sale of Web Summit assets.

An email summarizing his findings in early 2018 would reference his connections with Foley.

'Post the Deirdre Foley incident he admits he has taken money to represent other people,' Dave said in the email to Paddy and a lawyer working with Web Summit.

'He refused to name who these are and says they were not competing and was for "pocket money" … He refused to admit he did anything wrong in this incident,' he added.

Claims that Daire sold access to the company while he was a director would later form the basis of Paddy's defence against his oppression allegations.

There was undoubtedly a quid pro quo aspect to many of the company's dealings with both clients and the media. Journalists who had built up positive relationships with the company and its PR team were given access to high-profile speakers and many, in turn, wrote glowing reviews of its events.

This was a form of horse trading that both Paddy and Daire engaged in, especially within Irish media during the early years.

A number of sources from within the company confirmed that C-suite executives in top tier partner firms were often offered the chance to speak on a Web Summit stage. This arrangement was built into the package deal they entered into, a deal that often involved them sponsoring a fancy dinner or cocktail hour. They also received free tickets and invitations to private Web Summit events.

The challenge for the team tasked with finding the high-profile speakers was to ensure that each stage featured a mix of what one former staffer termed the 'dull as dishwater' executives and people with more star power.

The so-called 'speaker directors' were tasked with finding themes within the various talks that they could use to blend the more and the less interesting people together with.

As Daire had been among the most senior people dealing with a lot of the high-value clients, particularly during his tenure with F.ounders, he was well versed in being a concierge of sorts for the company.

Part of this was evidenced in emails displaying how he dealt with the rich and famous, such as when he tried to get Evan Spiegel, CEO of Snapchat, to attend Web Summit in 2014.

As previously explained, the policy was not to cover the cost of flights for speakers but exceptions were made for those who were regarded as extremely valuable.

'Perhaps it might make sense for Evan to fly direct from SF to Dublin and back to SF via NY. We have a number of flat-bed business class seats for key speakers and we'd be more than happy to help Evan make it to Dublin,' Daire wrote to the company's head of communications.

'We'd love to have Evan in conversation with someone senior from *WSJ*, *Forbes*, *Fortune*, *Wired*, *Guardian*, *Times*, CNBC, CNN, if he was able to make it,' he added, rattling off various well-known business people he said could 'vouch for us'.

This email exchange was exhibited as part of Paddy's attempt to show that Daire was doing side work with Goodwood, a client he did PR work for in 2015.

An email to the Snapchat head of comms that year, from his personal email account, invited Spiegel to an event at Goodwood House hosted by Lord March, who owned the Goodwood Estate in West Sussex. The event was being held as part of the Festival of Speed, which is held on the estate and self-described as the 'world's greatest celebration of motorsport and car culture'.

'As part of the event guests will enjoy unfettered access to the Goodwood estate and festival, a unique behind the scenes experience, access to drive previously unseen cars and the ability to fly a WWII era spitfire as well as a private dinner with Lord March in Goodwood house and an invitation to the Festival of Speed Ball,' Daire said in the email.

Aside from how they are used within the legal battles, the emails pull back the curtain on the behind-the-scenes work that fuels PR businesses in general.

In another exhibited email, Daire tells a client 'here's the deal'.

'I'll write an invite for you. I'll do the intro/get the email addresses for €1,500. If a speaker on the list confirms (an

A list speaker), I'd like a bonus of €2,500 per person. In other words, if Travis Kalanick, Tony Fadell and Sean Parker say they're interested, then you get world-class speakers where Vodafone "wet themselves" and I get a mere €9,000. If however I fail in securing them, I get just €1,500.'

Along with claims about selling access, Paddy alleges that Daire was engaged in separate consultancy contracts while working with Web Summit. Among the ones he chose to highlight was Boston Consulting Group (BCG), which was a sponsor of Web Summit and allegedly paid Hickey $10,000 a month in 2016.

He also takes aim at a former staffer who had been handling VIP attendees of F.ounders and who he claims Daire 'facilitated' the recruitment of from Web Summit 'in order to ensure the smooth operation of the BCG contract'. He has since attacked her online.

Along with it occurring during a time of mounting acrimony between the founders, Web Summit 2016 also took place during Donald Trump's shock electoral victory over Hilary Clinton to become the 45th President of the United States.

The 8 November election took place during Web Summit in Lisbon. Tech leaders gathered around a large screen erected in a backstage area of the Forum, an invite-only section for speakers and guests, to watch the count.

As more swing states turned red, the mood shifted from celebratory to dismal, and a number of those present were seen looking extremely morose. Among the heartbroken was Marcy Simon, Web Summit's US-based friend and PR guru. After that year's event, her involvement with the company would decline as issues with her alleged equity remained, according to her, unresolved.

When it became increasingly clear in the early morning hours of 9 November that Clinton would not become the first woman president of the United States, the few remaining attendees slowly gathered their belongings and moved listlessly back to their hotel rooms. One former Web Summit staffer recalls hearing a 'wail' from inside the Forum.

Attendees of Web Summit that year did not include just Democrat-donating Silicon Valley types, but diplomats working with the incumbent US President Barack Obama. The proximity of those orbiting the conference to the Obama administration was particularly palpable to attendees given that an event was hosted at the US Ambassador's residence ahead of polls closing thousands of miles away. 'The energy was electric and the outpouring of emotion was massive ... so many people around us were really invested in that outcome for the US,' a staffer recalled.

'There's a general sort of feverish energy that surrounds events, so it added to that. Was a very odd, strange experience.'

This absurdity of attendees at a technology conference treating the results of an election like it was an impending Armageddon was captured well by Sam Kriss in a piece for *The Atlantic* a few weeks later. Titled 'Watching the World Rot at Europe's Largest Tech Conference', the article chronicled how much of what is on display at a tech conference like Web Summit were elaborate get-rich-quick schemes as opposed to meaningful attempts to change the world.

Kriss said many of those he spoke to at the event had the 'hunted, hungry, over-caffeinated look of someone possessed' and exhibiting at the conference does not improve the very high probability that a start-up will fail.

'Web Summit is where humanity rushes towards its extinction,' he stated at one point.

Paddy called the article an 'amazing piece of writing'.

As Web Summit's celebrity grew, so did the status enjoyed by the three founders and in particular Paddy and Daire who were fond of rubbing shoulders with the rich and famous.

At this stage they had amassed a decade of experience of being pseudo-handlers for tech billionaires, famous Hollywood actors and human rights activists. But it was not just Daire and Paddy that dealt with the company's high-fliers because, by 2016, there were numerous senior staffers within Web Summit who handled lucrative accounts.

A culture of excess and wildness had formed within the company, which some ex-staffers said was a reaction to the individuals it was interacting with on a regular basis.

Ahead of the first event in Lisbon in 2016, news broke that Shervin Pishevar was facing a lawsuit from Brogan BamBrogan, who co-founded Hyperloop One with him in 2014. Hyperloop One is a high-speed transportation start-up dreamed up by Elon Musk which aims to revolutionize train travel in the USA. A lawsuit between tech founders may be a tale as old as time but the details in the Hyperloop One were unbelievably bizarre.

Among them was the claim that in retaliation for informing company investors of alleged breaches, Afshin Pishevar, Shervin's brother and another defendant, 'strolled through Hyperloop One's office and placed a hangman's noose on BamBrogan's chair'.

'Hyperloop One's security cameras captured it all,' it added, with a photo purporting to be from the security cameras included in the legal filings.

The suit also claimed that Hyperloop One was being 'strangled by the mismanagement and greed of the venture capitalists who control the company'.

'Those in control of the company continually use the work of the team to augment their personal brands, enhance their romantic lives and line their pockets (and those of their family members),' it added.

The reference to romantic lives referred to a claim in the lawsuit that Pishevar began dating the company's PR executive and 'increased her salary from $15,000 to $40,000 a month, more than any employee in the company'.

'When their subsequent wedding engagement fell through, he finally heeded suggestions that her work was worth little and terminated the arrangement,' it added.

In a statement to *Wired*, the company's lawyers called the lawsuit 'unfortunate and delusional' and said the plaintiffs 'tried to stage a coup and failed' and promised 'a swift and potent legal response'.

The reason that news of the lawsuit caused such a stir in Web Summit when it broke in the summer of 2016 was because so many of the characters involved were known to the company. Both BamBrogan and Pishevar attended Web Summit 2015 in Dublin and according to a staffer, a publicist, who was also in attendance, regaled a small group with a story about how she had recently been to Richard Branson's Necker island.

And in this way, even if they worked for a small Irish company, some Web Summit staffers were conditioned to think that they could end up in similar opulent situations.

For some, it was not just the possibility of finding oneself at a fancy dinner or in a luxury hotel, but the sense of belonging in circles of power and influence that the company promoted as enticing.

As someone who worked on some of the company's more exclusive events recalled, it was not uncommon to feel bewildered leaving a dinner with UN leaders, or a famous celebrity's house for an afterparty. It was, they said, a more extreme form of imposter syndrome because of the fact that many staffers were barely making enough to support their modest lifestyles at home let alone gallivant abroad.

A tale which became gossip fodder among Web Summit staff involved a party Daire hosted at the Coachella festival which gave VIP access to some of the company's loyal partners in the USA. It was pitched as a business opportunity but it was a party-heavy junket which featured a boozy brunch in an Airbnb near the festival site in southern California.

The story which made its way back to Ireland was that a VIP ticket that was intended for one of the Collison brothers was mistakenly taken by a Web Summit employee on the trip. When Collison arrived by helicopter to find the ticket had been taken, the team scrambled (successfully) to find him another one.

As much as it was full of new business plans and opportunities abroad, the period between 2016 and 2017 was an extremely turbulent time for the relationships between the three Web Summit founders.

At varying stages during their lives as colleagues, the alliances between the three would change and shift. For a significant period of time, especially around the 2016 conference, Dave and Paddy frequently messaged each other to bitch about Daire. They were not alone, as Daire and Dave often bitched about Paddy over the years, and Daire and Paddy had more than one rant over Dave. These notoriously changeable two-against-one relationships would flip flop as the years went on before landing in an alliance between Dave and Daire as the rows turned legal.

In supporting each other's legal cases, Dave and Daire united against Paddy, something the CEO would claim he found remarkable. 'This is because of the trenchant criticism Mr Kelly made of Mr Hickey's performance with the company over a number of years,' Paddy states in his affidavit.

Someone who worked with the company for a number of years remarked to me that the founder trio regularly experienced these dynamic shifts, describing the three men as 'moving magnets'.

'Sometimes they come together against one, and then they split up and are against each other, it's not like a consistent thing, often two will gang up on another one at different points for a certain argument but that won't mean that they'll have each other for the next argument,' they added.

If Paddy and Dave were aligned at the time on giving out about Daire, they were vehemently at odds in how they believed the company should be run and what its future would look like. This became very apparent in June 2017 when Paddy sparred with Irish journalists who, in covering that he was bringing MoneyConf, its fintech-dedicated spin-off event, to Dublin the following year, characterized Web Summit's 2015 departure in ways he was unhappy with.

'Are you smoking crack?' he asked Richard Chambers, a Virgin Media reporter. He also referred to Philip Boucher Hayes, an RTE journalist he would clash with repeatedly in years to come, as a 'fearless muckraker'.

Later that day and in response to these tweets, Dave messaged Paddy to warn that he would personally be careful confronting journalists. The pair were both in Madrid for that year's MoneyConf event.

'Hornet's nest,' Dave said to Paddy.

'Yup,' Paddy replied.

Switching topics, Dave then said that he knew in his heart he 'can't do this anymore'.

'Can we agree a transition plan and come to an amicable finish after seven years, will be good timing? ... I just need to agree it with you so I can pragmatically start to look for a new job.'

Paddy then launched into a long description about how he was 'so passionate' about contributing to make Ireland a better place.

'I can't sit by in the position that I am and do nothing. I can't shirk doing something because it will irk some well-heeled people in Ireland ... it's easy to just duck my head. Easy to just focus on building a business around the world. Easy to live comfortably. And I understand why it's the sensible and reasonable thing to do. But I'd end up living a life of regrets ... And of course I want to work everything out for you ...'

'That's fine,' Dave replied. 'It's not ended how I would have liked but whatever.'

'I've no idea how I will figure out how to do this alone,' Paddy said.

Another point of contention waiting to boil over at this

period of time was the prospect of outside investment and a potential sale of the company. Dave was in favour while Paddy was opposed.

On 23 February 2017, Dave told Daire that he was 'just honestly fucking wrecked'.

'Tell me about it. Sell the thing!' Daire replied.

A few hours later, Dave told Paddy that the all-consuming nature of the work was taking its toll on him stress wise 'and will no doubt affect my health long term'.

'For me, it has been a big struggle over the last seven years. We have not lived it up and have worked solid. The prospect of a positive financial outcome has been the trade I have made on all of the above. I have sacrificed building a career in an area I am more suited to.'

During the start of that year, a process of engagement began between Web Summit and Ascential, the B2B media company, where it was contemplated that the latter would invest money.

Dave said that this would have likely resulted in large sums being paid to him, Daire and Paddy as shareholders. He wanted Paddy to move on the deal or at the very least see what kind of an offer it would result in.

Patrick Murphy, who had been working on Web Summit's first VC fund, engaged with Ascential on behalf of Web Summit at the start of the year, but before a formal offer was received Paddy emailed the company's chief executive in March stating: 'Really appreciate all the time you guys have given us. We won't be able to progress with Ascential. Looking forward to staying in touch. Paddy.'

Dave was extremely upset after reading Paddy's email which he regarded as a 'unilateral' decision. Later that day he messaged Paddy asking why he emailed the company with a decision without consulting him.

Paddy replied that he was 'proud of what we've built together' but that they wanted different things.

'I want to continue building, but you want to sell and/or leave. Or at least that is my impression. I am more than happy doing this and will continue to be until I believe far greater value can be realized or run it as a perfectly normal and profitable business … I do not want a distressed sale or similar.'

Dave pushed back hard to Paddy's message, responding: 'Why not get the offer? It's not distressed getting that. You can spurn them then. I have built nothing, you have made that clear. You own the company.'

Paddy said Dave has been unhappy 'for a long time' working with him and constantly said events did not suit him. 'Unless we are aligned I think it will mostly just fester. I am proud of what we've built together and I just wish you were prouder and happier.'

Still not letting the issue go, Dave asked Paddy why he was not upfront in his previous messages.

'You said if we get an offer it changes etc. Why not at least see the offer? And wait 48 hours? Then you can say, hey not interesting and move on as you wish. When you are a director in a company with personal liabilities you could at least expect to be given a heads up.'

Paddy told Dave that it was 'the best decision for the company'.

The subject matter of this message exchange would go on to be repeated between the two men for many years to come. Dave would say in his affidavit that although Ascential had not formally ascribed a valuation at the time he estimated the company was worth in the region of €100 million–€300 million at this time.

Paddy strongly defended the decision to refuse the offer, saying it was pushed by Dave and Patrick Murphy, despite him 'having no involvement in Web Summit'.

'The prospective buyer bombarded the company with irrelevant questions absorbing executive time,' Paddy said. 'I was the largest shareholder and any transaction absolutely required my agreement and that was my right. What I can say is that I did not feel the Ascential offer would ultimately materialize at anything like Mr Hickey has indicated and I did not feel at that time that it was in the interests of the company to proceed.'

Amid the chaos of his increasingly troubled working relationship with Dave and Daire, Paddy was hard at work lobbying the Irish government to allow him to legally change the surname of his son, Cloud.

He wanted it to become a combination of his and Faye's surnames. Finally after months of wrangling, he arrived in the office beaming with news that it had done the deed: his first-born son would be granted the made-up surname. He is said to have regularly complained about the bureaucratic nightmare he encountered in making this happen.

Paddy's efforts to rail against what he saw as Ireland's backward political system only intensified in the years after the conference moved to Lisbon.

And so did his sparring with journalists. Among his favourites in 2017 appeared to be Mark Paul from the *Irish Times*, who he referred to as 'neutered' in his reporting during an argument over whether the term 'muckraker' was derogatory.

Philip Boucher Hayes of RTE was another, although it would be a while before they hit their stride in clashing at press conferences or in interviews.

Paddy's animosity with other media would intensify in the years ahead and lead him to his current viewpoint that the media hate him because they are 'embarrassed' by their work, which he points out as flawed. He seems unable to consider whether the relationship would be improved had he not used a carrot and stick approach for the better part of a decade.

Chapter 11

A FLOWER THAT NEVER FADES

'Weeks like this one we just had, I miss you,' Paddy told Daire in a text message on 17 August 2018.

It was Friday afternoon after a long week of Web Summit being in the news, and being the news. The message came just two days after Paddy had announced publicly that Web Summit would be rescinding an invitation for Marine Le Pen, the far-right French politician, to attend that year's conference in Lisbon. Then the leader of the National Rally party, Le Pen was invited to speak at the conference on the topics that gained her notoriety in Europe: her staunchly pro-nationalist views and anti-immigration rhetoric. As a figure likely to say controversial things onstage, the reasons for inviting her were both to drive eyeballs, especially those from outside the world of tech, and to increase the chances of Web Summit making international headlines.

These decisions are usually made months earlier by the team assigned with securing top speakers for the conference who devise 'wish lists' with the big names they want to secure. But the announcement that Le Pen was in the line-up seemed to happen quietly that month, and to the surprise of some Web Summit staff. These lists were usually vetted by senior staff, including Paddy himself if the speaker was significant enough. And Le Pen would have been the guest that year with the most polemic views.

It was a tried and trusted strategy for the conference, which had by then platformed speakers like Peter Thiel, the libertarian venture-capitalist and co-founder of PayPal, and Nigel Farage, the former leader of Ukip.

Thiel's appearance at Web Summit 2014 came years before his role in financing a multi-million-dollar lawsuit taken out by Hulk Hogan against Gawker over a sex tape was publicly known. The lawsuit, which resulted in Gawker going bankrupt after it was ordered to pay Hogan $115 million, was widely seen as being bankrolled by Thiel over anger that Gawker outed him as gay in 2007 and he stated that he feared others would experience worse.

And despite Farage's appearance occurring in the wake of the Brexit vote, he didn't make conference's main stage and instead appeared at the Forum.

Regardless of how popular or controversial they were at the time of their Web Summit appearances, these men were used by Paddy in defending his decision to invite Le Pen just 24 hours before rescinding it. He said he strongly disagreed with their views, which he described in both cases as 'destructive'.

'But Peter Thiel and Nigel Farage articulate viewpoints, however offensive to some, that resonate with a sizeable and by many accounts growing portion of not just the Western world,' Paddy wrote in a blog post on Medium.

A day can be a long time in a public relations tornado, and the 24-hour period which followed on from his defensive blog post manifesto was filled with angry voices, some of which came from within Web Summit. From the outside, the decision may have seemed like a misstep from the start, but getting Le Pen to confirm as a guest was a huge coup for Web Summit and its team charged with finding those who will make headlines.

'They brought her in for all the right reasons, they wanted to have real people in on these issues, but there was so much backlash, including from people in the company who were uncomfortable with it,' one staffer from the time said.

Among those that he received advice from on the decision being misguided was Ed Brophy, then chief advisor to the minister for public expenditure, Paschal Donohoe, and someone Paddy would later troll repeatedly online. In a series of tweets the day after defending Le Pen's invitation, the whiplash that Paddy must have felt from the quick about-face was palpable.

'Based on advice we have received and the large reaction online overnight, [Le Pen's] presence is disrespectful in particular to our host country,' he tweeted. 'It is also disrespectful to some of the many tens of thousands of attendees who join us from around the world,' he added.

The remarkable aspect of this débâcle was that it was one of the rare times that Paddy, a businessman who thrives on putting others on the defensive, was caught on the back foot.

Given the sizeable comedown that Paddy was forced to make, it is unsurprising that he told Daire that he missed him.

Around the same time that the Le Pen controversy played out, Mike Harvey, the other man Paddy relied on to steady PR firestorms, departed the company after what numerous sources described as a 'fall from grace'. The specific reason for his departure is unclear, but one ex-staffer described it as 'death by a thousand cuts'.

The Le Pen controversy had blown over a few weeks later when news broke that the company had signed a new deal to keep Web Summit in Lisbon until 2028 for €110 million. It followed a tender process that involved cities including Berlin, Paris, London and Madrid bidding to host the event there. Of those bids, Paris was seen as a serious contender and discussions were at an advanced stage before they collapsed.

The 10-year Lisbon deal came with plans to expand the existing conference venue to accommodate increased attendee numbers. It also featured a €3 billion buyout clause, which was the amount Web Summit (or another host city) would be on the hook for, if it left Lisbon before the end of 10 years. A prohibitively expensive fee to break the contract was evidence of what a robust deal this was, and for Web Summit it also was proof of the hefty economic impact its presence provided.

News of the 10-year deal broke a month before that year's conference and acted as the perfect setup to show that the Web Summit brand had tangible value. The high hopes that Portuguese government officials had for what the conference was bringing to their capital were palpable. And these included public statements indicating that Web Summit was responsible for a second coming of sorts for Lisbon.

At the opening ceremony of that year's event, the mayor of Lisbon presented Paddy with a portrait of Ferdinand Magellan, the Portuguese explorer credited with leading the first fleet of ships to circumnavigate the globe in the 1500s. He said Magellan was a guy who came to Lisbon 500 years ago and 'at that time Lisbon was the centre of the world, with innovation, with science, with technology, [and] with the courage of discovering new worlds'.

'The world that Magellan helped us discover and build is the world somehow, that you, the new generations of the brightest people, entrepreneurs, the courageous, are discovering. Opening new routes, opening new frontiers, giving new worlds to the world. Five hundred years later, Lisbon now becomes the capital of the world because of you,' the mayor said from the stage.

At the same time that he had a senior politician crediting his company with putting the city he represented back on the map, Paddy was not-so-quietly raging that he had less than expected numbers in attendance from the Irish delegation.

He tweeted that Ireland was not able to 'formally participate' at that year's event.

'Enterprise Ireland also have an event in Dublin next week & have asked their start-ups to stay in Dublin,' he said.

'One member of the IDA and a senior advisor to [Enterprise Ireland] have ordinary attendee tickets. Door is always open of course.'

His claims caused indignation within the IDA, which wrote to David Kelly the week after to express its annoyance after it fielded a media query asking for a response to Paddy's tweets.

'Apart from neglecting to mention that we have three marketing executives attending, and however modest he may view our participation to be, IDA has the correct number of people attending this year following our commercial assessment of the usefulness of this event,' Kevin Sammon, IDA's then communications director, wrote in the email.

'I struggle to understand what the purpose of highlighting IDA Ireland's involvement in this manner is, and whether his company think it appropriate to do so? This comes on the back of another particularly regrettable incident in New Orleans during our sponsorship of Founders at Collision, which has been raised previously with [the company].'

The 'particularly regrettable' incident Sammon referred to had occurred earlier that year and involved Paddy slow-handclapping an IDA staff member while she was giving a speech to a room of about 80 people. The IDA had sponsored the gathering of mainly C-suite executives.

According to sources who were present for the incident, he introduced the woman by referring to her working for an agency that represents multinationals which 'do not pay tax'. When she began delivering a speech that touched on the work of the IDA, Paddy regarded this as an attempt to hijack a Web Summit event to market her own employer. Standing at the back of the room, he became incensed and whispered to some staffers that they should get her to stop talking. When that didn't work, he initiated a slow clap while walking toward the front before taking the microphone away. One former staffer recalled hearing him say 'that'll never happen again' to the room after the incident.

For the staffers present, the most awkward part was the aftermath of trying to tread a fine line between not apologizing for Paddy, because that would only anger him more, and showing empathy to the embarrassed IDA executive.

Paddy strongly refuted that this situation caused any issue with staff, telling me years later that it was 'one of their most proud moments' for some employees at the time.

'She kept talking for more than ten minutes. She wasn't even supposed to talk, they handed out all these gammy flyers,' he said, claiming the woman's actions were 'absolutely reprehensible'.

In mentioning the incident in his November email, Sammon noted that the IDA spent more than €700,000 on sponsorship of Web Summit events since 2009.

'Perhaps the firm has larger contracts now that make IDA Ireland's contribution and goodwill expendable,' he said. 'Whatever is going on, I can think of no other commercial arrangement that we have entered into with a conference organizer that causes us the same issues. If we are to consider any future relationship I will need written assurances that the nature of our participation will not be made the subject of public comment by your founder in future.'

Dave received the email while he was on leave following the birth of one of his children. He told Sammon in reply that he would engage with him on his return.

A few months later a draft email would be sent by Paddy to David that was intended to be used in reply to Sammon, except David would never send it. It cited a line from Sammon's initial email which said that the IDA would need 'written assurances' that Paddy would not continue to post negatively about the agency if it was to continue its relationship with the conference.

Web Summit, the email stated, does not offer a 'hush money' system for government agencies.

It was, in one respect, a throwback to Paddy's infamous 2015 *Morning Ireland* interview where he first referred publicly to claims of 'hush money' and the IDA. But it was an escalation of these sentiments which sought to completely cut ties with the agency.

'Our company reserves the right to comment on the actions or inactions of any of our commercial partners, past or present,' the draft email, written in the third person, said. 'Paddy has in particular been very forthright with his views on many of our commercial partners including energy utilities, car manufacturers, technology companies, financial institutions, nation states and then some more … Having engaged a large group of stakeholders in Ireland we have decided stepping back fully from working with the IDA is the best course of action. However, as we end our relationship with the IDA, we are going to dramatically scale the promotion of Ireland at all our events.'

In a separate email a few minutes later, Paddy told David that he would 'get someone internally just to drop a note to EI …'

'Web Summit will no longer be able to work with Enterprise Ireland across any of our events. Moving forward, and after consulting many stakeholders in Ireland, Web Summit will construct huge exhibition stands at all its events and use them to promote both Irish start-ups and Ireland as a destination for FDI.'

Even though Dave would never forward on these emails, sent to him in early 2019, the email cold war was far from over.

A few months later, Paddy would have a legal letter sent to the IDA directly from Vincent & Beatty, the Dublin 2 solicitor firm he frequently uses. Written directly to Sammon, it was titled merely 'Re: Our Client: Paddy Cosgrave'.

The letter said the law firm had been instructed that at a meeting in Toronto, on 23 May, 'an American based tech company CEO' told Paddy that Sammon had allegedly informed them that he was currently 'under investigation by An Garda Siochana'.

'The clear implication of this statement is that Paddy Cosgrave is engaged in some form of criminal activity,' the letter, which Paddy sent me in 2022, stated.

'This statement is wholly unfounded, incorrect, has no substance, and is defamatory,' it added.

The letter asked for confirmation in writing that the statement would be withdrawn and a formal apology provided.

The IDA never responded to this letter due to it reportedly ending up in Sammon's spam folder.

The draft email also said that IDA financial backing has only been in relation to being a 'minor' commercial partner. This is still the line taken by the company.

It began with some vomit. A select number of VIPs were flown by helicopter from Hong Kong to Macau for an exclusive invite-only evening at the Four Seasons Hotel on the city's glitzy Las Vegas-style Cotai Strip.

The two-day-long event, held as part of the company's 2018 RISE festival, would wine and dine some of the world's most well-known founders, CEOs and company presidents.

It was unbearably hot, with temperatures rising to 34 degrees Celsius and 76 per cent humidity.

For the guests who did not make the list of helicopter-attendees, their journey involved a 55-minute ferry to the former Portuguese territory. The ferry was the chosen mode of transport because a 34-mile bridge connecting Hong Kong and Macau, which reportedly cost $20 billion and took nine years to build, would not open to the public until later that year.

The weather in the region that year, when RISE was held, was impacted by a powerful typhoon system lashing eastern Taiwan with strong winds and heavy rain. While the weather held up on the journey over, the ferry still involved a bit too much movement for some, and according to sources, lots of sea-sickness.

The reason Macau was chosen as a location to host the F.ounders event was because its reputation as the 'Las Vegas of Asia' meant it was the perfect setting for rich and powerful tech founders to be wined and dined.

The RISE event in 2018 was held at the Hong Kong Convention and Exhibition Centre and featured a number of very prominent speakers, including Carrie Lam, then HK chief executive. In discussion with CBNC she discussed the role of politics in technology, a delicate subject given the simmering pro-democracy unrest that was growing in the territory.

There were nerves among some staffers about containing any negative publicity, especially given that there was a cohort of Hong Kong-based media in attendance who would have been highly critical of Lam's policies.

Given that Web Summit was increasingly relying on high-value contracts with cities which pay to host the conference, ensuring these trips went smoothly was important. Along with the €11 million a year contract with

Portugal, Web Summit secured around €4.5 million from Toronto as part of an initial contract to host Collision there. It sought to increase this to a level on par with the value of the Lisbon contract for a three-year period, but the announcement made in 2023 was for a one-year extension.

A major benefit of having Toronto as a host city was that it was a direct flight away for most American VCs and investors. Rich tech bros hate connecting flights – a factor which made getting to New Orleans for a quick trip less attractive. For those coming from farther afield, Web Summit also learned that a host city should never be more than two flights away from anywhere in the world.

Added to the Toronto deal are those Web Summit would sign in later years with Rio de Janeiro in Brazil and Qatar, to host the company's first-ever Middle East conference in early 2024. This deal was set to be its most lucrative and multiple sources said it amounted to around $20 million a year.

Paddy has said that he intends to return to Asia with RISE, which had been held in Hong Kong since 2015 but was cancelled in late 2019 after unrest arising from pro-democracy protests resulted in safety concerns. The company is scheduled to return to Hong Kong in 2025 but he has also indicated that branching more into Asia could be on the cards.

As a business model, having a city pay to host a conference like Web Summit is a dream come true for the company. It meant the company had a steady and reliable income stream rolling into its bank account before it had even sold a ticket. And having cities bid was an extremely lucrative way to tap into that model.

Along with the company's income stream becoming increasingly diversified, it was also in talks about securing third-party investment to facilitate additional expansion plans. As previously described, a deal with Ascential was on the table in 2017 but other potential investment opportunities were floated among the founders in the years following.

Both Daire and Dave made it clear at various points over the years that they wanted to sell, while Paddy resisted, outlining in granular detail that he wanted to 'continue building'. And this was how he phrased his outlook following the Ascential offer. A notable aspect of the exchange of messages Paddy exhibited to show his side on the issue was how precise and detailed the communication was.

He took the time to draft out an extensive explanation which he would later rely on in the legal cases as proof that his desires for the company have been consistent.

A number of sources have remarked that this was not unusual behaviour for Paddy, who would occasionally send long emails or texts on an issue despite it seeming left-field at the time.

As Web Summit was toying with taking on investment in exchange for a stake in the company, it was also considerably scaling up its events. The number of speakers at its events throughout the year had risen to around 3,000 by 2018, which was more than double what the company was sourcing a few years earlier.

Attendance at all of Web Summit's events, which by 2018 involved the flagship Lisbon conference, Collision in North America, RISE in Hong Kong, MoneyConf in Dublin and numerous spin-off events within these conferences, reportedly stood at over 100,000.

The company blew through cash that year as part of its expansion plans, with its accounts showing it made a modest post-tax profit of €18,500 that year compared to the over €3.1 million in 2017. This was the result of expenditure of over €17.5 million in administrative expenses, up from the €12.1 million spent the year before. It also hired rapidly, growing from 164 to 210 employees.

Paddy told the *Irish Independent* that the company did not intend to be profitable for many years to come. 'We're making a series of long-term bets, in particular on software,' he added, saying the hope was that it would pay off by 2028.

To deal with the additional workload, Web Summit also commenced a period of implementing various 'strategic changes'. Along with increasing its headcount, these included: opening an office in Lisbon, reviewing the company's manager to employee ratio, reviewing the demands on individual managers' time and mentorship of their employees, and the introduction of a 'quantitative approach' to measuring success in each of its divisions.

The foregoing is what Web Summit would tell the Workplace Relations Commission (WRC) ahead of the company being ordered to pay a former employee €90,000.

The case related to events that occurred in the summer of 2018 when the employment of a speaker director was terminated by reason of redundancy. The staffer alleged that his redundancy was 'pre-determined' and that he was 'shut out of the office, marginalized and isolated from his colleagues'. His lawyers said all of this 'had a damaging effect on his reputation' and they questioned whether his relationship with Paddy had anything to do with his termination.

The facts of the case, as described in an anonymized judgement, state that the director, who had been employed since 2014, was part of strategic changes which sought to rectify 'disconnect' between teams.

In order to address those, a position was advertised, both internally and externally, for head of speaker operations. After an external person was hired for this role, the director was informed by Ronan Mooney, Web Summit's head of HR, that his role was at risk of becoming redundant. He was offered an alternative role with the company, but this role paid €60,000, a considerable pay cut from his salary of €90,000.

A back and forth between Mooney and the former employee repeatedly used what the WRC found was an incorrect use of the term 'garden leave'.

'Garden leave' is a specific legal term used in employment contracts which refers to the notice period after an employee tenders their resignation. Mooney would tell the WRC that he had mistakenly used the term, but that his conversations with the staffer made it clear that he was not on notice of termination.

'I find this to be quite incredulous,' the WRC adjudicator would state in his conclusion. 'The Head of HR of an organization of the stature of the respondent organization not knowing what garden leave was?'

The director's lawyers would also raise their client's relationship with Paddy during the hearing of the case, saying they had 'run-ins'.

The €90,000 was not the only payout that Web Summit has made over the years as part of complaints from current or former staffers.

A written complaint of bullying and harassment made

against Paddy resulted in a 'substantial' confidential settlement from the company, according to a claim Daire would make in his legal case. Although anonymized in legal filings, I would later reach out to this woman on LinkedIn asking if she wanted to talk about what happened. She never responded.

A Web Summit staffer told me they were aware I had reached out because the woman involved had informed the company and that the incident had been resolved to her satisfaction.

Multiple staffers who did speak anonymously for this book said they signed NDAs following their termination or resignation.

Another allegation made by Daire was that a separate female staff member had a panic attack and fainted due to being 'publicly chastised' by Paddy about the number of chairs set up for an event.

Paddy disputed that he was directly to blame for her panic attack, saying that he sent her a message nine hours before which included the line: 'I cannot express how disappointed I am at the utter disorganization, the complete breach of basic design principles ...'

He said he acknowledged the message was 'strong in its terms' but Web Summit was successful 'because of the high standards that we keep: all staff know this'. He also said Dave had previously blamed Daire for the circumstances which led up to the fainting.

The claims in the legal cases are far from the only issues that certain staff have had with Paddy.

In the course of researching this book, multiple former staffers, none of which include Dave, Daire, or any of those they referenced in legal filings, described being belittled by

Paddy. A number said they sought therapy after leaving Web Summit as a result of what they described as a work environment which damaged their confidence.

Paddy had 'that ability to build you up to the outside world as exceptional, and tear you down to just enough that you lose your sense of worth, but never feel able to leave,' was how one former staffer phrased it. Similar sentiments were echoed by others. Multiple people described Paddy losing his temper at them, including raising his voice and using offensive or demeaning language. I have seen written evidence of him cursing in a work discussion with a former junior staffer.

While the focus of many ex-staffers was often on Paddy, some of those I spoke with did not have nice things to say about Daire or Dave. A number said Daire was rarely seen in the office since he had been living in New York since about 2013, but that when he was present he did not engage with many of the staff. Someone who worked closely with him for a number of years said he was 'a pain in the ass in lots of ways', but generally easy to deal with. Dave was described by many as seeming aloof and disinterested.

Some of those who spoke highly of Paddy as an inspiring leader or said they got along with him noted that there were many others who had a tough time. It was remarked by sources who were fond of Paddy that if he did not like you, he could make your life 'very uncomfortable'. Acting on emotion or making 'knee jerk' decisions was remarked on by others.

'Paddy thinks he's quite Machiavellian, but he's very transparent. He overestimates his intellectual heft; he wants to be seen as a renaissance man basically but I don't think that he is, he's incredibly talented at persuading people, he can project a vision and has confidence,' another said.

Paddy's temper, which has been described as 'explosive', was remarked on by many ex-employees.

'The morning of the event or the evening before, at this point the production team would have been putting final touches, and the most dreaded moment was when Paddy would walk around, point at signs, colours clashing, things in the wrong place, finite details, shouting about stuff,' one person said.

Shouting in the office was something many ex-employees remarked on, with one person describing Paddy as being liable to 'go nuclear' if he became upset. 'He didn't apologise for it … I think he saw it as nothing,' one person said about being shouted at by Paddy.

Against all of these claims is the fact that a number of Web Summit staff have left the company only to return a few years later. Chris Murphy, a smiley, long-serving and party-loving staffer, left the company and came back, twice. He is said to have departed the company this year, but did not respond to a query on why this was the case.

Others have remained for over five years, and speak highly of the company and of Paddy as a boss.

Employees like these have been something Paddy had repeatedly cited in the years since the bullying claims were levelled at him in Dave and Daire's litigation. Indeed, I have met a number of those boomerang or long-serving employees at various Web Summit events and they are proud of the company. While some whisper that they do not agree with many of Paddy's actions or behaviours, they defend him and what he has achieved.

Paddy has understandably been keen to ensure that the bullying claims do not stick as that would jeopardize his chances of recruiting top-tier staff in future. When I raised the bullying allegations levelled by Dave and Daire during a 2022 interview with him, he referred to those who had bad experiences as 'cracked eggs'.

'Along the way, in any company that's employed hundreds of people, are there cracked eggs? Do toes get trampled on? Do people get pissed off? Do people feel they're under-recognized? Overworked? That's always going to happen. That happens absolutely everywhere.'

He said the overwhelming pattern was 'diametrically opposed' to what has been alleged.

There is also a significant cohort of long-serving Web Summit staff, many of which started as interns or in entry-level positions and carved a niche for themselves.

By creating and developing what effectively became their own departments, these employees have become invaluable to the operation of the company.

At the top of the list of these long-serving and loyal employees are those which make up its board of directors, including Mike Sexton, chief marketing technology officer, and Nida Shah, its chief operations officer. Before he resigned in February 2024, Sexton had been there for a decade. Shah has also been there for over 10 years but she resigned as a director in June 2024.

The company's senior leadership also includes Craig Becker, its chief events officer, who is quite a visionary in his own right with an impressive résumé that includes being involved in Live 8, the Brit Awards, the London 2012 Summer Olympics and the FIFA Club World Cup.

It is undeniable that Web Summit gave many smart and

talented young people their first start; it opened doors in a way that other companies without access to extensive travel and learning opportunities cannot.

The company, and its tight-knit cohort of staffers, also looked after its own when they fell on hard times. When an employee needed to take a year off for health issues, Web Summit paid them full wages the entire time. It also provided help and support to staff after a 29-year-old employee died of cancer after a long illness. His colleagues helped promote a charity drive which still operates to this day.

A long-serving staffer who experienced a bereavement said Paddy was adamant that he take off as much time as he wanted. The person described him as someone who does show up for people. 'He always said "Your family comes first, you deal with that, and you'll come back better,"' they remarked.

Another former staffer who faced a near-death experience following the explosion in Beirut in August 2020 said Paddy reached out in the immediate aftermath with offers of help. 'All he said was, "What do you need, what can I do for you?"' he recounted.

The man, who was injured after his apartment was destroyed by the blast, told Paddy that he needed help securing a visa for his wife as they had just gotten married. 'I just worked in sales, I had been gone for a year and a half. I was not a high value or influential person for him, I think he saw an opportunity to help someone that he knew,' the man told me.

'It wasn't actually Paddy who got us sorted in the end, it was a guy called Barry O'Brien,' he added. He remains grateful for the outreach and for O'Brien coming to his aid.

The irony in that is both that the man only knew O'Brien through Web Summit, and that O'Brien, described more later, has long been an adversary of Paddy's.

Some hires were excellent while some others crashed and burned, a trend visible in many start-ups, but at Web Summit it did appear that Paddy had a tendency to occasionally be taken in by people who he would later claim were toxic to the company's culture.

Someone who worked at the company for many years remarked to me once that Paddy had a habit of hiring really unsuitable staff because he was easily swayed by pretence. This, they indicated, made him a bad judge of character.

Occasionally he hits the jackpot with someone who is worth their weight in gold to the company. Sexton, Becker, Shah and PG, who honed his skills in the start-up team, were all among these talented and long-serving employees. The quality uniting them is their staunch loyalty to both Paddy and the company.

'Make no mistake, the people who work closely with him now know what he's like … they have weighed up the pros and cons,' a source said.

'A lot of those people that are in senior leadership positions or are long-term cornerstones, the company would really miss them because they hold so much knowledge,' they added.

Along with mulling over how to handle a simmering row with the IDA, dealing with blowback over the Le Pen incident and steering the company towards its most lucrative deals yet, Paddy also spent 2018 helping Amaranthine come to life.

Named after a flower that never fades, the venture capital fund was set to harness Web Summit's inside knowledge of the world's best emerging start-ups and the company would be an investor in the fund to the tune of $2 million.

When Amaranthine was established in 2018, Silicon Valley Bank (SVB) was also a banking service provider of the fund. The company also sponsored many Web Summit and Founders events over the years, to the tune of hundreds of thousands of dollars.

Paddy took a shine to a young VC partner named Patrick Murphy who had been working for Universal Music Group in San Francisco. The corporate VC he managed was founded in 2014 and featured a portfolio of 30 investments.

Patrick met Dave and Daire when the pair were travelling to the USA ahead of setting up the fund. The pair also frequently met with Barry O'Brien, a former Irish diplomat who worked with the VC team at SVB. With an office on Sand Hill Road, regarded as mecca in the VC world, O'Brien has been a major connector over the last 12 years he has lived there.

But, according to multiple people who know both men, the pair have irreparably fallen out in more recent years, something which, on Paddy's side, is believed to relate to O'Brien's friendship with Murphy, who Paddy would later sue, and his refusal to sever ties with Paddy's co-founders after the fallouts.

Originally from Dundalk, Murphy has an American-sounding accent after years of life in the USA. When he joined the company, he gave a town hall presentation which included a potted history of Web Summit, to the amusement of some staffers well versed in the company's past.

The $30 million Amaranthine Fund I included limited partners (LPs) such as O'Brien, Draper Esprit PLC, Railpen and others, $2 million from Manders Terrace and $250,000 from Murphy. There was a capital call of $500,000 from Manders Terrace in 2018, and the balance was to be paid in $250,000 instalments until 2021.

According to Web Summit's 2018 accounts, the agreement meant that Manders Terrace held a 33.33 per cent share of Amaranthine LLC and would incur the salary costs of those working on the fund in exchange for an annual management fee. It was also entitled to 30 per cent carried interest, or share of any realized profits.

Early literature for the fund stated 'we run the world's largest tech conferences and have the widest network in global technology today'.

'We use our network to pick the world's top tech founders who join us to learn from each other & go onto greatness. Amaranthine invests collaboratively in these founders, pursuing the biggest global opportunities in tech.'

Not long after it was formed, Amaranthine found itself at the centre of what became another of Paddy's manufactured PR stunts, although he did not intend for the fund for be involved.

By late 2018 and early 2019, Paddy had developed a habit of tweeting increasingly pointed political views which he then promoted either on his own account or through Web Summit's Twitter page.

The practice of paying to promote content or run political ads was something he had been doing since at least early 2016 when he paid to run Facebook ads about Section 110s. These are special purpose vehicles (SPVs) which paid no Irish taxes and were accused for years of facilitating widespread tax avoidance.

The law in relation to Section 110s changed in 2016 to ensure that those holding Irish property assets were subject to a 25 per cent tax on profits related to the mortgages held. Paddy saw his paid Facebook ads ahead of the 2016 budget as helping to push the issue into the public domain and he was keen to repeat the experiment.

In November 2018, Web Summit promoted one of Paddy's tweets which accused Fine Gael of enabling a new form of feudalism by exempting certain large funds and property owners from tax. The tweet contained a Soundcloud link which featured him making a speech on the subject. A number of Twitter users questioned why Web Summit was promoting the tweet.

The following year, Paddy set up a Facebook page with the name 'The Irish Tax Agency', a fictitious entity that was critical of Ireland's corporate tax regime. The website linked to the page stated that it was created 'for educational purposes to help inform European citizens on new tax structures in Ireland'.

'Ireland has helped companies avoid billions in taxes since 2015,' a headline on the homepage stated.

Links to Wikipedia articles on various corporate structures including Section 110s, and entities called ICAVs, which pay minimal or no tax, were also provided on the site. It also had a link to a UN report condemning Ireland's 'preferential tax laws' and weak tenant protections.

At the bottom, a number was provided for those who wish to 'speak to an Irish Government press officer'.

Paddy claimed he spent €20,000 on Facebook ads highlighting the website's content, a sum he described at the time as 'very small' given that it involved highlighting what he said was a serious issue.

After Paddy was revealed to be involved, Facebook removed the page for violating its policies, with a spokeswoman saying it violated its policies against impersonation.

The move against pages which lacked transparency occurred in the wake of the fallout from the Cambridge Analytica scandal. Transparency advocates also took issue with the page given that it operated with anonymity before Paddy was discovered to be behind it.

After the page was taken down, Paddy posted a screenshot on Twitter of the account's performance to show that it reached 1.4 million people in the week it was promoted, with the implication being that his ruse had worked.

At a press conference he held in Ranelagh the following day, Paddy presented what he announced would be a €1,000 prize to the Irish journalist who acted as 'top handmaiden' to foreign property funds.

Wearing a bright white shirt and squinting through dark framed glasses into the Spring sun, Paddy said he wanted to present RTE's Philip Boucher Hayes, who he called 'PBH', with the prize. With numerous journalists and photographers surrounding him, there was, to Paddy's delight, an enormous element of spectacle to the occasion.

'As the head of investigations for RTE, I think he's done an exceptional job, failing to talk about the elephant comprehensively in the room, it's only €500, it's not the full prize,' Paddy said, standing next to the journalist and posing with the envelope to ensure the moment would be captured on film.

Boucher Hayes refused the money and later said that Paddy must not be a regular listener of RTE since he counted at least 30 recent Drivetime programmes on tax avoidance entities.

But it was the questioning that Paddy faced from Boucher Hayes after he attempted his award presentation which brought the tax affairs of Amaranthine, based in the US state of Delaware, into the spotlight.

'There is an element of hypocrisy in what you are advocating now because you yourself are availing of the same tax avoidance structures with your company,' Boucher Hayes said.

Still holding the 'elephant prize' envelope containing €500, Paddy said he was availing of tax avoidance structures 'by merely establishing companies in Ireland'.

When asked why he chose to set up Amaranthine in Delaware as opposed to California, where Patrick Murphy and many of the fund's LPs were based, Paddy said it was the 'standard procedure' to choose the east-coast state.

'Is it not a tax advantageous procedure for setting up venture capital funds?' Boucher Hayes inquired.

'These types of arguments are not permitted at the level of a secondary school debating competition,' Paddy responded.

Around the same time that Paddy was holding court with journalists in Ranelagh to push his fake Facebook page, an anonymous Wikipedia user known as 'BritishFinance' was making thousands of edits to entries about Ireland, the IDA and various elements of the state's tax regime.

At the time, the user had made over 40,000 edits to various pages on this subject and others. Many speculated that Paddy was behind the account given the suspicious overlap of his campaign, the Wikipedia edits, and a cryptic tweet he posted earlier that month about the IDA 'secretly paying people' to edit articles about itself. Indeed, even the Wikipedia pages that Paddy linked to on the Irish Tax Agency website were heavily edited by BritishFinance.

A number of government sources told me they still believed he was the person who had operated that account, or that at the very least he had been in contact with them.

Paddy has vehemently denied being behind the account or knowing who was. But the claim about the IDA paying to edit pages turned out to be true, as the *Business Post* reported a week later, noting that this happened on pages about the agency and Martin Shanahan, its then chief executive.

What was revealed was a war of Wikipedia edits between the IDA's Kevin Sammon, who had clashed with Paddy only the year before, and the BritishFinance Wikipedia editor.

With the username IDAComms, Sammon had edited Shanahan's page but later had his username blocked after being accused of being a 'sock puppet' Wikipedia editor.

The IDA then hired an external communications firm to help with the edits which also got flagged by Wikipedia for potentially being in breach of its mandatory paid editing disclosure requirements.

These potential conflicts of interest were described as 'an especially egregious type of COI [conflict of interest]; the Wikimedia Foundation regards it as a "black hat" practice akin to Black Hat SEO'.

It was a link to this notice that Paddy tweeted in April 2019. And although he said at the time that he was 'not particularly interested in these types of shenanigans', he tweeted about the episode three more times in the months that followed. Each time, he repeated the 'black hat' phrase used in the notice.

Despite initially feigning boredom, the issue was one he had been trying to firm up for a long time.

Nearly a year prior, he tweeted 'If true this is pure gold: Has anyone heard rumours that the Irish Government paid people to edit Wikipedia pages on tax havens or unfavourable mentions related to our tax policies?' In the previously referenced draft email he allegedly wanted Dave to send to the IDA in January 2019, he also referred to a 'clandestine' global communications campaign which he noted had 'not broken into the public domain'.

It was an issue that Paddy regularly traded gossip on, and spurred those around him to see if they could find out more. Ahead of his tweet in which he also claimed to be disinterested in the matter, he indicated the day before that he had firmed up his theory.

All of this is to say that Wikipedia that year had allowed him to land a public blow on an agency he so desperately wanted to embarrass.

Just a few months later, Paddy would welcome Katherine Maher, then CEO of the Wikimedia Foundation, which hosts Wikipedia, to the Web Summit stage, for the first time. In a previous role as chief communications officer with Wikimedia, she too tweeted about 'black hat' practices. In May 2019 she also tagged The North Face brand in a tweet about how Wikipedia 'doesn't exist for you to SEO hack your way to the top'.

'The future is not a solo act,' Maher said from the Web Summit stage that year. 'It will take all of us working together.'

These words would be immortalized as the closing lines of a video made to commemorate 10 years of Web Summit, released at the start of 2020. Maher was not seen or named in the two-minute clip, which Paddy shared online by commenting that it had been laden with 'dozens of Easter eggs'.

In the background that summer, Paddy was also working hard to realize another objective of his: making Daire resign from his directorship of Manders Terrace, the firm's parent company.

A back and forth discussion had been ongoing between Daire and Patrick Kirwan, Web Summit's chief financial officer, since March of that year. The communications intensified in the weeks that followed as Daire did not take up Kirwan's offer to meet regarding the specific issue of his directorship. He also repeatedly cited his own concerns with the alleged lack of corporate governance in the company.

'As I mentioned I have been looking to get better corporate governance structures in place in the company for some time and look forward to this happening under your watch. I'm not sure what else there should be to discuss,' Daire said after Kirwan offered to meet him in New York.

A more formal letter from Paddy followed: 'At this stage it makes sense for you to resign as a director of the various entities and that is the outcome that I want. I believe that this is in the interests of the companies and indeed, your own best interests. Needless to say, this does not affect your shareholding or your status as a founding member of Web Summit. Obviously, we would hope to manage your resignation in a manner that would impact on you and the company as favourably as possible.'

This continued for a number of months, culminating in a telephone conversation between Daire and Kirwan in July in which the former alleged he was told that he would be removed as a director if he did not step down.

A board meeting was set for August which Daire feared would involve him being removed, an embarrassing potential outcome he wanted to avoid.

That month, Daire also got married to his long-term partner in a 12-bedroom castle in the south of France.

In an email sent to Paddy and Dave during his honeymoon, he finally threw in the towel on his directorship.

'Paddy and David, Sometimes it's hard to let go ... See the attached documents that show my resignation as secretary and director of the various entities. This should bring to an end any disagreements we have had ... I wish you both and indeed Web Summit the best of luck into the future.'

After his resignation as director, Daire continued to grow his successful PR business, but he held on strongly to a sense of belonging and ownership with regards Web Summit. As recently as mid-2023, nearly two years since the lawsuits began, his Twitter banner picture was a wide angle shot of a Web Summit event with Paddy onstage in the distance.

The characterization that Daire had been trying unsuccessfully to improve corporate governance has been strongly rejected by Paddy. In his version of events, Daire's resignation was sought as a result of the alleged access-selling that he and Dave became aware of.

He outlines in detail in his affidavit how he and Dave had discussed Daire's removal as a director for years before the summer of 2019.

'It was very disappointing that I could not rely on Mr Kelly to follow through on what was a simple job that Mr Kirwan was able to complete so efficiently,' Paddy said, framing Daire's departure as something which had been building for many years.

'Everything that happened, happened, because of choices made by Mr Hickey. Once he "got off the train", so to speak, "the train left the station" and it therefore became difficult for him to get back on.'

A few months later, whistleblower Edward Snowden appeared by video link from Russia to deliver the conference's keynote address. Wearing a charcoal suit in front of a dark grey background Snowden outlined a dystopian future of surveillance during his 20-minute conversation with British journalist James Ball.

'The internet is global, the law is not the only thing that can protect you, technology is not the only thing that can protect you, we are the only thing that can protect us, and the only way to protect anyone is to protect everyone. Thank you and stay free,' he said.

Returning to the stage after Snowden's presentation, Paddy said 'wasn't that fantastic' before plugging the company's new swag store which claimed to be stocking his wife's €800 jumpers.

'If you wanted to get a T-shirt or a number of other little gifts, just go to swag.websummit.com' he said with a smile, himself wearing a Web Summit branded T-shirt.

The topic of Web Summit swag had become much more than just shameless merchandise plug before he made the remark onstage. After noticing that the pricey jumpers were for sale on the website, a number of media reports followed on how people were confused and 'shocked' at the choice of merchandise for a tech conference. 'This just underscores how tech conferences like this are for the rich and are exclusionary to founders without easy access to liquid capital. This is a symptom of a larger issue,' one Twitter user said.

A BBC report on how the jumpers were snapped up, as evidenced by 'sold out' captions on the items, featured a quote from Paddy confirming that all 12 on offer were bought. The story was also covered on BBC radio.

He would later admit lying to the BBC journalists, telling me that they were never actually for sale on the website.

'We were just having fun,' he told me. He also later implied the reporters were in on the stunt.

Jane Wakefield, the BBC technology reporter who covered the piece, had this to say about the episode when I met her at Web Summit 2023: 'I remember talking to Paddy about the jumpers story. I didn't particularly want to cover it, as I thought it was a bit fluffy (excuse the pun) but my editor was keen as it was all over Twitter, mainly outrage at the cost. Paddy and I chatted about how they were made in Donegal by his wife, and other women. To find out now the whole thing was a pack of lies, is extraordinary and for him to suggest the BBC knew it was all made up is ridiculous.'

Chapter 12

THE LEO THING

Tech founders, politicians and random celebrities are mingling backstage on opening night of Web Summit 2021 as Noel Toolan eyes the scene in wonder.

As the first in-person gathering since the Covid-19 pandemic, the conference has pulled off what was unthinkable only a year before. It has brought together tens of thousands of people, hundreds of VCs and a smattering of top-tier speakers including comedian Amy Poehler, scientist and web inventor Sir Tim Berners-Lee, and Facebook whistleblower Frances Haugen.

Sitting in a large holding pen where VIP guests sip wine and nibble on food, Noel Toolan, a Web Summit veteran, looks on with awe.

As a long-time supporter of the conference, he has used it as a stage to showcase his intangible wares in the art of brand marketing. Toolan is extremely clever, and skilled at bringing ideas to life. His résumé includes years developing the immensely successful marketing campaign behind Baileys and Tourism Ireland, and Toolan has been credited as the man who placed Ireland on the map as a holiday destination. 'The creative architect of Tourism Brand Ireland, one of the first tourism marketing concepts to attempt to brand a country,' was how the *Irish Times* phrased it in 1997.

It was because of this legacy that Paddy tried to forge a connection with him in the very early years of the company and why he was later hired on consultancy contracts to help Web Summit hone its identity.

Over the years, he has become a sounding board for Paddy and garnered himself a rare place among those who have not fallen out with the co-founder despite being encouraged to take a side in various fallouts. He also maintained congenial relationships with Daire and Dave, or at least he had until the lawsuits unleashed a permanent state of miserable acrimony between the trio.

But waiting for the opening of Web Summit to formally commence, Toolan could think only of what a beautiful brand-making opportunity that moment was. The stage was set, the world was travelling again, the pandemic was receding, the 'great coming back' had happened and all that was required was for someone to grab it with both hands.

Paddy walks through the Forum, preparing to go onstage and officially open the conference, and Toolan wishes him well.

'Wow, you got through it, it's like it never changed,' Toolan recalls telling him.

Paddy seemed distracted, which was not unexpected ahead of opening night. But instead of bursting with pride at how they had managed to get to this point, Toolan recalls his reply was to ask if he had been following the news.

'I genuinely thought what, had something happened? And then … [it was] the Leo thing,' he tells me.

The 'Leo thing' refers to a story which broke in the *Village* magazine, a left-wing publication run by barrister Michael Smith, about how Leo Varadkar leaked a draft confidential document to a friend in 2019. Then Taoiseach, Varadkar had leaked a copy of the proposed GP contract agreed with the Irish Medical Organisation to Dr Maitiú Ó Tuathail, the president of a rival organization.

The *Village* covered the story in October 2020 with a front page that read: 'Leo Varadkar, lawbreaker'. It alleged that the leak had breached the Official Secrets Act and 'may also be a crime' under the Corruption Act.

The story came to light after Paddy introduced Chay Bowes, then a Dublin-based healthcare entrepreneur, to Smith, editor of the *Village* magazine. And after it was published, he promoted the story on his personal Twitter account as well as via Web Summit's account.

In early 2021, Twitter blocked Web Summit from promoting Paddy's political tweets, which included references to Varadkar's 'reported law-breaking', after stating that they broke its content policy. But by Web Summit 2021, Paddy had tweeted over 40 times from his personal account using the hashtag #LeotheLeak. And on 1 November, right before introducing headline speaker Haugen onto Web Summit's main stage, he highlighted the Varadkar story to the opening night crowd.

On large screens facing out into Lisbon's Altice Arena, images of the *Village* magazine cover describing Varadkar as a 'law breaker' were displayed and Paddy invited Bowes, Smith and John Tye, co-founder of Whistleblower Aid, to join him onstage. (Tye's organization was credited by

Paddy as helping play a 'seminal role' in the emergence of evidence that led to the downfalls of Jeffrey Epstein and Harvey Weinstein.)

'This tiny organization was only founded in 2017 but already its impact on our world has been earth shattering,' he said from the stage.

'In 2020, Whistleblower Aid created their first outpost in Europe in Ireland. The very first Irish whistleblower that John Tye, the co-founder of Whistleblower Aid, advised was an entrepreneur called Chay Bowes ... The guidance Whistleblower Aid provided to Chay and the work of Michael Smith have triggered the longest criminal investigation into a senior political figure in decades in Ireland,' he added.

After the men joined him onstage, Paddy said: 'What you have done, Chay in particular, has taken incredible courage'.

'I'd like to ask ... everybody to give them a huge round of applause for what they've achieved. Thanks so much, guys.'

To many of those present in the arena, the moment was a non-event because they had no idea who the people being described were or why this issue was being flagged by the CEO of a tech event during an opening night ceremony. Many in the stadium were confused to the point of boredom, turning to their phones as a distraction or gazing around the room in wonder. It fizzled out as quickly as it began, occupying less than three minutes of the opening ceremony, but to Paddy it was a statement, made as loud as possible, and using the physical space he and hundreds of others had worked tirelessly to make a world-class stage.

And to some Irish attendees, and Toolan in particular, it was a flashpoint.

'Brand Web Summit' and 'Brand Paddy' may have frequently converged in the past, overlapping online or spilling out at work events, but this was an intersection of unprecedented proportions. It highlighted what remains one of the Paddy's biggest weaknesses: the inability to draw a line between the two identities or, more specifically, to remove his personal interests from the platform. This is because, to him, the platform has only ever been improved by his personal interests.

'I was a bit floored, but no one around me seemed to notice or care. There were a few furrowed brows, but for the most part it just seemed to pass people by,' one Irish person in attendance remarked.

The so-called 'Leo the Leak story' was a significant political story in Ireland, and one which dominated headlines at various points throughout 2021. It was also one which Paddy played a large role in promoting and in acting as a connector between the various players involved.

Around this time, he was also funding Whistleblower Aid to help it establish an outpost in Ireland, allegedly wiring it around €25,000 in mid-2020 and telling David Kelly that he planned to raise up to €475,000 to support the work. The funding relationship was not clear when Paddy began to promote its work online.

'I am handing over the gathering of information from whistleblowers to the most credible international organization there probably is. Their team will manage it all, and spin up a campaign specifically for Ireland,' he said in a message to Dave.

After news of the organization's work landed a front-page story in the *Irish Examiner*, Paddy was ecstatic, praising the paper and pitting himself as a saviour to the nation's media.

'It took an arrogant, narcissistic tech bro ticket tout to help sniff out cronyism at the very top of Irish society in basically a week,' he tweeted.

Paddy had become very close to Bowes by the time the story broke, saying that he connected with him in the early days of the Covid-19 pandemic. The pandemic acted as an incubator for Paddy's activism in spite of his business nearly going bust. He was diligent when it came to observing social distancing and quarantine rules, but the impulse to attack landed him in hot water more than once.

For example, he tweeted that doctor Maitiu Ó Tuathail was involved in 'spin and deception' and implied this was leading to unnecessary death. The tweet ended up at the centre of a High Court defamation action taken against Paddy by Ó Tuathail, with the former paying €10,000 to settle the case and tweeting an apology.

Paddy also picked a Twitter fight with Paul Reid, then director general of the Health Service Executive (HSE), with similar accusations to those levelled at Ó Tuathail.

Unlike most of those he attempts to goad into a fight, Reid quoted his tweet and issued one of his own, saying, 'I don't do spin and aim to be straight with the public. You have your view and I have my responsibilities as CEO of @ HSELive which I cherish. Throwing rocks from the sideline doesn't help anyone.'

Other senior health care officials came under similar scrutiny from Paddy. But Paddy was not out to be 'hurling from the ditch all of a sudden' as he told Reid in March

2020. Instead, he indicated that he was looking for some credit for trying to 'help Ireland prepare'.

In March 2020, Paddy incorrectly tweeted that four nurses had died at a time when he was railing against the government's response to the virus. When the Irish Nurses and Midwives Organisation, the HSE and the country's chief medical officer dismissed this as fake news, Paddy accused them of spin.

His tweet received significant criticism off and online, including from doctors and nurses who said it caused unnecessary stress and panic among frontline staff.

It was not until June that Paddy tweeted an 'unreserved' apology after Pat Phelan, the businessman, posted that he had received the information but that the sources were wrong.

When I asked Paddy about what many regarded as a wilful dissemination of misinformation, during an interview in the summer of 2022, he said that he 'fully' believes the claim he made was true. He said he had tried to get the data to prove his claim but had been unable to, and that he only apologized because it 'seemed like the right thing to do'.

A few days later, he sent me screenshots of texts which depicted WhatsApp conversations between him and a person he said worked for the HSE at the time. The messages mainly concerned the delivery of the PPE shipment that Paddy had helped facilitate, but they touched on details regarding a nurse who had allegedly died. The individual in the messages asked him for the information to be kept in confidence.

During the pandemic, Paddy donated €1 million from Web Summit to ChangeX, an Irish platform which he said would identify and fund projects aimed at strengthening the country's response to Covid-19. He also connected Chinese donors to the Irish government regarding the PPE shortage and he organized PPE to be donated by Alibaba for frontline healthcare workers in Ireland.

'I think doing something radical also buys immense trust and understanding with staff,' Paddy told Dave in entertaining the donation idea. 'We will get more than a month's gain in productivity out of people,' he added, referring to staff costs at the time being around €1 million a month.

The €1 million donation really irked Dave, who alleged in legal filings that the decision was ultimately made unilaterally and that he could 'do nothing to dissuade him [Paddy] from proceeding with it'.

Dave wrote to Patrick Kirwan, the company's chief financial officer: 'He is making the assessment that we can survive the million. And that it buys great goodwill etc. I just don't agree with taking the risk … It's mismanagement. I am livid.'

Kirwan, who had joined the company in 2018, told Dave that 'separation between PC and Company is not here'.

'Company is PC,' Dave replied.

Paddy refuted the claim that Dave was not consulted, and said he explained his 'rationale' for the 'radical' move a couple of days prior to making the announcement.

'There was a further external business rationale that this would assist Web Summit in the creation of positive brand sentiment and improve the company's standing in the eyes of the tech community, which is highly socially aware,' Paddy said in reply to Dave's concerns in legal filings.

'I have no doubt that making this donation was the right thing for Web Summit to do in the context of the Covid 19 crisis in March 2020,' he added.

As for the PPE donation, Paddy felt quite resentful because the plane carrying the goods 'sat on the ground for days' in Liège, Belgium. In the end, it arrived 'with scarce a mention or thank you from the Gov/HSE,' he tweeted months later.

The ordeal weighed on his mind for years and so when the topic turned to the four [not] dead nurses in a discussion with me in the summer of 2022, he initially refused to admit that he was wrong and turned the tables to why I was even asking the question, when I could have focused on the PPE delivery.

In a subsequent discussion it became clear that even when he concedes that he might be wrong, he still believes he is right.

'Let's say on the nurses, if I was wrong, why was I concerned about it? Why? Because I thought frontline healthcare workers were being fucking ignored,' he said.

'It's like, oh my god, guys can you stop, just for this one national emergency,' he added, referring to the 'politicians and technocrats' who were busy 'spinning'.

When I told him that he cannot expect to get a pass on being wrong just because his intentions were right, he changed the subject.

The Covid-19 pandemic put Web Summit under immense strain, both financially and existentially. It was unclear when and, at some stages if, the world would return to large in-person gatherings of the kind that the company depended on to survive.

As the future of in-person events remained completely unknown at the time, Web Summit's ability to survive was predicated on whether it could adapt and how long it could hang on for. Although it had attempted a pivot to virtual events, these were far less lucrative and failed to offer the material benefits the conference provided such as chance encounters and general banter.

The effect of this would hit hard on its bank account, which recorded a €5.3 million loss and a drop in turnover from €48 million in 2019 to just €17 million in 2020. The equity attributable to owners of the company was just €7.7 million at the year-end 2020, compared to €13 million just 12 months before.

Dave was particularly affected by the stress of the firm's precarious financial position and its prospects of surviving the pandemic. In a document entitled 'Working Scenarios', which he began drafting in the autumn of 2020, he forecasted that Web Summit could lose €13 million the following year and bring in only €11.2 million.

Paddy alleged that Dave never shared his prediction with the company, but hearing or seeing Dave worry about money or the company's financial position was a common occurrence for staffers at the time.

'Web Summit almost went bust in 2020,' Paddy would write in a LinkedIn post in June 2022, adding that it 'came close to catastrophe'.

'It was without doubt the most stressful year I've ever experienced. And I'm sure that was the same for almost everyone at Web Summit,' he wrote.

'Looking back, these were huge gambles for us – by far the biggest in our history. But we trusted ourselves and all that led us to that point. Somehow our gambles paid off.

We knew that our goal wasn't to succeed in surviving the moment, but in putting ourselves in the best possible position to grow into the future, post-pandemic. And we did.'

The reflection may have been with the benefit of hindsight and having the vastly improved 2021 numbers to rely on.

According to someone who spoke with him over the course of 2020, he appeared more interested in discussing Leo Varadkar and the government's pandemic response than how Web Summit would dig itself out of the financial hole it was tumbling into. Another said that he repeatedly boasted that he was going to bring down the Taoiseach because he was 'sitting on nukes' and that, when Varadkar did not resign in the months after the story, it 'put him into a rage'. Staffers said casual work discussions could frequently lead to the subject of Varadkar.

Based on his Twitter activity alone, 2020 was like a fever dream for Paddy cut with brief interruptions to criticize Irish politicians, the media and post landscape pictures from his walks. Like a number of others who became experts in various fields following the onset of the pandemic, he was flooding his feed with studies, stats, documents and letters to share what he regarded as valuable information, or use the information to lash out at those in power.

There were two main additions to his life that year, with the most notable being Chay Bowes. Described by someone who knew him for years as a 'Walter Mitty sort', Bowes was a confidant to Paddy and the pair quickly developer a relationship as friends.

Along with being a VIP guest of Web Summit in 2021, when he was brought onstage, he also attended in 2022, when he was overheard describing himself as Paddy's 'chief strategist' to a stranger on a plane to Lisbon. Paddy tweeted that Bowes was 'Nominee for Irish Person of the Year'.

The bond between them was developed while devising what to do with the evidence Bowes had obtained regarding Varadkar's leaking of a confidential document. The evidence was gathered through Bowes' work with the National Association of General Practitioners (NAGP) – the now-defunct organization that was led by Ó Tuathail. Through this work he had access to internal communications and was a member of group message threads involving other doctors when the leaked document was discussed. The *Village* magazine story published excerpts from a message thread as well as an embarrassing message from Ó Tuathail where he wrote: 'To be fair, Leo always delivers'.

Afterwards Paddy and Bowes set their sights on other ventures, including Health Reform Ireland, an 'evidence-based think-tank' that would provide critiques of the healthcare system. The entity was (and remains) based in Tramway House, where the Web Summit HQ is located. Its website invites people to become a member for €9.50 to 'access monthly seminars with world leading experts on health systems'.

A self-described 'public-interest advocate' and former member of the Army Medical Corps, Bowes has a wide variety of interests, in particular a fascination with fire-arms. He collects antique guns and in early 2020 applied to get planning permission for a firing range at a site in the foothills of the Dublin mountains. The proposed development was refused permission.

For many years Bowes worked as a phlebotomist, a person who takes blood samples from people for testing.

He enjoyed enormous success in a venture he launched called Tara Healthcare, which provided community-based solutions aimed at avoiding hospital overcrowding.

In 2007, the company received an annual budget of over €6 million from the HSE to provide at-home services, but the health service ended its contract with the venture a couple of years later.

Bowes showed up to the launch of the book *Pandemonium: Power, Politics and Ireland's Pandemic* by journalists Jack Horgan-Jones and Hugh O'Connell. Standing next to me at the back of the room on a staircase, he shouted 'Fake News!' on his way out as the launch got underway.

The most striking development in his career came in mid-2022 when he moved to Russia and later began working as a correspondent with RT, a Russian state-controlled media outlet which has been banned in the EU following the country's invasion of Ukraine. Bowes has appeared in RT clips circulated on social media from where he is listed as a correspondent. He regularly posts videos on social media from Moscow, extolling the virtues of life in Russia.

A frequent critic of the USA and NATO, Bowes has, like Paddy, used his social media account to attack Irish politicians, media and private enterprise. Along with his primary account, he has been linked to a number of other Twitter accounts and launched a High Court defamation case over allegations he tweeted homophobic views from one of them.

Bowes, in describing on a podcast how Ireland has an 'LGBT+' narrative, which he said was 'fine', recounted how there were 'plenty of gay people' in Russia.

'I mean I actually got thrown out of a gay bar about 10 days ago for being not gay enough,' he added.

Paddy has similarly made references to gay men and made sexual innuendos online. In a post which garnered significant criticism, Paddy tweeted a picture of Varadkar and Ó Tuathail at a gay pride event, writing 'Was there more than one favour? [eyes emoji]'.

In early 2022, Paddy hit out at journalists and politicians he said have 'peddled a conspiracy' that Bowes was a 'Russian stooge'.

Since Bowes has taken up the role with RT, Paddy has been less vocal on social media about praising him, but the pair are believed to still be in touch as friends.

While Paddy has been keen to describe his role in the Leo the Leak story as more akin to a background character (making connections, introductions, etc), Bowes has painted him as having a more active role in the process.

Speaking on YouTube to Tara Reade, the woman who accused Joe Biden of sexually assaulting her and then defected to Russia, Bowes, referring to himself and Paddy, said 'we exposed the Irish prime minister's corruption through the *Village* magazine, we wrote about it'.

In this interview, Bowes also said, through the Leo the Leak story, he and Paddy established Ditch Media, the company behind the investigative journalist news site, The Ditch.

On one of the last occasions I saw Paddy in person, in the Web Summit office for an event a few days before he would ultimately resign as CEO, he told me that I should talk to Michael Smith of the *Village* magazine for the book.

'He might say good things,' Paddy said.

When I asked Smith if he would speak, he said he needed to chat to Paddy first and then, even if he was approving of the concept, he said he needed to reflect on it from his own point of view. He wondered whether, as a friend of Paddy's and as a journalist, his primary obligation was 'to the truth' or to his friend.

'I have to think all that stuff through, I don't know if Paddy would have thought it through, either,' he told me in a call.

A few weeks later he declined the offer of speaking, saying Paddy was 'not enthusiastic' and that he thought it best not to talk to me about him 'because he is a friend'.

The mention of friendship was striking to me because when Paddy described Smith to me at a Web Summit event two years prior, he praised his work as a journalist and said: 'He holds everybody to account; he's nobody's friend.'

The Leo the Leak story would not be the end of the involvement of Ó Tuathail, who had settled the defamation case he had against Paddy in April before the *Village* story was published that Autumn.

In early 2021, Paddy also messaged Ó Tuathail, saying it was time that he 'opened up'. 'Let's be clear: you're completely full of shit. That said you've an opportunity to either do something decent and to a point save your reputation, or you can allow yourself and your reputation to be burned to the ground,' Paddy wrote.

'Paddy. Leave me alone. Please. Find someone else's life to destroy,' he responded.

* * *

The other significant addition to Paddy's life in 2020 was Adam Connon, who joined Web Summit as its 'general counsel', or in-house lawyer, in January of that year.

Connon is figure with a colourful past, with previous jobs including solicitor for a London law firm that waged a campaign to save an Irish pub, lawyer to Niall Harbison, then of LovinDublin, a website known for listicles and food reviews, and manager at Brown Thomas, an upmarket department store.

With thick-framed spectacles, which Paddy has referred to as his 'little lawyer glasses', Connon cuts a shy figure living in Paddy's shadow. But he is a trusted member of staff who has amassed considerable responsibility.

Like a number of other 30-something-year-old men in Paddy's life, he is a fan of skinny jeans. His voice, thick with a south Dublin accent, features an unusual combination of both gravelly and nasally tones. He enjoys digressing frequently in long conversations.

Prior to joining Web Summit, he was general counsel for the Jamie Oliver Group, working through the high-profile collapse which resulted in around 1,000 job losses.

The lawyer has a profound level of respect and admiration for Paddy, refusing to make a negative comment when his boss is not around. This has resulted in him occasionally occupying an ostracized position among some long-serving staffers who regard him as too devoutly loyal.

I once told Connon he was 'The Hand', implying the role of the aide to the king in *Game of Thrones*, but he didn't get the reference.

In many ways, Connon's 'trusted advisor' relationship with Paddy is the type that well-paid lawyers strive to cultivate with a client. He may be uncomfortable with the public pressure that Paddy inadvertently drags him into, but he seems to be enjoying the ride.

A difficulty for Connon is that while he is an ideal employee, committed to the work and to the ethos of Paddy's leadership, his boss's impulsive tendencies are at odds with his more cautious demeanour.

I've had a front row seat to some of this, such as when, following a rather outlandish remark that I dubbed untrue, Connon tried to gloss over the issue by repeatedly saying his boss was 'obviously joking'. Paddy, sitting adjacent, insisted he was not.

Connon has had significant involvement in the ongoing lawsuits, including helping manage the company's discovery process for the ones involving the co-founders and keeping Paddy updated on its progress. He has also appeared as a character in the case involving David Kelly, whose final Web Summit years overlapped with the start of Connon's tenure.

Dave alleged he wrote to Connon to inquire whether there was a risk the company could be sued for the activity if one of Paddy's tweets was defamatory.

'It's strange as on a weekly basis he's asking me about defamation of such and such tweet he wants to promote – and without exception I've explained to him they are all defamatory – then he hasn't tweeted a single one of those,' Connon replied.

'But then there are all these Leo ones he doesn't ask me about,' he added.

A revealing conversation between Paddy and Bowes, which the former recorded and shared with Dave, is also exhibited in his lawsuit. In it, Paddy refers to Connon providing him with assistance on his tweeting.

'The odd time I'll send out a tweet, my legal counsel, chief legal counsel, whatever his name is, will be like, will normally be like, yeah, that's fine. That's fine,' Paddy tells Bowes in the call.

It is undoubtable that Connon spins a lot of plates in Web Summit which go beyond typical general counsel roles. In 2022, he helped Paddy and Web Summit organize a response to the Ukraine war with Techfugees and assisted some of those fleeing the war deal with Irish bureaucracy on arrival.

But chief among the side projects, and the one which has garnered the most attention, is Ditch Media Limited, the company behind The Ditch website. The site, which launched in April 2021, is a left-wing news outlet that has focused much of its investigations on uncovering alleged criminality or, at the very least, embarrassing errors committed by those in power.

It has had enormous success in this regard, with its reporting leading to the resignations of junior ministers Robert Troy and Damien English, as well as the deputy chair of An Bord Pleanála Paul Hyde. As a result of what its reporting uncovered, Hyde was sentenced to two months in jail for making false or misleading declarations, but he got this punishment reduced to a suspended sentence and a €6,000 fine on appeal.

'Maybe you'll call us hurlers,' The Ditch website states. (Its name and catchphrase are taken from the sport of hurling and relates to an Irish expression meaning a person who offers unsolicited criticism about something they are not involved in.)

Until late 2023, Connon had a prominent role in its development and operation as a 33 per cent shareholder. He acquired the shareholding from Chay Bowes, who previously held a third of The Ditch. He also presented the company's accounts to the Companies Registration Office and his personal Twitter account, which has since been deleted, included the phrase 'also a bit of ditch' with a hurling emoji.

The two journalists behind The Ditch website are Eoghan McNeill and Roman Shortall, who were both paid by Web Summit for their work.

McNeill, a Donegal native, has been a long-term Web Summit staffer and worked for the company since 2015, minus a year when he lived in China and worked for *China Daily*, a state-owned English-language newspaper. He has left political leanings reminiscent of student politics, recently describing Fidel Castro's Cuban revolution as 'one of the most personally inspiring'.

Shortall worked as a legal assistant in a solicitors' office for many years before also operating a recruitment service which was aimed at Romanians looking for work in Ireland. He made headlines in Ireland after going on *Liveline* to highlight that his child benefit was taken away after he was quizzed by gardai and social welfare officers while boarding a flight to Romania at Dublin airport. Shortall also made headlines in early 2023 when he was ordered by a judge to vacate a home over nearly €50,000 in unpaid rent. He said he 'withheld' a portion of the rent following a dispute with the landlord, an unlimited company.

As a result of not having extensive contacts and sources, their initial work involved scouring planning applications, land registry documents and other open-source material for stories. As tips from the public began to flood in, it soon involved chasing down leads alleging corruption in county councils, government agencies and in the Dail.

In its early years, Paddy repeatedly denied having editorial control over the venture, merely being a 'patron', and 'one of hundreds'. But some of the correspondence exhibited in Dave's lawsuit shows him having a more active role in investigative work before The Ditch launched.

'Eoghan is also out the door with legitimate whistleblowers across all sorts of areas. A very good legal mind has joined the effort,' Paddy said to Dave at the end of 2020.

A few months later he told his co-founder that 'Eoghan and I have been working with a sort of activist lawyer for about the last six months'.

'He's very, very good. I am going to hire him to continue working on the HSE stuff and other bits. In time he may also be a reasonable resource for legal stuff. He's not a deal maker type, but instead a more wonkish type who knows how to nail organizations or countries on finer points of law,' Paddy added.

In person, the pair of founding Ditch journalists are quite different: Shortall is soft-spoken and demurred while McNeill is more abrasive and up for a fight.

The latter is in line with the brand The Ditch is cultivating as it strives to be an anti-establishment news source, taking down those the 'mainstream media' are too scared or lazy to go after, as they see it.

Despite regularly gloating about how those in power regard them with disdain, Shortall applied for and was awarded Newcomer of the Year at the Law Society's justice media awards in 2023. The news was not acknowledged by The Ditch on its active Twitter feed.

A criticism of the website is that some of the offences it alleges against its subjects, such as having an expired motor tax, appear to be unworthy of the heavy-handed language used to narrate them. It has also been criticized for initially publishing the stories under pseudonyms and providing little information as to who was behind the venture.

Paddy's skill at manipulating the media has been recognized by some readers in how the stories sometimes unfold. The content, teased out over a number of days, achieves significant traction by allowing a revelation to drip out into the public domain.

Citing the controversy around Robert Troy, who resigned following reports from The Ditch, a source said they could see Paddy in the promotional style of the material.

'It was day one, release things, and then have him deny them, and then release more – that's smart, it shows a savvy media mind at work,' he added.

Although Bowes did a lot of work in promoting The Ditch during his tenure as a director, and even after, his association with the outlet became increasingly problematic for the lads, especially once he moved to Moscow and began working for the Russian State.

After Bowes resigned as a director and transferred his shareholding to a company controlled by Connon, it was hoped that any past connection between Bowes and The Ditch would be quashed. But just a few months later, Tánaiste Micheál Martin would lash out at the website on the floor of the Dail, citing how Bowes was a founding member and the Russian ambassador was 'full of praise' for him.

The outburst came after weeks of stories about Niall Collins, a Fianna Fáil colleague of Martin's, who The Ditch had reported about a sale of land he voted on which was ultimately bought by his wife. In this coverage, it reported that Collins had lied about his home ownership in a planning application. The TD maintained that 'no law was broken'.

Martin described The Ditch as a 'political organization' which was not independent 'by any stretch of the imagination'.

'Nor should anyone even suggest that it is because if you read all the tweets of Paddy Cosgrave or Chay Bowes in respect of me or other political leaders on this side of the House it is clear that their agenda is to take down the Government,' Martin said.

'That is fine and they are entitled to have that, but I understand what it is and I am not going to facilitate it every week, in and out here in Dáil Éireann.'

The Tanaiste also remarked, in questioning where funding for The Ditch was coming from, that he was alarmed that the Russian ambassador in Ireland had recently praised Bowes.

'A few weeks ago, on 9 April, Chay Bowes turned up on RT India, where a caption referred to him as a *Russia Today* correspondent. That is what is behind The Ditch lads,' he added.

The sight of Martin attacking a news website on the floor of the Irish parliament, and using the privilege afforded to politicians in this setting to say what he wanted without fear of a defamation lawsuit, was shocking on many levels. Until that moment, it had not been clear to the general public that the deputy leader of the country, or the government in general, was that profoundly bothered by The Ditch.

Their stories garnered significant engagement on Twitter, and, as previously noted, resulted in tangible real-life consequences for some subjects. But in many cases it seemed like the online content existed in its own echo chamber, reinforcing the views of those who have already made up their mind about those in power.

Paddy reacted with outrage, sending a complaint to the Clerk of the Dáil that the Tanaiste had breached a standing order and that his reputation had been 'adversely affected' by the comments. But privately he knew that Martin losing his temper, and showing that the The Ditch was indeed needling those in power, was extremely beneficial to the brand.

'Web Summit is funding journalism. Meanwhile, the Tánaiste is attacking journalism cheered on by a half dozen bootlicking Irish tech bros who seem to think corruption & fraud are just fine. We all see you,' Paddy tweeted shortly after the ordeal.

A source who has engaged with Paddy for years said his ongoing goal of getting a strong reaction, annoying the government, and being relevant was achieved by Martin's remarks.

'I'd say his happiest day was when Micheál Martin attacked him in the Dail. I'd say that was his best ever day,' they added.

In a departure from how the public reacts to his usual tirades, Paddy had important groups like the National Union of Journalists (NUJ), a number of well-known campaigners, and academics on his side. The NUJ released a statement denouncing Martin's comments.

'The media operates within the constraints of extremely restrictive defamation laws,' Séamus Dooley, NUJ secretary, said in a statement.

'Politicians who wish to challenge the accuracy, efficacy

or bona fides of any journalist or media organisation should do so within the same constraints and without the protection of Oireachtas privilege,' he added.

As a result of the back and forth, which made headlines for days on end, McNeill and Shortall were also thrust into the spotlight in ways they had never been before. In an interview with RTÉ the weekend after Martin's remarks, McNeil defended the outlet and denounced the criticisms. He also revealed that along with 'four figure' donations received from the general public, Web Summit had agreed to put up 'about €1 million' toward the website.

A few weeks after the funding relationship was made public, Shortall used the name 'Sugar Paddy' to describe his backer while addressing journalism students.

The funding commitment was not the only connection between Web Summit and The Ditch. As previously described, Connon owned a third of the shares, while McNeill and Shortall were originally Web Summit employees. Despite working primarily for The Ditch in its early years, they both maintained connections with the conference company, including attending and in some cases working at events.

McNeil said in the interview that he and Shortall have full editorial control over the website, and Paddy has similarly told me that he has no editorial interference in The Ditch. But a few weeks later, in his own RTÉ interview and after being confronted with a question on whether his credibility was undermined by his tweets, Paddy appeared to give himself a more central role when he said: 'I think the stories that I've been involved in amount to the most substantive journalism undertaken in this country in a very, very long period of time.'

Prior to The Ditch, Paddy toyed with other media enterprises he might fund or establish. At one stage, he tried to hire an Irish journalist to work on a new media venture within Web Summit. In early 2020, after pledging to establish €100,000 in bursaries for student journalists over the next 10 years, Paddy told the *University Times* in a direct message that 'a healthy media, or 4th estate, is a prerequisite of a healthy society'.

'No doubt in the first year there will be kinks to iron out, but hopefully in time it might in some very small way help student journalists. It's just an idea at this point, but committed to turning it into something,' he added. The bursary was never established and a meeting with the then *University Times* editor did not materialize.

McNeill has indicated that the outlet severed ties with Bowes because of his views on the war in Ukraine, saying the issue became a 'bone of contention'.

Shortall has also publicly distanced himself from Bowes' views about the war. But Paddy, their main backer and promoter, has been less forthright about ditching Bowes.

Just days after he and his media start-up were publicly sparring with the government over its identity, Paddy was in Rio de Janeiro, Brazil, for Web Summit's first foray into Latin America.

Held at the Riocentro, the largest exhibition centre in Latin America, and one of the venues for the 2016 Olympics, Web Summit Rio was the first time the flagship brand name was being used outside of Europe. It drew a number of big-name speakers including Ayo Tometi of the Black Lives Matters movement, Nikolay Storonsky, Revolut's founder, and Amrapali Gan, the chief executive of OnlyFans.

At a press conference, Paddy addressed The Ditch controversy, saying it was 'quite despicable that, without evidence, it can be implied that attempts to highlight corruption in government is seen as some kind of Russian-backed campaign'. He likened it to 'something Donald Trump might do'.

In Rio he became annoyed at a Twitter account which was posting critically about a queue issue at the conference as well as others which lambasted the WiFi and sound quality.

As much as he enjoys revelling in the drama when it suits him, Paddy aggressively played down the criticism to enjoy his company's first pep rally in South America.

'Some Irish haters are relying on a Twitter account with 0 followers to try hatchet what is one of Ireland's greatest brands & success stories. The WiFi worked, the speakers were [fire emoji] & today, opening day, is buzzing with 91 countries,' he tweeted.

Sitting in Ryan's on Parkgate Street, a Victorian pub near Dublin's Phoenix Park, Noel Toolan's eyes light up as memories of some of the more unusual episodes in Web Summit's recent history are recounted.

For him, the 'Leo the Leak' moment at Web Summit 2021 is top of the list among those he has witnessed in person.

From his perspective, the 2021 event was among the most important, if not the most important, in Web Summit's history as a company because it showed that the business had come back from the brink.

'Here you are at the most important moment probably of the entire story, and it's not off the cuff, there's a video!'

he says, referring to the images displayed on screens in the arena.

'That really got me. I thought he might say something, [but] that was bizarre,' he adds.

Toolan says he has seen 'that sort of fixation' before, characterizing it as something which appears minor to Web Summit's customer base, but which then distracts from 'the brand'.

He is in his usual stride meeting me here on a weekday afternoon in December. He was up at 5 a.m. having recently attended the Slush tech and start-up conference in Helsinki, before a full day of travelling by boat and plane followed by a remote conference appearance in his car. And after this chat, he's getting back in the car to be in Sligo for dinnertime.

Much like Paddy, Toolan has boundless energy and it's not hard to see how the two of them have got along for years. He radiates positivity when he discusses what the trio of founders – and he credits each of them with establishing the company – did to promote it in the early years.

Speaking in short bursts and frequently name dropping, he uses his hands to traverse the space between us and illustrate the past decade of Web Summit moments. Toolan is a natural performer and the monologue is extremely entertaining, interrupted only by his laughter.

'Birch, Zennstrom, Dorsey, the guys from Angry Birds, kind of Finnish guys going "we're quite a breakthrough but this is very, this is very unusual," and then yeah, we're meeting the president of the country. Mary MacAleese, and Enda played with them ... Number 10 talking to Tony Blair ...' he says.

'[The early Web Summit team] this is the way they behaved, and they scaled it, and if you do those things, if you go to a start-up ecosystem, close your eyes and listen, you could be in Lisbon, Helsinki or Hong Kong, this is transferable ... big guys will come in, local guys, bit of language, maybe, who cares ... There's all that kind of natural stuff that happens, done professionally, can really work. The guys were real, they had no limit on their horizon, they were great natural connectors, and maybe there's an Irish thing there, I think there is, we're good at this, and they were driven, they worked really, really hard, and they bumbled into things, and they weren't organized ... but it worked, and one of the reasons it worked was the combination of the naivety, in a positive way, the ambition, no we're going to have the best marketing people in a room together and it'll work, and if it doesn't work we'll make it better, some of the early stuff was almost comical but they kind of got away with it, they said we'll do it better the next time, but people came back.'

Web Summit, he says, required a 'zany, break through, irreverent, break down walls, and break the rules approach'.

'It wasn't just about breaking things. Paddy built something very different and built it on a number of concepts that were pretty unique, and have held through and were core to the brand like this idea of engineering serendipity.'

The last phrase has been a crucial slogan for Web Summit and used throughout the years as a launchpad when attempting to devise ways to describe what the company was selling. Staff from earlier years recall the phrase being splattered on a white board, which remains at the back of the Dartry office to this day, albeit with much of the marker text faded.

As a slogan, it was the essence of the brand, Toolan explained, noting that Paddy came up with it.

'It's the great singular idea that stitches it together – the idea of so-called random meetings with people where the business is really done,' he says.

'They lived it at hand-to-hand combat, "we're on our way to the studio", "we're on our way to see the President", and it was fantastic to see,' he adds.

Toolan and I met for the first time only a few weeks prior to this coffee date, in Lisbon for Web Summit 2023, the first in the company's history without Paddy in attendance.

I had been chasing him for weeks, digging for his views in conversations with others and speculating that Paddy was turning to him for advice amid the fallout from the controversy generated by his comments on Israel and Palestine.

It is an interesting moment to be chatting to him, in a rare window of time when Paddy is not chief of the company and so it feels like his thoughts are more reflective of the bigger picture.

Toolan holds extremely high opinions of Paddy, casually referring to him as a 'genius' and an 'innovator' whose professional views he respected. But as much as he eulogizes Paddy, he's also pointed in his criticisms, even though he might not mean them to be as critical as they sound.

In the wake of Paddy's departure as chief executive, Web Summit, Toolan says, is now 'detoxed' and from a practical perspective he wants the company to shake itself free from what he sees as onerous sub-brands. These include

Collision, its North American event, and RISE, its Asian event.

A one-world Web Summit umbrella is the way forward, and Toolan wants the company to market each event based on the city and the year, similar to the model used by the Olympics.

While I'm interested in his marketing plans, I find his use of the word 'detoxed' far more peculiar, given that it implies the company was toxic with Paddy at the helm.

'I've never witnessed, I've heard of it, and I know it has happened … and it wasn't nice,' he says, when asked about Paddy's ability to hurt those around him with his words or his actions. He refers to the behaviour as appearing to be aimed at getting retribution for a perceived wrongdoing, but says they typically engage on lighter subjects.

'Anytime Paddy talks to me he is great fun, he is absolutely interested in learning stuff … and preaching, but it's great craic to talk to him,' he adds.

Toolan is not fazed by the concerns raised by many of Paddy's critics that the company's reputation will struggle to recover while he remains the majority owner.

In a way which conveys he has had this conversation with many others in recent weeks, he describes how most people don't know or don't care that the Innocent brand of smoothies is owned by Coca-Cola.

'Ownership is funny like that,' he adds.

He says that the company can create huge value in the wake of Paddy's departure, especially if it can navigate the upcoming event in Qatar delicately.

Web Summit, he explains, is at a make or break moment, but it seems from the way he finishes our chat that he thinks the same about Paddy.

'I hope Paddy comes back and brings his fabulous, considerable skill and that he's learned his lesson on his toxic behaviour, and hopefully that's corrected, and that he's big enough to, and I don't know that, but it would be great if he was big enough to say ah yeah, I was illogical about it, and I would say that to him if he asked me, you know, okay, you're damaged, you need to fix it, rise, Lazarus, it can be done, but you have to mean it, you have to really mean it, you can't just say it, you have to behave differently, and is he capable of that? I don't know. I can't answer that question.

'I remember when I met his kid, Cloud, I thought oh my god, Paddy, you have your own brand, you have a sub brand, and he's going yeah, yeah ... but he didn't change that much. The people close to him say that's just Paddy, that's just the way he is.'

Chapter 13

THE FALLOUT

In a final phone call, Dave told Paddy that he had recently cried as their relationship fell into ruin.

It was the end of March 2021 and the pair had spent weeks engaged in a series of tense communications about Daire, Patrick Murphy and the future of Amaranthine. A few days before, Dave had resigned as a Web Summit director.

After 25 years, many of which included sharing important life moments and helping to grow a successful business, the partnership appeared terminal.

'You've broken me as a man. You've broken me as a human being,' he told Paddy. 'I cried last week, like after you tried to tell me that I owed you for the fund, I owed you for this, I can't take that shit,' he added.

Despite already being aware of concerns regarding Dave's mental health over what was turning into a vicious and public row, Paddy's response was 'but it's true'.

'How is it not true? How is it not true that you basically got entirely dicked over by Patrick. I spotted it and sorted it out.'

This 13-minute conversation, which was referred to by both Paddy and Dave in their legal cases, marked a moment when years of unrest finally turned irrevocably poisonous.

During the call, Paddy hit Dave with the claim, which he would repeat in his affidavit, that he had allegedly mismanaged a sexual harassment complaint against Daire, and that he was allegedly shutting Web Summit out of conversations regarding a second fund.

Dave accuses Paddy of attempting to 'play dirty' to which he responds 'the only person that's playing dirty, my friend, is you'.

After over two decades of being the less outspoken person in the relationship, Dave tells Paddy that he's a 'highly good manipulator'.

'Undermine me and make me question myself, question my judgement. Try and rattle me, great, go for it,' Dave says. 'I'll literally go to town and tell the world … about how you've manipulated me. How you've bullied me, how you've diminished my self-worth.'

'And with the fund, tell me exactly what happened with the fund?' Paddy asks in reply.

'You have to win, right?' Dave says. 'Like this is your playbook, right?'

Despite this conversation being exhibited in the form of a written transcript, it is hard to avoid how devastating it was for their relationship and how it would set in motion a cascade of life-changing events.

Why Paddy and Dave got to this point is one of the most heavily contested aspects of their entire falling out. It's almost impossible to tease out the legal points in their argument without uncovering some of the more emotional elements to the dispute.

The crux of the row is whether Paddy and Web Summit were cut out of a potential second fund and whether Dave began soliciting investment in a follow-on fund prior to when he said he did.

Just six months after the final 13-minute conversation, Paddy filed the California lawsuit, making a string of allegations against David Kelly and Patrick Murphy, the fund manager whom Dave had gone on to partner with. By this time, the pair seemed too far gone to sit at a table with some of the best mediators in San Francisco, although that was floated as an option.

Paddy demanded a jury trial to deal with the issues and sought injunctions against his former colleagues as well as damages and a disgorgement of all 'improper' profits.

In Paddy's US lawsuit, he alleges that Dave and Patrick Murphy 'secretly' established an investment fund he claims benefited from its association with the Web Summit, but from which the company and Paddy were excluded.

Dave and Patrick strongly deny the claims, alleging instead that Paddy decided against having Web Summit be involved in a second fund, and that the first fund was 'not Web Summit's fund'.

Paddy alleged that they told him they did not intend to raise a new fund, that they did not solicit for a new fund from existing LPs, and that they did not intend to use Web Summit's data in relation to their new fund.

'All of these representations were false,' the lawsuit claimed.

'These claims arise from a plan hatched by Murphy and [Dave] to deceive Web Summit and Mr Cosgrave, breach an agreement with them, and secretly establish a follow-on fund that improperly usurped Web Summit's brand, resources and assets,' it also claimed.

Paddy wanted the case to go to trial because he wanted the allegations aired in open court. He also wanted to draw attention to what he felt were damaging allegations and being bound by a confidential form of dispute resolution would not facilitate that.

This became clear after Dave and Patrick moved to have the case kicked to arbitration. Katherine Farrell, a Web Summit spokeswoman dealing with media queries regarding the legal actions, released a statement saying that this would place the proceedings 'behind closed doors'.

'David Kelly continues to attempt to distract and deflect from the serious cases he faces in the US and in Ireland,' she added.

Dave and Patrick's lawyers argued that Paddy had previously agreed to arbitrate disputes and was prevented from litigating his claims. Ethan Schulman, a judge of the Superior Court of California, agreed.

The existence of parallel US proceedings meant that Kelly and Murphy instructed lawyers across the water.

Patrick Gunn, a partner in Cooley LLP, a San Francisco-based law firm, said in a July 2021 letter that since the breakdown in the parties' relationship no investors had understood either that Paddy or Web Summit was involved 'in any way' in any new venture by his clients.

'Web Summit has also demanded the names of all investors in the new fund and all communications between my clients and investors concerning it. As an initial matter, I note that Mr Cosgrave already knows the investors who have contributed the overwhelming majority of capital to the new fund and has communicated with them directly about their involvement,' Gunn wrote.

Gunn's reference to Paddy knowing and contacting the new fund's investors related to email communications he sent to their fund's LPs in May 2021.

In one of these emails, Paddy stated that he was informed by a third party that Patrick repeatedly described Dave as a 'gullible imbecile' and generally described him as 'an easy person to manipulate'.

In another email, which Dave alleged he sent to some LPs, including his father-in-law, Paddy claimed to be quoting Dave's own words that Patrick 'pressurized' Dave into signing 'a peculiar legal document'.

'What Dave signed immediately reduced Dave's carry in Fund I to ZERO, assigning an assumed 80 per cent carry to Patrick,' Paddy alleged in the email.

Dave said the allegations made in both emails were untrue and 'constituted a transparent act of attempted sabotage'.

It would transpire, Dave alleged, that the person who made the claims about Patrick's alleged remarks about Dave was Peter O'Malley, an early Web Summit employee who Paddy once regarded as a protégé. Dave alleged that O'Malley outed himself as the individual behind the claims in a text message conversation which featured the line 'I'm sure the Titanic have comfortable deckchairs.'

Agitated by the claims made by Paddy in their phone call, Dave made contact with a number of Web Summit employees to test out the veracity of the allegation that he was under investigation for mishandling a complaint about Daire.

He said in his affidavit that he was told by two senior staffers that no investigation was taking place.

'What Mr Cosgrave stated to me was false and had been invented by him', he added.

On 18 March 2021, Dave verbally resigned as a Web Summit director because, he alleged, his relationship with Paddy had become 'irremediably toxic'.

In an email acknowledging this, Paddy said: 'David, As per your request for a clean break, I recognise that you've resigned as a director with immediate effect and will be leaving the fund as soon as is practical. I'd like to catch up separately in person and will also write to thank you for everything … something I can't stress enough. It's the privilege of a lifetime.'

Dave claimed that he never stated he was going to leave the fund and Paddy was placing it there to create an alleged false documentary record.

He told Patrick Kirwan, the company's chief financial officer, shortly after things began to dramatically unravel: 'I am going to have to start taking legal advice. That stuff is not good for my health.'

Kirwan replied: 'Hey David, was chatting to PC and mentioned I was catching up with you. He would much prefer that we move all discussion to email between us three to try and resolve this as best as possible. I am here to help and going to email may be the best course to get this wrapped up.'

Dave had been on edge and not in a good place for weeks. At one stage he blocked Paddy's number on his phone. He also received advances from mutual contacts attempting to act as mediators. Some of these individuals Dave spoke with during this period recorded the conversations and sent them to Paddy, who would later rely on them as evidence that Dave's claims of oppression were allegedly unfounded.

In an email from late May 2021, Paddy tells Dave that he had just listened to two 'lengthy phone recordings of you to friends'.

'David, the things I have heard you say are beyond reality. I know this is not you. And while you will not listen to me, I am nevertheless going to say it: I do not think you are in a good place and I am urging you to seek professional help,' Paddy added.

In one of the interventions, a mutual friend named Sam Hunt, who knew Paddy and Dave from school, allegedly said Paddy would buy his shareholding for €1.25 million if he committed to ceasing his involvement with Murphy.

'It's like do I want to buy into Paddy's threats or move on with my new fund?' Dave asked Hunt.

'Agree on all fronts, except I think the threats are real and he will be relentless,' he added.

Hunt would later make a strong attempt to talk Paddy down from launching the lawsuits, asking whether he could not 'rise above it' and whether, when someone is reading his eulogy one day, he will be proud of how he had acted now.

'I think you are being overly destructive and are being the least sensible person right now. I think you just leave it go. You will be able to focus on creating value not wrecking people's lives,' Hunt said in a message to Paddy in May 2021, forwarded to and exhibited by Dave.

After meeting Hunt at Web Summit 2023 and bringing up these message exchanges, I asked him if he would speak with me for the book. He said he did not want to be involved but suggested that I try to be fair to Paddy. 'While no doubt he has his flaws, he comes from a place of strong integrity and high ethical standards,' Hunt said.

As has been referenced at various points, the lawsuits brought with them a series of increasingly inflammatory claims on all sides.

But among the most bizarre occurred just as things were falling apart between Paddy and Dave on the fund, when a mention of alleged *kompromat*, a Russian term for 'damaging information', was made by Paddy to Dave.

In Dave's version of events, Paddy initially made reference to what would become known as the *kompromat* in 2019 when he was allegedly strategizing on how to get Daire to resign as a director. This allegedly concerned photos of Dave on his stag weekend taken by Daire, which the former described as a 'fabrication'.

Paddy alleged that he 'heard rumours' that Daire held *kompromat* on Dave and that Daire had shown him an 'embarrassing' photograph of Dave. He referred to this in legal filings after stating that he was concerned as to why Dave 'appeared to be so reluctant to remove [Daire] as a director'.

This reference would resurface in a text message from Paddy to Dave in the weeks leading up to the latter's formal resignation in 2021.

'I've seen the *kompromat* you're so worried about. It's nothing. Can you share me on all files related to Amaranthine. I want to start talking to LPs about this split,' Paddy wrote.

Upset by the message, Dave replied, 'Call me. I can't live like this genuinely wired differently. Happy to introduce you to whomever on LPs. Find it bullshit saying *kompro-*

mat … At this stage in my life with three kids I don't need messages on a Saturday morning suggesting you have seen some sort of *kompromat* on me. But if you want to blow me up please just go for it.'

By August of 2021, the legal letters were intensifying and Paddy was inching toward filing a breach of fiduciary duties case against Dave in the Irish High Court.

An initial letter to Dave from Clark Hill, the law firm Paddy instructed for the lawsuits with his co-founders, spanned 13 pages long.

'You have failed to act in good faith and without the required loyalty to the company,' Paddy's 3 August 2021 legal missive stated. 'This correspondence provides you with due warning that proceedings will be issued by the company and by Mr Cosgrave against you, seeking, amongst other things, an account, damages, and injunctive relief, should you fail to comply with the undertakings set out below within a period of two weeks.'

The letter made a number of demands, including that Dave resign immediately from his new fund, unwind the investments made by any LP in that fund, and agree to make a public statement. It described how the pair had a long-standing relationship and that Web Summit was built to its successful position 'as a quasi-partnership' between the two.

'Your recent actions have been in clear breach of the relationship of trust and mutuality that flows from a quasi-partnership and in those circumstances, you are liable not only to the company but also to Mr Cosgrave personally,' it added.

Those practising in litigation often say that pre-action correspondence, or early legal letters fired back and forth before a case is filed, can be the most vitriolic because the goal is to heap pressure on the opposing party. In this case, the heat in the communication was exacerbated by the history between Dave and Paddy.

A reply, which came a few weeks later from Dillon Eustace, said that Dave refutes and denies all the allegations made by Paddy. 'It appears from the outset that much of the content of the letter is based on either a complete misunderstanding of the relationships between the various parties referred to in your letter or a complete and wilful disregard for those relationships, as well as the basic facts, legal documents and rights underpinning them,' it said.

The letter also threw out a few of its own bombshell claims which would form the basis for Dave's alleged oppression case.

'A clear pattern of behaviour by Mr Cosgrave whereby whenever our client did not agree with Mr Cosgrave, or when he questioned or queried his actions, Mr Cosgrave's response was to make up untrue allegations about him, to threaten him, and to essentially do whatever he deemed appropriate to pressurize our client into towing the line,' it added.

After the cases were filed in the Irish High Court in the autumn of 2021, headlines with many of the more salacious details became a regular occurrence for the next six months.

In November of that year, Daire rowed in with a minority oppression case of his own, alleging that Paddy displayed 'disreputable conduct' which has undermined the Web Summit brand and that a concerted strategy led by Paddy forced him out of the company.

His legal papers contained a number of allegations such as that Paddy waged a campaign against Denis O'Brien, the millionaire businessman who is alleged to have donated more than €200,000 to Web Summit in the past. Daire alleged Paddy had flown multiple times on O'Brien's private jet before beginning to attack the businessman on Twitter after forming the view that he was supporting the Dublin Tech Summit. Paddy, Daire alleged, has 'maintained numerous petty vendettas against business or political figures by whom he feels slighted or underappreciated, which he seeks to disguise as principled political stances.'

The gloves were well and truly off and it seemed that the appetite to understand why the former friends had fallen so foul of each other was insatiable. Shareholder oppression type cases, like the ones launched by Dave and Daire, are referred to by lawyers as corporate versions of bitter family law disputes.

In a replying affidavit filed in early 2022, Paddy issued his most substantive response to much of the allegations levelled at that point by Daire and Dave. In one of the colder passages, he denied the pair were ever co-founders at all, saying he provided them with the 'vanity title' as a 'soother'.

He also denied the existence of a profit-sharing agreement, which both Dave and Daire had claimed was in place from the early years of the company. And he levelled a litany of allegations of his own, portraying both men as ineffectual workers who repeatedly wronged him and the company.

While the lawsuits put unprecedented pressure on the co-founders, they also exposed dozens of Web Summit employees, current and former, to questioning – a fact that became increasingly uncomfortable as time went on.

Shortly after the cases were launched, an email went out from Connon to former staffers asking them to complete a discovery questionnaire because they may have information relevant to the proceedings. It asked various questions regarding what desktop and laptop computers were used during the period of employment and whether any devices may contain documents relevant to the proceedings.

'Considering the issues in the litigation (which can be explained to you), covering the time period between 2010 and 2021, what documents, both hardcopy and electronic, do you have or might have had, which are relevant to the matter?' it said.

Given the optional nature of the questionnaire, and the fact that most people understandably do not want to be involved in litigation for a former employer, a number of recipients did not respond or did not end up completing the questionnaire.

As it faced up to a large-scale discovery process, Web Summit initiated a trawl through its own email archives. Among the items it found was one which would eventually result in another former Web Summit employee becoming involved in a lawsuit.

In the spring of 2022, Paddy posted a series of tweets which alleged that Mark O'Toole, who worked for Daire at the time, had taken a large database of media contacts from Web Summit before he left the company in 2015. The basis for this was a forwarded email from Mark's Web Summit email address to his Gmail address.

A month before Paddy began tweeting about it, Connon had written to O'Toole alleging that forwarding the database was a 'breach of data protection law'.

'Bearing in mind the highly competitive nature of Web Summit's business, it considers any actions by employees which are in breach of contractual obligations and which may result in damage to the business of Web Summit as extremely serious,' the letter stated.

It also threatened the possibility of proceedings being issued and the company required O'Toole to retain 'email, texts, business plans, diary entries, and minutes of meetings originating from Web Summit property'.

A series of tweets containing serious allegations were then issued by Paddy while O'Toole consulted with lawyers on potential defamation proceedings arising from them.

Around this time, Paddy began sending me screenshots of legal correspondence between O'Toole and Lavelle Partners, the law firm he was engaging with. I was confused as to how Paddy had obtained this correspondence, but received no definitive response from him to my queries.

It transpired that O'Toole had been forwarding the emails to one of Daire's old Web Summit-related email addresses, instead of the one he was currenting using with 150Bond. And as Paddy had long ago engineered that emails to this account would be forwarded to him, O'Toole's legal correspondence was flowing freely into the inbox of the former boss who was allegedly defaming him.

A letter threatening a lawsuit was issued in April, with lawyers for O'Toole saying the content of Paddy's tweets was 'malicious defamation'. The case, launched in April 2022, remains live.

It was not just ex-Web Summit employees who were being pulled into what was beginning to look like endless litigation. Friends of the founder trio were also thrust into the spotlight, including Trevor White, a long-time friend of

Paddy's, who Daire alleged was paid €50,000 by Paddy, using Web Summit money, for a 0.25 per cent stake in Camile Thai, the takeaway business, at a time when White was experiencing financial difficulties.

White currently operates the Little Museum of Dublin, which is located at 15 St Stephen's Green, the same building where Paddy and Daire began their political outreach venture Rock the Vote nearly two decades ago. He is also a major connector and has been the organizer of an unofficial annual club for, as he terms it, 'a bunch of white cisgender middle-aged men'. Dubbed the 'Pecker Dunne Memorial Lunch', named after the late banjo-playing folk music performer, the gathering occurred at posh Dublin restaurants (the Pearl brasserie being a repeat venue) for what White has described in an email invite as an 'annual exhibition of peacock-feathers, five-cent wisdom and bonhomie'.

Invitees have previously included Brendan O'Connor, the *Sunday Independent* columnist, Michael Smith, of the *Village* magazine, Nick Webb, the journalist, Sebastian Hamilton, a journalist turned tech public affairs advisor who Paddy hired, Paul Hayes, the tech PR guru, Simon O'Connor, of the Museum of Literature Ireland, Cillian Fennel, a former *Late Late Show* producer turned advisor, Marco Herbst, chief executive of Evercam, Ed Brophy, former government advisor turned head of public policy for Amazon, and Paddy.

In one of the emails, reference is made to Trevor's Camile Thai stake, with Max McGuinness, a Trinity College Dublin academic and son of Paul McGuinness, U2's manager, stating that he was 'eager to discover how a Thai food franchise seemed to acquire a price-earnings ratio greater than Tesla's'.

In another chain, mention is made of Michael Smith's proposed purchase of Coollattin House in County Wicklow, with White floating that members of the 'fellowship' could invest €100,000 each so they could buy the house as 'a venue for Pecker-type activities'.

After I made inquiries as to who ended up purchasing the house, Smith got wind and sent me an over 550-word message on WhatsApp saying I was 'embarrassing' myself, that I should 'be careful' about implicating my employer with 'wild questions', and threatening to sue me. Much of his anger appeared to be directed at what he regarded as a suggestion that Paddy was providing him with funding, which he strongly refuted. There is no such suggestion.

In early 2024, I dropped into the Little Museum to see if Trevor White would speak with me about his relationship with Paddy, leaving my name and number behind. He sent me a written quote by text message and said he would not be commenting further.

It stated, among other remarks, that he wished Paddy would stay off social media and that to read Paddy's critics was to recognize that 'many of them are just establishment shills, particularly those who pose as moral titans'.

'I find it laughable when his left-wing worldview is characterised as hypocritical, as if liberals should be banned from running international businesses,' he added.

White was far from the only non-Web Summit employee to come up in the litigation. Paddy's wife Faye has also been referred to. She weighed in on the cases after Dave cited her jumpers in his affidavit.

In reporting on his legal filings, the *Irish Times* said Dave claimed the decision to sell the jumpers attracted negative publicity, 'overshadowing the event itself'. (This line was not included in his affidavit and has since been removed from the article.)

'For years, I've been championing the humble Aran sweater,' Faye posted on her Instagram in front of a series of pictures of her and Paddy in the jumpers. 'So today when I read that my lovely jumpers managed to over-shadow a 70,000-person global tech conference ... I knew I was on the right path #paygarmentworkers.'

As the discovery process continued to unfold, a number of long-serving staffers were also identified by Paddy's lawyers as custodians or 'key custodians' of data. This meant that their WhatsApp and Slack messages, emails and other documents were open to being scoured over by lawyers for potential nuggets through which to argue their various cases.

The lawsuits mean that senior Web Summit staffers, and in particular those who sit on its board of directors, are liable to be called as witnesses in the case if it proceeds to a full hearing. This possibility was said to cause significant stress to some of them.

'Your chosen profession, your field of expertise is now a battlefield in Russia's war against Ukraine, a battleground between good and evil and some of the specialists in Russia have made their choice to be aggressors and murderers,' Olena Zelenska, the First Lady of Ukraine, told a packed arena on the opening night of Web Summit 2022.

The words were not typical of those spoken from a Web Summit stage. Ukraine had been thrust into a war since February of that year – a conflict which had claimed over 10,000 civilian lives by the time Zelenska stepped onstage in Lisbon.

In her speech, Zelenska also gave a nod to Bellingcat, a multi-award-winning investigative news outlet founded by Eliot Higgins, a British journalist, in 2014. She credited the outlet with uncovering how Russian IT specialists were playing an active part in Russia's attacks on Ukrainian cities.

Bellingcat has been behind a number of the most pertinent investigative projects of the last decade, including deep dives into the downing of Malaysia Airlines MH370 and the attempted murder of Alexei Navalny.

And just two weeks before Zelenska mentioned Higgins onstage at Web Summit, he had indicated his intention of boycotting the conference.

The controversy arose after the line-up that year featured two journalists from the Grayzone, a far-left news outlet which has been accused of spreading Russian propaganda. Issue was also taken with Noam Chomsky, the American linguist who has been criticized for his views on the war, being featured as a speaker.

A flurry of posts appeared online as part of a public attempt to heap pressure on Web Summit to de-platform the trio of speakers. In the background, Ukrainian representatives and PR professionals were privately pleading with the company to row back on its decision.

Ukraine was a recent entrant to Web Summit but its national presence became among the most enthusiastic of the international delegations. It began attending the conference as a collective entity in 2021 when it brought 14 start-ups with help from donors such as Civilian Research and Development Foundation (CRDF) Global.

Olesia Malovana, a co-founder of Ukrainian Hub, an NGO, said it was collectively decided by various organizations, including her own, and the country's Ministry of Digital Transformation, to work towards securing Zelenska as a speaker in 2022. She said the First Lady's speech, along with the spotlight on Ukrainian start-ups by their presence at Web Summit, promoted the country's 'resilience' and bucked a trend of backers getting cold feet when it came to putting money into start-ups.

'They can see that nothing, [not] even the war, can stop our businesses and destroy our goals and objectives, because we are really strong in this situation,' she said.

The appearance of the two Grayzone journalists, as well as Chomsky, on the programme released a couple of weeks from the conference caused upset within the Ukrainian start-up community, and the wider network.

Malovana said it was a challenge to lobby Web Summit to amend the programme given how close it was to opening night, but they received help from PR representatives at IT companies, as well as from PR Army. The latter is a collection of volunteer communication specialists who came together after the war to counter the parallel information war being waged online.

She said the process was difficult and felt like 'fighting' with the organizers at various points and pleading with them to understand the importance of the issue. Along with Web Summit's speakers team, Paddy was directly contacted.

In the end, Malovana says they were happy with the outcome, their pavilion was a popular spot at the conference and 'a lot of people just came and said that they are really supportive of Ukraine'.

While the Grayzone reporters were removed from their speaking engagements, they were still invited to a private dinner hosted by Paddy at JNcQUOI, a fine dining restaurant near Lisbon's Bairro Alto neighbourhood. Attendees were mainly close friends, his immediate family, as well as reporters like Michael Smith, of the *Village* magazine, and Nick Webb, the *Sunday Times* columnist. The dinner took place less than 24 hours after Zelenska's address.

When asked about this at a press conference the following day, Paddy reiterated his wish that Web Summit 'be like Switzerland,' a place where different voices can be heard.

The episode in Lisbon was not the first time that the Grayzone reporters had attended a Web Summit event. Earlier that year, they spoke on the 'Fourth Estate' stage in Collision in Toronto where they decried most of the media as 'activists for neo liberal capitalism'.

While Paddy was backstage sucking down on a Starbucks Frappuccino and comparing himself to philosophers in the lead-up to the French Revolution in conversation with me, the Grayzone journalists hit out at government-funded think-tanks and coverage of the 6 January attack on the US capital.

After the interview concluded, the journalists were said to have been asking for a copy of the segment but the 16-minute clip was never uploaded to Web Summit's social media accounts or referenced in any promotional posts other than a schedule note advising its time.

Then, three weeks later, a clip of the interview was uploaded to Grayzone's YouTube account with a caption that it was delivered 'before a hostile audience filled with members of the corporate press'. The video has nearly 100,000 views and its value to Grayzone's anti-establishment brand is clear.

Chapter 14

QATAR? 'YEAH, IT'S A BUSINESS'

In the spring of 2023, Web Summit announced that it was going to Qatar for its first event in the Middle East. The event, held at the Doha Exhibition and Convention Centre, was to welcome over 10,000 people and the deal was extremely lucrative – said to be upwards of €20 million.

Hot on the heels of the FIFA World Cup which was marred by controversy for being hosted by a country with well-documented human rights abuses, Web Summit's news was met with scepticism.

Qatari law calls for a prison sentence of one to three years for 'inducing or seducing a male or a female in any way to commit illegal or immoral actions'. It also calls for the same punishment for whoever is 'instigating' or 'seducing' a male to 'commit sodomy'.

Football fans at the FIFA World Cup in Qatar said they were refused entry to matches while wearing rainbow symbols, and multiple teams abandoned plans to wear rainbow armbands due to concerns that they would be sanctioned.

Paddy acted unphased when I met him shortly after the announcement to discuss the move and how the conference could maintain its integrity.

When I asked if his speakers would be free to discuss topics of their choosing, or criticize the Qatari regime, he told me I should read a 1980s Noam Chomsky book about the media.

'The world is a complicated space, it's not a Disney movie,' he said.

In response to whether staff or attendees would be allowed to wear rainbows, he said: 'It's a region of 500 million people, we're not going to ignore it.'

The stated aim, and this was how Web Summit employees pitched the event to international speakers as well, was that it would 'help the region' and be a force for good in promoting change. Another phrase offered by Paddy by way of explainer was that 'the ethical value of one's pontifications is proportionate to their expected outcomes'. He used this to justify why he campaigned against corruption in Ireland but not in other jurisdictions willing to pay him millions to stage his event.

Many of those who know him well are confident that he genuinely believes it's worthwhile to rail against any perceived wrongdoing by those in power at home. Ireland is a small pool, and he sees himself as a big fish, albeit one who feels aggrieved for not being celebrated any more.

But PR aside, he is also a shrewd businessman who saw an open goal when it came to a lucrative income stream. When I asked if the value of the deal, which he refused to disclose at the time, contributed to the decision, he said, 'Yeah, it's a business.'

In a WhatsApp message later, in a reference to The Ditch website, he said: 'Now Web Summit can fund ten new Ditches.'

Qatar was no stranger to Web Summit events, and had attended with trade delegations for most of the last five years. This was along with Saudi Arabia, Oman and the UAE, which were in the running to host the country's first Middle East event.

In a statement announcing the deal, Mohammed bin Ali bin Mohammed Al Mannai, Qatar's minister of communications and information technology, said attendees will have the chance to experience 'Qatar's vibrant culture'.

A well-placed source said some staffers were sceptical about the decision and were concerned about how it would be perceived. These concerns were said to have been discussed internally among staff.

Around this time, Paddy's online vitriol spilled out into the real world when he confronted Mark O'Toole, who sued him for defamation a year before, and another former Web Summit employee that he had previously doxed. In early 2021, Paddy had posted a photo and the personal mobile phone number of the former Web Summit employee online in a since-deleted tweet which made serious allegations about him.

He took issue with the employee after he began working for the VC fund involving Dave and Patrick Murphy, and Paddy alleged that he had stolen from Web Summit. Mark and the former employee were at Dogpatch Labs in Dublin together when Paddy saw them and began filming on his phone, making allegations while he stood less than a metre away.

Although Paddy had become extremely fond of unmasking the identity of anonymous Twitter accounts connected to business people or civil servants, online activity targeted at former Web Summit employees has existed and continued in the background as well.

When I told him that his doxing was akin to social media vigilantism, and that it had the power to cause real damage to people and their safety, he claimed it was 'public service journalism'.

When asked who should hold him to account when he is wrong, he said that he gets it 'overwhelmingly right' and is 'righter than almost all of the media put together'.

His reputation as someone fond of doxing people online came under scrutiny when he posted a long statement lashing out at the *Irish Times* for publishing the address of his new home in Donegal.

In late 2022, Paddy and Faye purchased a €1.8 million home in the county, near one of the nicest blue flag beaches in Ireland. The purchase of the house, which has no mortgage on it, occurred in the same year that Web Summit advanced an over €1 million directors' loan.

In reporting on the purchase the *Irish Times* included a photo of the house and its exact location. Paddy sent legal letters asking for the article to be removed. In a statement he released on social media, he said that an armed intruder broke into his Dublin home following the publication of his address by the *Sunday Times* in a previous story. He said he had to install security cameras, that the experience was traumatic and he asked the *Irish Times* to 'consider their actions'.

A few months later he also claimed that he had to travel with 'a three-person private security team – all former military personnel'. He blamed Irish journalists, Fine Gael and Fianna Fail for fuelling these attacks.

Shortly after the Qatar deal was announced, the Web Summit lawsuits were in and out of the High Court as a discovery process dragged on.

The legal teams for the three founders had beefed up considerably, and along with senior and junior barristers they all had a team of in-house solicitors working around the clock on various preliminary matters.

Much of my exposure to the case came from being in court on the occasions it was listed 'for mention', which is when the lawyers give the judge an update on the progress, or lack thereof, in the cases.

Bernard Dunleavy, Web Summit and Paddy's senior counsel, typically did the talking for the company during these instances, but he works with barrister Oliver Butler.

Dunleavy, Butler, as well as Kirby Tarrant and Elizabeth Burke of Clark Hill solicitors, were guests of Web Summit 2022, receiving 'chairperson' tickets, meaning they had full access to the conference's VIP areas. In a Twitter post after the event, Dunleavy posted pictures of his passes as well as one of Paddy speaking.

'That's the end of my first Web Summit and I have to say I can't remember attending a more energizing, more intriguing, more optimistic and downright buzzier event: believe the hype!' he wrote about his client.

Kelley Smith, Daire's senior counsel, instructed by Dentons, is part of a small cohort of women SCs practising in commercial law. She works with Brian Conroy, a barrister who moved up to senior counsel in 2023.

Dave has been represented by Frank Kennedy, a former Fianna Fáil councillor for Dublin city. Michael Cush SC, one of the most well-known barristers in the Law Library, was instructed early on in the case but has not been in court for the majority of its preliminary listings.

In mid-2023, an issue arose about emails which had apparently been deleted by Dave just two days before the parties were due to exchange documents in May. He said it occurred 'in a moment of panic'.

A row also ensued after Dave floated a 'hypothesis' that Web Summit had remotely deleted the material. Dunleavy said this was 'doubled down' on despite no evidence being provided and that his client was not capable of remotely deleting material held by a third party.

The deleted emails meant that forensic e-discovery experts had to attempt to recover the content, and it resulted in additional days in the High Court providing updates to the judge on the progress.

Mr Justice Denis McDonald, who has been presiding over the cases in the High Court's commercial list, said he did not understand why Dave had only highlighted the issue around the time that discovery was due given that he had initially retrieved the emails in October 2021. He said he was 'not impressed'.

Continuous delays in the discovery process meant that the cases were only inching toward a full hearing as the costs continued to increase. Each time a legal missive was sent between Clark Hill, Dentons and Dillon Eustace, and every day the cases were listed in court, the fees charged by the various solicitors and barristers rose. And as many of the cases were being fought and defended by Manders Terrace, Web Summit's parent company, the business has been paying for the legal fees incurred in the co-founder lawsuits.

Also that summer, the list of boomerang Web Summit employees grew with news that Rich Forde, who worked in PR for the firm between 2015 and 2018, had rejoined. Forde was rehired on what multiple sources said he told them was a six figure salary and a sign-on bonus to be vice president of start-up relations. Part of the job was to build bridges with those in the Irish tech world who had been affected by the acrimony, especially that levelled by Paddy at those who failed to take a side following the lawsuits.

In many ways there was no better man for the job. Forde is easy-going and likes to be friends with everyone. But despite admiring Paddy from afar during the years he was gone from the company, he was astutely aware of how sour things could become.

The reason for this was because of Forde's friendship with Bobby Healy, founder of Manna Drone Delivery. Like a number of business people and journalists, Healy championed Paddy and the Web Summit for many years. His drone delivery company received backing from Amaranthine and Healy was a speaker at Web Summit 2021.

But after Paddy showed up to his large house in a leafy south Dublin suburb with a trove of documents he had compiled ahead of the lawsuits, things went south. Paddy 'cancelled' Healy from Web Summit 2022 arising from what he described as his decision to 'turn a blind eye' to the alleged issues he was presented with.

At the heart of this were documents which essentially consist of Paddy's description of the past few years and every alleged wrongdoing by his co-founders and other employees.

Written in the third person, he has presented a lever arch file of documentation to tech founders and journalists over the years. At one stage Paddy messaged a journalist he had shown the material to in a Dublin café to remind them that they had seen it and that it was 'all on camera'.

Paddy has repeatedly taken very public issue with journalists who have been presented with the material but who have not reported on its detailed contents. The dichotomy being that if you were a good journalist you would be reporting on the issues as he sees them.

Dave and Daire have referred to the existence of a so-called 'dossier' in their legal papers, but Paddy has refuted Daire's characterisation and said there was 'no such dossier'.

Forde was acutely aware of how the lawsuits were driving a wedge between friends of Web Summit, as well as Paddy and former allies.

The turmoil caused by Healy and Paddy's falling out was difficult because he maintained a close friendship with the drone deliveryman and an amicable relationship with his former boss.

Ahead of agreeing to his employment contract, Forde sought assurances from friends, and, crucially, from Paddy in writing the terms under which he was accepting the role and that he would be unimpeded by his boss's politics.

In his typical style of making self-knowing jokes, Paddy addressed guests at a Web Summit event just days before his resignation by jokingly referring to Rich as a 'total fucking traitor' who had previously left the company.

'But I found stuff about him and I started to hold it against him and brought him back here,' he added, laughing.

The other major hire around this time was Sebastian Hamilton, the former group editor of the *Irish Daily Mail*, Daire's old boss, and, along with Paddy, an invitee of the 'Pecker Dunne' dinner club.

He joined Web Summit from Revolut, where he had been head of public affairs Europe at the fintech, and took up the role at Web Summit as head of group public affairs. Since taking up the job, he has been a very active cheerleader of Web Summit on LinkedIn.

But Hamilton was only about six weeks in the door when Paddy issued a series of tweets that would cause an international affairs firestorm and lead to dozens of high-profile attendees cancelling their attendance. Hamilton was actually off work for part of the week that Paddy's backtrack, apology and subsequent resignation occurred.

I was approached about Hamilton's role by Ronan Mooney, Web Summit's head of HR, in a LinkedIn message in the summer of 2023. I told him that I was not interested but that I would happily chat with him for the book any time. He politely declined.

Shortly after this my relationship with Paddy, which by then mainly consisted of him messaging me with prompts on who I should contact to uncover details of alleged fraud, drastically soured.

He took issue with me referring to him as controversial and volatile in a message with a third party, which was screenshot and shared with him. We had a heated argument at the end of July 2023 where he accused me of covering up alleged fraud, which he has said involved many others outside his co-founders. I told him that I was not writing a book to settle all his scores.

The timing of Paddy's tweets on Israel, as well as where they occurred, were what made them highly damaging for Web Summit.

On the same day as the 7 October attacks which killed more than 1,200 people, mostly civilians, Paddy was in Doha doing early media engagements and meeting with officials ahead of the inaugural event the following year.

Qatar has been a long-time supporter of and has had enormous influence over Hamas, including being a financial backer of the extremist anti-Israel military group responsible for the massacre on 7 October.

On the evening of 7 October, Paddy shared a graph on the number of deaths of both Israelis and Palestinians in the conflict since 2008. That post has since been deleted.

Also that day, he shared a video of him doing media engagements while in Qatar, saying he was 'Chatting in Qatar about Ireland's Minister Niall Collins. And @ websummitqatar next February.'

The following day, as the death toll figure was still climbing, he tweeted a video from the stands of the Qatar grand prix, saying 'it's very loud'.

He also shared a video from inside the lobby of the Fairmont Doha Hotel which boasts the world's tallest chandelier: a 56-metre crystal sculpture that lights up with different colours.

Toward the end of the following week, he shared the tweet which has been credited with causing his downfall and which received huge levels of engagement online.

'War crimes are war crimes even when committed by allies, and should be called out for what they are,' he added.

The backlash was swift as the tweet went viral.

Despite repeating the phrase with the line 'I will not relent', he also doubled down by stating how 'In the last 24 hours, while nine investors cancelled, 35 new investors registered. Two media cancelled but more than 50 media requested media passes. Oh and somehow we sold more tickets than any other Monday in 2023.' This post has since been deleted.

A number of tech sources based in the USA said that while the damage was done once people started noticing his earlier posts and likes, it was this later tweet which really dug the boot in.

'That did untold damage, that was a death knell,' a US-based VC tells me.

An American-Israeli VC who cancelled his attendance at Web Summit after Paddy's comments said something similar. 'If after the first post, he would have said, no that's not what I meant, I think it would have died down. I think what pissed people off was that he continued to talk about how he's correct.'

'It's not like people noticed it right away, nobody cared about what Paddy said on 7 October or 8 October, but it was him saying, no we sold more tickets. Stuff like that really pissed people off,' he added.

Talia Rafaeli, a partner at KOMPAS, a VC firm based in Copenhagen, Denmark, had been attending Web Summit events for over half a decade when she made the decision to cancel her participation at the 2023 event. Rafaeli, who lives in Tel Aviv, said the conference had been 'huge' for the tech ecosystem in Israel and firms there had supported the event by sending hundreds of start-ups over the years. She said that was why Paddy's tweets in the initial days after 7 October felt like such a 'huge insult' given that he remained silent on the deaths caused by Hamas.

'When the pain was so raw, everybody here knows someone who was either killed or kidnapped or very, very seriously affected,' she tells me. 'It's such a raw open wound,' she adds.

The momentum for Israeli firms to boycott the conference quickly grew as Paddy's posts were shared on WhatsApp groups and as more high-profile VC figures posted critically online.

A real blow for the company came after Scott Galloway, an extremely high-profile marketing expert and NYU academic, cancelled his appearance as a keynote speaker. Not only that but he discussed the decision to step away on the Pivot podcast with Kara Swisher and called Paddy a 'terrible leader'.

Web Summit had been chasing Galloway, who Paddy held in high esteem, for years and had tried to get him as a keynote for Web Summit 2022.

Speaking with Swisher, who had attended previous Web Summit events and was equally critical of Paddy's remarks, Galloway described Paddy's tweets as 'being an apologist for terrorism'.

'He is putting a lot of people's economic livelihood in the cross hair of his grandstanding and political beliefs. That's not what a CEO does,' Galloway said.

'I see Twitter as nothing but kerosene that is ready to be poured on our worst instincts, and he got caught in that. And I do believe we need to move, and I hope we teach people this in high school, in an era with social media with a network of facts where there's a 24/7 camera on your life, that we become slow to judge and quick to forget,' he added.

Toward the end of the segment, the academic became audibly emotional describing what the ordeal stirred up in him. A source close to Web Summit told me that hearing Galloway cry at the end of the segment was when it really became clear that the problem facing the company was much deeper than initially appreciated.

Another source said that Paddy had initially asked some in his inner circle of staff whether he should resign as the heat was beginning to build, but was told not to. They were said to have wondered afterwards whether Paddy was testing them.

In the end, the decision was made by Paddy and the resignation statement was issued on Saturday 21 October 2023. A number of his closest advisors in the company said they were unaware of the decision, and had been briefing media that morning on the previously agreed line that he was 'not going anywhere'.

Despite the apology and resignation, Paddy appears to firmly believes in what he said and does not regard it as something he should have had to apologize for. Like tweeting wrongly about dead nurses, many expect Paddy to state that his apology was more about doing what seemed like the right thing in the moment.

It has also been remarked on by numerous sources that Paddy was unprepared for the backlash because he had acted with a perceived impunity for years. He had attacked the most senior members of government on a sometimes daily basis, lambasted the country's media, embarrassed former staff, and accused his enemies of serious crimes, all while successfully running Web Summit with few consequences.

Someone said it was almost like his Twitter activity lived in a parallel world to his professional activity, but that the 'hubris' this created left him exposed to something unexpected.

'He thought he was like Icarus and he could fly close to the sun … I think he felt that he knew what the line was and then he got caught out,' was how someone in the tech world phrased it.

Paddy's own remarks to Chay Bowes years previously are also highly relevant to how he was so blindsided by the level of blowback he received. In discussing how he has a business where '99.9 per cent' of the revenue comes from everywhere else in the world, 'I can pretty much say whatever the fuck I want and there's so little consequence.'

'You know, I'll be chatting to the managing editor of the *New York Times* or something like that and they'll be like "I've seen your Twitter, good stuff" and I'm like, yeah, yeah, nobody cares. People outside Ireland don't care about that stuff. It's just totally irrelevant. And so I have that freedom that a lot of other people just don't have. And so I feel some type of obligation just to at least rattle cages,' he said in a 2020 phone call referenced in the lawsuits.

When someone later expressed frustration that years of hard work were evaporated or severely under threat because of his comments, they said his response was to emphasize how he was right.

There were a number of deeply ironic aspects of the entire episode, including that the messaging of Paddy's tweets was not unlike those being expressed by leading political figures in Ireland, including Leo Varadkar.

After years of railing against almost every utterance from Varadkar, Paddy found himself in agreement (at least in principle) with the Fine Gael leader while he was spiralling toward his own downfall.

Another ironic aspect was that Paddy's sentiments were shared by a number of his most virulent critics, including some of the former employees who spoke to me for this book. Many said they regarded it as among the least controversial things he had ever said and they wondered why more issue was not taken with his years of online trolling.

'I agree with him, hate to say it,' one said after Paddy resigned. Others said the ordeal was the first time they felt bad for him. In the weeks after he stepped down, Paddy received an outpouring of messages in support of his stance and sympathy for the predicament he found himself in – including from some prominent figures he had previously sparred with.

One high-profile speaker, who agreed to speak on the condition of anonymity, said they thought Paddy's comments were 'distasteful' but they appreciated his apology and thought the resignation was appropriate. 'I faced pressure from folks who disagreed with Paddy's comments to pull out. Ultimately, once others started to pull out and my events were cancelled, the conference no longer seemed like it was worth the time and headache,' they added.

The exodus happened as a domino effect within the top-tier partner companies, with a senior tech source saying it became a matter of leaving to avoid the potential PR disaster that staying on would create.

After a six-week hiatus from Twitter, Paddy returned with posts which indicated that he believed he was the victim of a coordinated smear campaign. As evidence of this he relied on a report, published on Substack, which alleged that senior figures in Silicon Valley worked with the Israeli government to disseminate pro-Israel content. It cited a series of slides dubbed 'Israel advocacy during war' which featured a number of his tweets and included advice like 'show their inconsistencies'. The claims of coordination were denied.

Paddy later threatened to sue Amit Karp, a senior executive at Bessemer Partners, alleging that he was a part of a campaign to damage him. At the time of writing, he has yet to take any legal action against Karp.

Just 10 days after Paddy's resignation, Web Summit announced the appointment of Katherine Maher as its new CEO.

She had not had a full-time CEO role since she left the Wikimedia Foundation in 2021, a year when Internal Revenuc Services (IRS) data shows she received more than $623,000 in a severance payment from the foundation. She had been on the board of a number of companies including Signal, the encrypted messaging platform, and had also been a member of the Foreign Affairs Policy Board (FAPB) within the US Department of State. Launched in 2011, the FAPB provides 'independent, informed advice' to the Secretary of State on matters relating to US foreign policy.

Interestingly Antony Blinken, the current US Secretary of State that Maher was advising, was cited by Paddy in his apology as someone he 'tried' to emulate in the remarks he was criticized for. He also quoted Blinken to defend criticism of Web Summit's decision to sign a lucrative deal to host an event in Qatar next year.

'Like the US government, Web Summit believes in working with regional and global partners – including Qatar – to encourage the dialogue and communication on which peace depends,' he said.

The apology was widely criticized and Paddy resigned days later.

Maher is exactly the type of CEO you want to hire in a crisis. Originally from Connecticut and the daughter of a Democratic senator, Maher graduated *magna cum laude* with a bachelor's degree in Middle Eastern and Islamic studies from NYU. Polished and confident, she rarely stumbles over her words and speaks in full sentences not cluttered by filler phrases or sounds. Her enthusiasm is effervescent albeit slightly saccharine. She is described on the World Economic Forum's website as 'culturally fluent and always curious'.

On the opening night of Web Summit 2023, she went onstage in front of tens of thousands of people and did what many of the company's senior staffers have done over the years – she addressed a controversy of Paddy's making.

'If you know Paddy, you know that he's always been outspoken on stage and online,' she told the crowd, seeming slightly nervous as she found her feet during these remarks. She received a round of applause for recognizing the right to freedom of expression.

'We expect plenty of debate on the stages in the days to come, but I also want to acknowledge that having a right to free expression and considering the weight of your words are two very different things.'

Maher's opening night speech was part of a whirlwind

performance at Web Summit 2023, a feat all the more impressive given that she was only in the job a few weeks at that point. But a number of sources said she seemed significantly less involved than Paddy. The fact that she lived in New York during her stint as CEO also led a number of Web Summit staff to regard her as being far less hands-on than Paddy.

In the few months that she was at the helm, Maher attempted to draw a line in the sand between her tenure and that of her predecessor. Among the big-picture decisions she made was to sever the company's funding relationship with The Ditch. While sources said there was a plan in place to do this at a later time, the decision was brought forward after the news outlet had tweeted out a mocking apology for its support for Palestine in November. It said that upon reflection, it 'decided it would like to apologize to: nobody'. The tweet was deleted shortly after, but the damage was regarded as being done.

Shortly after it was posted, a call was made telling the hurlers that the funding was going to be cut. But given that the €1 million in funding pledged from Web Summit to The Ditch was over a five-year period, the first €200,000 is believed to have been already budgeted out of its 2023 accounts.

Maher told the *Irish Times* that she did 'not see the business alignment between Web Summit and having an independent media outlet that is affiliated with it, particularly one that is quite focused on Ireland'.

'This to me felt like this was a project of the previous CEO, and with the desire to move the company back towards a focus on what happens in the rooms and on the stages, it just didn't make sense,' she added.

But after only three months in the job, Maher announced in early 2024 that she was leaving to take up the role as chief of National Public Radio (NPR) in the USA.

It was undoubtedly a better job, not just for NPR's prestige as a media organization in the USA but also when the country was heading into what many predicted would be the most divisive presidential election ever. As a private company which receives significant public funds, the interview process for CEO of a company like NPR would have taken months, although it remains unclear when she was approached about the role.

John Lansing, its former CEO, announced publicly in September that he would be stepping down by the end of the year, with the board saying at the time that it would then begin its search for a successor.

Maher worked through the first Web Summit Qatar, and officially stepped down from her CEO role on 1 March 2024. But she remains on the board of directors, an arrangement sources said was agreed as part of her recruitment package – believed to be worth in the high six-figures.

At the time of writing, the NPR website listed her Web Summit directorship in the past tense, and the company did not respond to a query on why this was.

Another headache for the company in the weeks immediately after Paddy resigned was a video created by senior figures in the Israeli tech community criticizing Paddy for his comments.

The video was posted on YouTube and Twitter by Ran Harnevo, a high-profile Israeli entrepreneur and former president of AOL. He is a part of a political activist network of Israeli founders and tech industry veterans who have protested on a variety of issues, including controversial judicial reforms in Israel.

'We attended Web Summit in droves, and we will never do it again,' Harnevo said in the video. 'Fortunately, many brave tech leaders and tech companies from all over the world joined us.'

But a few days after it was posted, and shared by a number of prominent American figures like Bill Ackman, the hedge fund manager, and Jonathan Greenblatt, chief executive of the Anti-Defamation League, it was removed from the platforms after Web Summit filed a copyright infringement complaint. Adam Connon said the video incorporated Web Summit's official 2023 trailer.

Harnevo made a new version of the video and shared that instead, telling me that because Paddy had apologized, the 'battle' over a copyright claim reflected poorly on him and Web Summit.

The video was one small part of the onslaught that Web Summit was facing which catapulted the Irish tech company into the throes of a raging culture war. In many respects, it was a battle over the definition of 'liberal' in an increasingly polarized world. And as the viral video implied, Web Summit was now at the centre of an 'us versus them' world stage.

The feeling of being under attack from prominent figures online emboldened Web Summit staffers, many of whom agreed with Paddy's stance, even if they were annoyed at how it affected their livelihood.

A senior Web Summit staffer mocked the video and those who were involved in its creation to me at the time.

Regardless of how much of a strong front they presented ahead of the conference, being in the news on a weekly and sometimes daily basis was exhausting for staff. The constant scrutiny, coupled with the feeling that fighting back was almost pointless, put many Web Summit employees on edge.

After queries were sent in from two Irish newspapers, including the *Business Post*, as to whether Maher and Paddy were friends before she was hired, a letter was sent by Adam Connon threatening legal action. It took issue with the questions being asked and said at least one 'crosses the line from legitimate journalism into defamation'.

'Please be advised that Ms Maher's appointment processes are conducted with the utmost integrity by the board of directors of Web Summit,' Connon said. 'We demand that any articles that you publish refrain from making any defamatory statements or implications about Ms Maher, the Board, or the business. We would also urge you to consider the potential harm that could be caused by any misogynistic commentary or insinuations in your reporting.'

Maher defended the letters during a frosty press conference at Web Summit two weeks later. She said she had met Paddy 'exactly twice' before taking the role and she regarded any implication to the contrary as 'frankly offensive'.

In the aftermath of Paddy's resignation and the loss of senior sponsor partners, another big problem for the company was Web Summit Ventures, its VC fund. Although the enterprise, which was to consist of two $20 million funds, initially had the backing of a number of high-profile LPs, at least one asked to have their money removed and refused to commit additional capital.

Backers of the fund included a number of well-known Jewish Americans including Sean Rad, founder of Tinder,

Jon Soberg, managing partner of MS&AD Ventures, a corporate venture capital firm, and Rob Frohwein, CEO of Cabbage. The latter was the one who publicly stated that he asked for his money back. Soberg did not respond to queries on whether he remained an investor and attempts to contact Rad did not result in a reply.

As of the last end-of-year funding round, Web Summit Ventures had raised just over $5 million, although it is not clear how much of that came from the committed money pledged by Web Summit itself. A number of Israeli firms have also refused to accept investment from the Web Summit fund.

In the weeks after Paddy's resignation, Dave and Daire wrote to the board of directors, which consisted of multiple senior staffers, urging that an independent sales process be commenced. 'Until the company is controlled by persons independent of Mr Cosgrave and until Mr Cosgrave severs all association with Web Summit, it is my strong view that support for the company and by consequence its value, will continue to fall into sharp decline,' Daire said in an email exhibited to the High Court.

'I therefore call upon the board to consider as a matter of urgency the appointment of an investment banking firm to advise and initiate a sales process for the sale of Web Summit,' he added.

In an email a couple of weeks later, Dave and Daire said it appeared that Paddy was acting as a 'de-facto director and/or a shadow director'. The email said this was likely to have potentially very serious legal consequences for him and the other directors.

It also called into question Maher's independence, saying that it was 'incredible' that a company of Web Summit's size could run a candidate selection process for its leader in less than a week. Similar remarks were made about Damian Kimmelman, who had then been recently appointed to the board and who the co-founders alleged had known Paddy for over 10 years. Kimmelman is a frequent supporter of Paddy on Twitter, including liking his tweets which attack the co-founders, former staffers and the Irish media.

The first-ever Web Summit Qatar took place in late February 2024 at the Doha Exhibition and Convention Centre. Operationally, it was seamless and among the smoother of Web Summit's events, with the tens of millions the Qatari government poured into its success a factor in how well it ran.

Given that the embers from the PR fire over his Israel tweets were still simmering, Paddy was well aware of the sensitivities around the Qatar event. A message on a WhatsApp group for founders around the time of his resignation captured the disgust which the Qatar event had in the minds of many Israeli VCs and Jewish Americans in the tech community.

'I love you all and I loved Paddy for facilitating it, but I was blind to who he is. The two-faced greed of speaking about international law when he's organizing a conference where 6,500 foreign workers died while building sports stadiums, and is a funder of those that intentionally and happily killed 1,500 people, is just staggering to me,' one group member said in October.

But a lot had changed in the rhetoric since the weeks after the post on 7 October, and Israel had come under fire by leaders far more influential than Paddy. By the time Web Summit Qatar had kicked off, Israel's offensive against

Gaza had killed nearly 30,000 people and the country had been the subject of a trial before the International Court of Justice.

Still, there was a lot resting on Web Summit's contracts with American tech companies, especially those centred around its Collision conference scheduled for June in Toronto. Paddy flew into Doha for meetings but avoided being photographed in any official conference material by heading back to Ireland the evening before opening night. For Web Summit's inaugural Qatar conference, Sheikh Mohammed bin Abdulrahman bin Jassim Al Thani, Qatar's prime minister, announced a $1 billion VC fund through the country's investment arm. On stage, American talk show host Trevor Noah spoke as a headliner, as did Queen Rania of Jordan.

As for the host country, the population of Qatar includes around 300,000 nationals and around 2 million migrant workers, although the true number of nationals is unclear given that women and political dissidents can lose citizenship for a variety of reasons. Power is extremely consolidated among a small group of citizens, but Qatar is unique among many Arab states in that it has managed to remain an ally of the USA while also retaining long-held diplomatic links with groups and countries outside the US orbit like Hamas and Iran. Mustafa Qadri, CEO of Equidem Research and Consulting, a human rights not-for-profit organization, said this helped contribute to the country's reputation as a 'third-way' state.

Ahead of the FIFA World Cup 2022, Equidem conducted an in-depth investigation which exposed the extent of human rights abuses of migrants in the country. It also helped reveal the royal family's links to the construction companies building the stadiums where thousands of migrants died.

Qadri is not familiar with Web Summit but he said that these types of partnerships were common and part of Qatar's aim to cultivate a form of corporate liberalism. 'If you go there and are in some way in dialogue or in partnership with Qatari interests, you have the red carpet rolled out, it doesn't seem to be all that conservative,' he said. 'But once you get past that, it's actually a very repressive society. It's a bit more subtle in the way that it controls. You don't see as many cases of political dissidents being repressed, as you see in the Emirates and Bahrain or Saudi. In fact, the citizens self-police a lot. So in fact, a lot of that repression is invisible.'

Similar remarks were made by Isobel Archer, a senior migrant rights researcher with the Business & Human Rights Resource Centre, a London-based group which tracks over 9,000 companies worldwide. She said the concept of sports washing, where states attempt to camouflage human rights abuses by hosting internationally recognized events, can also be applied to events in the tech world. 'All of that serves to present a very flashy distraction, located in the respectability of international business to conceal these other issues. And there will undoubtedly have been workers at risk of abuse actually at the Web Summit event, because we know the general trend is there are only very few companies operating who are truly taking meaningful steps to protect migrant workers in practice,' Archer told me.

Those who have known and supported Paddy for years were unphased when asked about allegations of hypocrisy in relation to the Qatar event. One said Paddy was a businessman who was just making money at the end of the day. 'He can create a profile and platform in these places and use that platform for a change,' he said. 'I don't think Paddy not running Web Summit in Qatar is going to make any change to their regime.'

A number of those who attended said it was an impressive conference, both in terms of how it ran and in how much attention was paid to smaller details. A large firework display concluded the final night in front of the event's hashtag illuminated in the sky.

Chapter 15

THE PARTY'S OVER. OR IS IT?

On the fourth day of 2024, Paddy, Daire and Dave sat together in a room for the first time in over six years and talked.

It was a cold, dry day in Dublin when they met, in the identical place where it all began. But this was a far cry from 15 years ago, although even those meetings were often less than amicable. Now the three Web Summit co-founders were embroiled in contentious litigation, with no clear end in sight.

Daire and Dave had called this extraordinary general meeting, which shareholders who hold more than 10 per cent of the company can convene, to propose a series of resolutions. It had been over two months since Paddy stepped down, and there was a sense that some kind of compromise was possible. Or at least more of a sense than there had been in the two years since the litigation began.

Indeed, just a month prior to this meeting, the High Court was hearing glimmers of hope that the preliminary trial matters which had been dragging on were nearing an end, and that a hearing date would soon be secured.

'Everyone wants to wrap it up,' Bernard Dunleavy, Paddy's senior counsel, said. It was the first time in the history of the lawsuits that some sense of like-mindedness was felt between the parties. Certain motions were being agreed or 'abandoned' without the need for a hearing, and there was a feeling that maybe, just maybe, Katherine Maher's leadership of Web Summit would result in a speedier resolution of the toxic quarrelling.

The resolutions proposed by Daire and Dave included that the sale of the company would be explored, that an independent consultant would be appointed and that there would be a prohibition on the use of company money to fund the legal expenses of its shareholders. The pair also sought to have a nominee appointed to the board.

Using prepared remarks, they did a lot of the talking, with Paddy sitting and listening. He voted down each resolution, a decision that was within his rights as an 81 per cent shareholder, but one which nonetheless seemed heavy handed for anyone attempting to convey an iota of compromise.

The rowing was far from over and, in many ways, it was only just heating up again.

Paddy may have been stood down from the company for months but he had made appearances at the office, regaling staff with his latest outrage at the government or at more salacious details emerging from the legal process. The litigation had been among his preferred topics of conversation and an almost unavoidable discussion for anyone who crossed his path, including near-strangers who chatted to him casually or bumped into him on the street.

The interminably impatience he felt at waiting for more details to come out was obvious when screenshots of a companywide Slack message were disseminated to a select group of Irish journalists via a PR employee. In them Ronan Mooney, the company's head of HR, provided an 'update' to staff on the court proceedings following an exchange of discovery between the parties. The journalists who received the screenshots (among whom I was not included) felt it was a transparent attempt to get new material which had not yet been before a judge, and which they could not verify, into the public domain.

Months later, Paddy's lawyers joined the long list of those who have had to apologise for him when this 'deeply regrettable' Slack message was brought to the High Court's attention by Dave and Daire's legal team.

Paddy was reminded 'in stark terms', his lawyers said, of the importance of complying with the undertaking he gave to the court to not disclose information received from discovery for any purpose other than the litigation at hand. His lawyers said Mooney sent the Slack message 'on the direct instructions of Mr Cosgrave' and accepts not questioning the instructions to send it was a 'significant error' of judgement.

Despite Paddy's de-throning a few months prior, 2024 was set to be a big year for the company. A year earlier, Paddy had said that there was a good chance the company would pass €100 million in revenue in 2024. 'That's not bad for a maligned little Irish company you know,' he said. 'It's a real business.'

The chance of that happening was not beyond the realm of possibilities. In the financial accounts for 2022 (released at the start of 2024) overall turnover stood at €52.5 million, up 65 per cent from the €31 million it generated in sales in 2021. And these figures were from before the company had secured its lucrative Qatar deal.

While revenue was rising, so too was spending, as these accounts showed an after-tax profit of €114,166, down 97 per cent on the €3.8 million net profit made by the company in 2021.

The accounts also showed that the events conference company spent nearly €20 million on wages and salaries in 2022, up almost 70 per cent from the €12 million in staff costs it incurred during 2021. This spike in employee costs occurred despite staff numbers decreasing slightly in 2022 to a headcount of less than 240.

Additionally, the company paid more than €3.5 million to its five directors in 2022, which consisted of Paddy, Mike Sexton, who has since resigned, Peter Gilmer, who resigned in early 2023, Nathan Hubbard, who resigned from the board later that year, and Nida Shah, its chief operating officer, who resigned in June 2024.

In a statement, CEO Katherine Maher said the company invested in pay increases for its staff in 2022 in recognition of 'their success' in guiding the company through the pandemic.

The start of 2024 was also when Paddy bucked a trend of something he said he would never do and sued for defamation. He issued defamation proceedings against Mediahuis, the publisher of the *Irish Independent* and the *Sunday Independent*, concerning what is understood to be captions in a video published online around the time he resigned. The video was a profile synopsis of his life and career to date.

In announcing the decision, Paddy said on Twitter that he was taking the step 'reluctantly' and only after what he said were 'persistent attempts' to avoid litigation. 'Any potential monetary settlements or awards will be donated to children's charities,' he wrote.

The lawsuit was a huge change of tack for Paddy, who has long been a vocal opponent to Ireland's defamation laws, which he has described as 'odious', 'chilling' and 'insane'.

In 2021 he posted on X that 'on a point of principle' he had never used Ireland's defamation laws to 'muzzle media'.

'But most business people do,' he added.

And in one of the last conversations we had together, after I expressed concern at what I regarded as threats of defamation from him, he told me, 'I'm never going to sue anyone for defamation because I don't believe in it.' He said I could be 'rest assured of that'.

To some onlookers the defamation case was Paddy drawing a line in the sand ahead of a planned return as CEO – a move which had been anticipated and expected for weeks since Katherine Maher's resignation announcement. So when Maher stepped down on 1 March 2024, Paddy waited in the wings before announcing his triumphant return in early April.

It was an entirely unsurprising move which some around him had been floating for months, even before Maher's departure announcement. And especially since Paddy appeared to regard the reason he stepped down to be not of his own making.

In a bizarre twist, Maher was less than a month into her role as CEO of NPR when she found herself the subject of criticism over her own tweets. The posts, which dated from years before she took up the job, included one which called

Donald Trump a racist and another which described a dream about going on a road trip with Kamala Harris and 'comparing nuts and baklava from roadside stands'. Numerous commentators questioned her independence and she was criticized by NPR's business editor, who was subsequently suspended and then resigned.

While Web Summit was in Brazil for its second annual conference in Rio, Paddy tweeted Elon Musk asking if he would speak remotely to attendees. Elon never replied to Paddy but he did weigh in on the Maher controversy, saying she 'hates the Constitution of the USA' and calling for NPR to be defunded. Only a month before, Paddy posted a glowing review of a trip to Space X, with a picture of a VIP pass and a bottle of the rocket company's own-brand Pinot Noir.

While silent online about Gaza after his return, Paddy continued his regular scheduled programming of lambasting the government, Irish media, his co-founders and various others in the tech world.

The vitriol has appeared to increase as he tweeted pictures of former staffers, calling them names and accusing them of being criminals. He also called Charlie Taylor, a well-regarded tech reporter and an excellent colleague of mine, a 'pig'. When Taylor asked senior staff in Web Summit who he engaged with on a regular basis, including Sebastian Hamilton, where they stood on the claim, he was met with radio silence.

As with many of Paddy's attacks, the strategy was not without consequences. A number of Irish tech entrepreneurs later declined a dinner invitation, saying that they thought Paddy's behaviour had become too toxic to associate with.

When Paddy appeared at an annual alumni dinner for Trinity College publications, those in attendance said he was in flying form, talking at length about his current interests, which included the court cases and Leo Varadkar.

Accompanied by Eoghan MacNeill, editor of The Ditch, Paddy talked up the work being done by the anti-establishment investigative website that Web Summit had funded. Numerous sources said he did not mention returning to Web Summit but a couple of days later he posted online that he was back. He referred to the time he had off giving him a chance to think about what he wanted Web Summit to be.

The questions facing Web Summit, such as whether and to what extent the biggest sponsors or most valued investors will return to its flagship event, remain. But even without them, the company will expand into new countries hungry for innovation and attention. Start-ups searching for partners, investors and customers, will flock to Web Summit in the hope that life-changing deals will be done there.

Paddy has made it clear for years that he wants to keep building Web Summit – and told me once he thought he had '40 years' left in him to help make Web Summit a so-called 'hidden champion'. These referred to medium-sized companies which are at the top of their game in their sector and are 'founder-led'.

While he clearly still has immense passion for the work – and many long-serving staffers are happy to have their energetic boss back in charge – it's hard not to wonder whether Paddy would ever know the right time to leave the party. And instead of looking back in awe at what he's accomplished, his reflections are heavily tainted by the long list of those he claims have wronged either him or the company.

In the meantime, the company and Paddy face the litigation, which is arguably the most existential challenge in its history.

The landscape of the lawsuits changed after his resignation, as evidenced by amended pleadings and additional discovery orders.

'In my view the reasons for the resignation of Mr Cosgrave are important,' Ms Justice Eileen Roberts said in a ruling which forces Web Summit to disclose any messages from third parties relating to Paddy's Israel posts. 'Where the alleged acts of oppression and where loss and damage to the company are hotly in dispute, documents which establish the circumstances of Mr Cosgrave's resignation as CEO are in my view both relevant and necessary to discover,' she added.

This summer the cases were allocated a nine-week hearing date beginning in March 2025, and, with each day in court costing each founder many thousands, the legal costs over nine weeks will be eye watering.

If the cases proceed to trial, as opposed to settling, they will be among the most contentious commercial lawsuits to get a full hearing in recent High Court memory. Like many litigants, Paddy, Daire and Dave want their day in court, but it is undeniable that each stands to lose a lot in the process, both financially and reputationally.

Daire and David want Paddy, as majority shareholder, to buy their shares, but for how much and whether a significant discount should be applied will form the thrust of the battle in the oppression proceedings. If directed to buy their shares, he may need outside investment.

Paddy is seeking damages in his directors duty lawsuit against Dave, claiming that his alleged breaches likely resulted in a $10 million loss to Web Summit. Some senior staffers at Web Summit feel the lawsuits will result in some sort of vindication for Paddy and the company.

As many sources have said throughout the process of writing this book, 'no one comes out looking well from this'. Many of those close to the various co-founders just want the lawsuits to go away. I have spent years talking to people about Paddy and the Web Summit in conversations which wavered from being glowingly positive to so negative that I could feel the agitation and anxiety of the person in front of me, or at the other end of a phone.

The question that has often come up in these discussions, in some shape or form, was whether Paddy's crusading was genuine, or part of a plot to undermine faith in societal institutions, for the sake of it. Many observers have speculated that it was for the sole purpose of wanting to set the world on fire and watch it burn down. The casual manner in which he talks about something as serious as suing his business partners and former friends, using company money he has spent years building, speaks volumes to support this theory.

'Petty squabbling is, if you can afford it, worth every penny,' was what he told friends in early 2022, referring to the live litigation and others he said he had in the pipeline. 'I'd highly recommend it. However, if you can't afford it, and are merely a middling millionaire or worse a centrist dad, you're deluded to ever involve yourself in such personally and professionally pointless tit for tats,' he added. The email was preceded by someone telling him there was 'plenty of banter down at the Law Library apparently', referring to his cases.

For Paddy, much of the rowing is 'banter'. I have been in his company when he has delighted in sending a Twitter missile and appears completely unphased by whether the decision was prudent or not. But on the other hand, there is no doubt that he believes what he is doing, or has done, is right and just.

'I find it particularly inexcusable of people that are highly educated and wealthy, that they say so little about things that they know to be so wrong inside the society of which they are a member,' he told me years ago. 'So I really feel a responsibility, that is grounded in some sense of what ethics really is, to do something about the things that I can have some impact on, however small that might be. And Ireland is one of those places where I think I can have some very, very small impact.'

When he resigned, I thought he might sell the company and go start something new to show the world that he wasn't a one-trick pony. But Paddy believes, rightly or wrongly, that the business needs him to thrive and that staying at the helm improves its chances of continued success. He also has far too much energy to stop working and too many perceived 'bad guys' to take down.

Aside from the deep acrimony he holds for his co-founders, Paddy is also resentful toward a long list of people he has known over the past decade or so. At some point, this list included at least 13 people he named in a message to me while questioning my ability as a journalist.

'Maybe you're just not good at digging or maybe you're just really good at blind eying their grim grifting and fraud,' he said in a message to me last year. 'It's actually hard to know.'

When I first became acquainted with Paddy, I told him it was only a matter of time before he 'turned' on me. He would put on a scary voice and repeat the claim back to me in a way which mocked the notion and diminished the possibility.

It then became clear that somewhere along the way Paddy became deeply angry at me for not seeing the past 15 years through the same lens as him. When I pressed him on whether he thought the story of his company was just about people who have allegedly wronged him, he said it was 'a' story.

When he was first told about this book, and how it was going to contain plenty of things he would not like, he seemed unphased, saying all 'protagonists' needed to be 'flawed' and that he hated 'sanitized' business books. I recall him saying he would sue me to 'boost book sales' while laughing. If he was joking then, it certainly has not felt like he is joking now.

He has since sent me a litany of aggressive messages, attacked me and my integrity online, instructed legal letters to be sent to my publishers, and likely by the time you are reading this, much more will have unfolded.

Even if all the fighting ends up being only fun for Paddy and not his 300-strong workforce or the business he leads, he's unlikely to stop any time soon.

ACKNOWLEDGEMENTS

I owe a debt of gratitude to the dozens of Web Summit staff, both current and former, who spoke to me for this book. In certain cases, the hours we spent talking seemed to help some unravel their own experiences or put shape on their thoughts about what it was all for. It certainly helped me to understand this story, and for that I am truly grateful.

I am also extremely grateful to the many others who shared their experiences of interacting with the company or its founders over the years. They all offered pointed and thoughtful insight about how this story fit into theirs and why it matters.

Conor Nagle, thank you for believing in this project and, most importantly, in me. It feels like a lifetime ago that I fired off that pitch email and when that you told me over coffee that I was the person to tell this story, and I will be eternally grateful for the advice you provided and the empathy you showed.

Joel Simons, thank you for guiding me through this process and bringing your calming energy to the entire experience. You helped me see this project as a living thing when I was too focused on tying a neat bow around it, and that was invaluable for me as a writer. A sincere thank you to the rest of the HarperCollins team, including Sarah, Patricia and Ameena, as well as Tom for his sublime editing skills and, of course, Kieran.

The process of writing this book, as I imagine is the same with most books, was a rollercoaster of emotions. I am overwhelmed with appreciation for all the people who prevented me from quitting which was, at numerous points, an almost certain outcome in my mind.

Chief among those is my friend and colleague Aaron Rogan, who talked me off many ledges and was always on hand to offer advice and (hopefully) free counselling. Let the record show that I thanked you in my book and you didn't thank me in yours, but at least I'm not petty enough to mention it.

Thanks to Killian Woods, my tremendous colleague, friend and mentee, for being a voice of reason on many occasions, as well as to Charlie Taylor, Ellie Donnelly, Daniel Murray, Barry J. Whyte, Peter O'Dwyer and the entire *Business Post* newsroom for bigging me up and slagging me off every step of the way. Thank you also to the newsroom editors, including Danny and Gillian, for being very supportive and understanding even when I was only half present at times.

So much gratitude to my beautiful friends for living this with me week on week, namely Rosanna Cooney, Beth Walsh, Jane Kupen, Lorraine Harmon, Neil Kenna, Shaunagh Devlin, Lauren McKenna, Ellen O'Riordan, and special thanks to La familia elegida: Caro, Lydian, Stephen, Delphina, Ana and Elise, for their boundless support and encouragement.

ACKNOWLEDGEMENTS

To my amazing in-laws Rita and Diarmaid, as well as James and Christina, thank you for listening, nodding and always making me feel very loved.

Thanks to the clever Emma Sanz for always taking me down a notch and not having a clue who or what this book is about.

To my wonderful Dad, who taught me to take leaps and face down challenges. To my unshakeable Mom, who taught me to be curious (nosey) and persistent (pushy) – I do this for you. You both may be many miles away, but I feel your unconditional love every single day.

Most of all, thank you to my husband Tommy, for putting up with endless rants, for seeing silver linings when I only saw clouds and for always making me feel like I can do anything. You are magnifishcent. I love you.

SOURCE MATERIAL

Much of the material in this book arose from reporting I've done over the past three years in my job as a journalist with the *Business Post*.

The anonymous quotes were largely sourced from off the record interviews with Web Summit staff, both current and former, or from documentary evidence, including texts and videos, provided to me by these individuals. In some cases, people consented to certain information being relayed as long as their names were not included.

There are also a number of on and off the record interviews with various individuals who played a role in the company's rise or in Paddy's life before and during Web Summit.

The dialogue from a town hall meeting comes from an audio recording which was held internally by the company and provided to me in early 2023.

The quotes from newspaper articles were largely sourced from Irish Newspaper Archive or from material obtained via microfilm readers at the National Library of Ireland.

The documents referred to in the lawsuits largely come from the grounding affidavits filed by each founder ahead of the cases being first opened, as well as the exhibits referenced in these. In Paddy's case, an affidavit replying to his co-founder's cases, which he was permitted to file in late 2021, is also relied on. Reference is also made to documents which were filed ahead of a discovery hearing last year and which were subject to an order of the High Court.

As flagged in the text, many of the quotes from Paddy stem from interviews he's given to me over the past two years or from messages he's sent to me and others.

The quotes from David and Daire come from their own claims in legal filings, or from radio, newspaper or podcast interviews they have given over the years.